Crafting Consensus

Crafting Consensus

Why Central Bankers Change their Speech and How Speech Changes the Economy

by

NICOLE BAERG
University of Essex

OXFORD
UNIVERSITY PRESS

OXFORD
UNIVERSITY PRESS

Oxford University Press is a department of the University of Oxford. It furthers the University's objective of excellence in research, scholarship, and education by publishing worldwide. Oxford is a registered trade mark of Oxford University Press in the UK and certain other countries.

Published in the United States of America by Oxford University Press
198 Madison Avenue, New York, NY 10016, United States of America.

CIP data is on file at the Library of Congress

ISBN 978–0–19–049948–8

1 3 5 7 9 8 6 4 2

Printed and bound by
Marquis, Canada

Contents

List of Figures ix
List of Tables xi
Acknowledgments xiii

1. Crafting Consensus 1
   1.1 The Girth of Greenspan's Briefcase 1
   1.2 Central Bankers as Wordsmiths 5
   1.3 The Statement-Writing Process 7
   1.4 The Importance of Committee Composition 10
   1.5 What Comes Next? 16

2. Monetary Policy Committees and Central Bank Communication 19
   2.1 Introduction 19
   2.2 Central Bank Committees and Institutional Design 25
      2.2.1 Committee Size 25
      2.2.2 Committee Composition 29
      2.2.3 Decision-Making Protocol 32
   2.3 Central Bank Communication 35
      2.3.1 How to Communicate? 35
      2.3.2 Formal Models of Political Communication 38
      2.3.3 Communication and Expectations 39
   2.4 Conclusion 42

3. A Model of Central Bank Communication 45
   3.1 Introduction 45
   3.2 The Model 49
      3.2.1 Strategic Vagueness 49
      3.2.2 Model Departures 52
      3.2.3 Actors 57
      3.2.4 Utility Functions 61
      3.2.5 Game Sequence 62
      3.2.6 Equilibrium 63

3.3 Disseminating Economic Information 69
3.4 Empirical Implications 72
3.5 Conclusion 73

4. Central Bank Committees and Political Communication 75
4.1 Introduction 75
4.2 Research Design 76
4.2.1 The Sample 77
4.2.2 Dependent Variables 83
4.2.3 Independent Variables 88
4.3 Empirical Model and Results 91
4.3.1 Results for Diversity on Policy Statement Uncertainty 92
4.3.2 Results for Diversity on Policy Editing 96
4.4 Conclusion 98

5. Central Bank Announcements and Inflation Expectations 101
5.1 Introduction 101
5.2 Origins of Inflation Expectations 103
5.3 Research Design 105
5.4 Data and Results 107
5.4.1 Dependent Variable: Posterior Inflation Expectations 107
5.4.2 Independent Variables 108
5.4.3 Descriptive Statistics 109
5.4.4 Regression Analysis 114
5.4.5 Sensitivity Analysis 116
5.5 Conclusion 118

6. Testing the Theory in Latin America 121
6.1 Introduction 121
6.2 Data and Analysis 125
6.2.1 Dependent Variable: Inflation 125
6.2.2 Independent Variables: Inflation Expectations 126
6.2.3 Information Precision 128
6.2.4 Control Variables 136
6.3 Main Results 138
6.4 Sensitivity Analysis 143
6.5 Conclusion 146

7. Putting It All Together 149
7.1 Summary of the Findings 150
7.2 Accountability and Transparency 155
7.3 Horizontal Accountability and Central Bank Appointments 157
7.4 Future Research 159
7.4.1 Rotational Voting 159
7.4.2 Qualifications 161
7.5 Applications beyond Central Banking 163
7.5.1 Judicial Politics 163
7.5.2 Corporate Governance 165
7.6 Final Thoughts 166

Appendix 169

References 185
Index 195

List of Figures

2.1. Policy changes in central bank communications and transparency from 1993 to 2015 for the US Federal Reserve. 20

2.2. Policy changes in central bank communications and transparency from 1993 to 2015 for a subsection of other national and supranational central banks, including the Bank of England (BOE), the European Central Bank (ECB), and the Bank of Japan (BOJ). 21

2.3. Changes in central bank transparency from 1998 to 2014 for select countries around the world by level of market development. 24

2.4. De facto MPC size. 28

2.5. MPC composition for diverse central banks. 31

2.6. MPC decision-making. 34

3.1. Higher and lower levels of communicated vagueness. 50

3.2. Differences in actors' preferences. 60

3.3. Preference differences according to bias and distance. 61

4.1. Opposing bias of chair and median based on all members. 89

4.2. Opposing bias of chair and median based on voting members. 90

5.1. Expected level of inflation (twelve months) by gender. 110

5.2. Expected level of inflation (twelve months) by age cohort. 111

5.3. Expected level of inflation (twelve months) by news readership. 112

5.4. Expected level of inflation by respondents in control and treatment groups. Group mean is indicated by the white diamond; the median is indicated by the black dot. 113

5.5. Persistence of the treatment effect. 113

5.6. Changes in prior beliefs by information precision. Those who get vague information (control group) have weightier priors than those who get more precise information (treatment group). 117

6.1. Global inflation rates (annual percentage CPI) in 1998. From the World Bank World Development Indicators (missing data in white). 122
6.2. Mean inflation expectations and annual inflation. 128
6.3. Density of newspaper articles by information precision. 134
6.4. Variation in information precision by country and over time. 135
6.5. Attenuation in Marginal Effect of Mean Expected Inflation. 141
6.6. Attenuation in Marginal Effect of Standard Deviation in Expected Inflation. 142

List of Tables

3.1. Notation 60
4.1. Effects of committee heterogeneity on uncertainty and certainty in FOMC statements: All members 92
4.2. Committee heterogeneity on uncertainty and certainty in FOMC statements: All members, fitted on the scale of the linear predictor 93
4.3. Effects of committee heterogeneity on uncertainty and certainty in FOMC statements: Voting members only 94
4.4. Committee heterogeneity on uncertainty and certainty in FOMC statements: Voting members, fitted on the scale of the linear predictor 94
4.5. Effects of distance on edits to the FOMC statements: All members 97
4.6. Effects of distance on edits to the FOMC statements: Voting members 98
5.1. Participant quotas 109
5.2. Effects of information on households' inflation expectations 115
5.3. Effect of information treatment on individuals' inflation expectations 118
6.1. Example inflation article from Reuters news 131
6.2. Machine versus human coding status by diagnostic test 132
6.3. Linear OLS regression model 139
6.4. Effect of information precision on inflation using both OLS and IV regression 144
A.1. Descriptive statistics for corpus of official FOMC policy statements adopted 169
A.2. Effects of committee heterogeneity on uncertainty (Finance Dictionary) in FOMC statements: All members 175
A.3. Effects of committee heterogeneity on uncertainty (Finance Dictionary) in FOMC statements: Voting members only 176

A.4. Effects of committee heterogeneity on uncertainty (LIWC) in FOMC statements: All members 177
A.5. Effects of committee heterogeneity on uncertainty (LIWC) in FOMC statements: Voting members only 178
A.6. Effects of committee heterogeneity on certainty and uncertainty (Longer FOMC Dictionary) in FOMC statements: All members 179
A.7. Effects of committee heterogeneity on certainty and uncertainty (Longer FOMC Dictionary) in FOMC statements: Voting members only 180
A.8. Frequency distribution ($N = 108$) 182
A.9. Frequency distribution by treatment group 183

Acknowledgments

Writing a book takes a long time and this one seemed to take especially long. One positive outcome of having taken so long is that this book is better than before and represents a lot of learning and development that has happened since finishing my PhD. It also reflects support from four different institutions, my academic community, and family and friends. While I tried to mention everyone I could here, I am sure that there are important omissions. So many people gave me feedback on this project over the years. Thanks so much for your support.

I am like most academics in that two large hurdles I have faced were getting through graduate school and getting a permanent job. Mark Hallerberg supported me in both these endeavours and in ways that changed my life (without being hyperbolic). Mark wrote letters for me, answered numerous emails and messages, read my drafts, wrote papers and grants with me, and was a stable force of support throughout my academic life and when I needed it most. The stability that he provided and his sponsorship of me and my work was encouragement that I needed and a *mitzvah*. I don't even know how to convey how thankful I am. I think he knows. I leave it at that.

In addition to providing most of my empirical training during my time at Emory University, Drew Linzer changed the way I think about data in a profound way. This allowed me to tackle new tools, such as text analysis and machine learning, on my own, and prepared me for teaching methods to students, which I honestly enjoy now that I have done it numerous times. I doubt that I would have had the courage to continue to tackle new tools in machine learning, hard or easy, never mind found it as manageable as I did without this training. I also appreciate that despite Drew's departure from academia, he continues to be a good friend and a positive reminder that life is a series of small choices about what you want to do and who you want to spend your time with and so we should all choose wisely and with an open heart.

Last but not least, Eric Reinhardt was a solid support for me while writing my PhD. He read drafts, taught me how to structure arguments and write to a broader audience, and also taught me how to find an actually interesting puzzle. As a first-generation student, it was often hard for me to know exactly what I was supposed to be doing during graduate school and what the norms were (and how often I was breaking them). This was especially true early on. Like Mark, I always felt that Eric had my back, was patient with me, and believed that my research had something of value to contribute to the conversation. I am very thankful for his support.

While attending Emory University, I was also very fortunate in that I found a home in the Research Department of the Federal Reserve Bank of Atlanta. There was no better place to be a student of political economy and monetary policy, especially during such an eventful time as during the US financial crisis. My deepest gratitude to Stephen Kay for keeping me gainfully employed throughout my graduate training, especially in the summers; reading my stuff; and being a constant and positive source of career support and guidance over the years. Despite rarely giving me his lunch and always giving it to Gustavo, Steve encouraged me to work on this book manuscript early on and encouraged me to send it to Oxford University Press after reading it a number of times and reassuring me that I did in fact have something of interest to say.

My thanks go to the research floor, including Julie Hotchkiss, Myriam Quispe-Agnoli, Pedro Silos, Federico Mandelman, Anastasios Karantounias, Eric Smith, Toni Braun, Will Roberds, and Tao Zha. My economics compatriots, Gustavo Canavire Bacarreza, Andy Balthrop, and Mzwandile Ginindza only made a little fun of me for not being an economist, but not too much, and I appreciate them for being my anchors to the world of economics graduate school during this time. I also appreciate the number of economists who walked through the research floor's doors whom I got to see present, meet, and talk to about my research, including but not limited to Martin Eichenbaum, Lawrence Christiano, Juan Rubio, Tom Sargent, Chris Sims, and Nobuhiro Kiyotaki. I will fondly remember the time that I did actually have to give my dissertation elevator pitch in an elevator to Tom Sargent and another time, while in the same elevator, someone cracked a joke, praying that the elevator's fundamentals were sound despite being in the peak of the US housing crisis.

My work at Emory and the Atlanta Fed paved the way for the continued methodological and substantive training that I undertook at the University of Mannheim. In particular, my colleagues while there are now two of my dearest friends—James Lo and Will Lowe. The Lo/we brothers are two excellent methodological wizards, whose insights and expertise in computational linguistics, scaling, and survey research and design, not to mention political science, provided a rigorous and supportive environment for me to keep trying my hand at new techniques and tools that helped advance my research in important and creative new directions once I had graduated. James was and remains an important "early reader" of my work and acts as a tough but constructive reviewer. Will's collaborations and "textpertise" was fun and even sometimes productive (ha!). I also thank Colin Krainin for contributing significantly to this manuscript and to my work generally. You will find Colin's math-print and theoretical ideas sprinkled throughout this book as well as in our joint paper. The rewriting of my dissertation model into the bargaining model that you find here in these pages is due to Colin. Finally, I thank Jakob Willisch, who is an excellent scholar in his own right and also an important reader of my work and a thinker alongside me while I work out problems. I also thank Alyssa Taylor, who was such a dutiful research assistant that she even edited this declaration when I sent it to her as a thank-you note.

I give special thanks to Britt Bolin, Matthias Haber, Stefan Maier, Keigo Tanabe, Kelsey Worboys, and Elisa Wirsching for important research assistance that contributed significantly to the construction of the manuscript. Thank you also to Holly Monteith and Kathy Kieva, who edited and indexed this book and Darick Ritter for the cover. Thank you also to Oxford University Press, my former editor Scott Paris for taking this book on, and David Pervin and James Cook for seeing it through. I also thank the three anonymous reviewers for making this book better.

Other people I am indebted to include (in no particular order) Jeff Frieden, Mark Brawley, Julia Gray, Jon Slapin, Mark Manger, Cesi Cruz, Imad Mansour, Emily Ritter, Michael Ehrmann, Thomas König, Thomas Bräuninger, Erica Owen, Peter Rosendorff, Cristina Bodea,

Christina Schnieder, Catherine DeVries, Stefanie Walter, Carolina Garriga, Bill Clark, Oli Proksch, Cheryl Schonhardt-Bailey, Mark Kayser, Rob O'Reilly, and Thomas Gschwend. I thank my many coworkers (past and present) at Essex and at Mannheim, who are great friends and colleagues, and who made living abroad fun and familiar.

Finally, thank you so much to my parents, Ron Baerg and Diane Baerg. Without you or your support this book would not be possible. I also thank my extended family: Tova Turin, Erez Turin; Gina, Dani, and Ari Turin; Rachel Turin, Shoshanna Rousseau, Marie Marcolli, and Bob Wilton. Finally, I thank my friends Zoya Shvartzman, Katy Stigers, Jacob Ricks, Maimi Niina, Jake Smith, Ran Oren, Etienne Noreau-Hebert, Jeff Spiers, Rebecca Elias, Catherine Fisher, Heather Dale, Sophia Fischer, Ivan Fischer, and Dmitri Fischer. I especially thank Jeff Spiers for making me feel impatient enough with the popular rhetoric on central banking during the crisis years that I ended up feeling like I actually had something useful to say. While at times I came across as arrogant and naive in my love for central banking, I think that this book shows that I care deeply about the practice of central banking and that I hope that people better understand the practice and art of central banking in today's modern economy.

Perhaps the best news is that I still find central banking fascinating and I continue to want to theorize and explain what exactly these institutions do and why. I believe this topic is timely, interesting, and meaningful. All errors, omissions, and limitations are my sole responsibility. I sincerely look forward to learning more along the way.

And now to the task of thanking my husband. This book is dedicated to you, Amos Turin, my love and my best friend. I am most thankful for your kindness, support, and unbridled encouragement of my career.

1
Crafting Consensus

Given that financial conditions [. . .] are particularly tied to the public's expectations regarding the future course of monetary policy, our effectiveness in promoting maximum employment and price stability is crucially dependent on conveying our policy strategy as clearly as possible.

—Federal Open Market Committee Minutes, September 2012

On these reports, let me say, first of all, it's fairly normal to disagree about things. It happens everywhere. Just read the recent statements about when to raise interest rates in the United States by members of the FOMC. It happens in the UK, it happens in Japan. So this is part of normal diversity.

—Mario Draghi, speaking on behalf of the European Central Bank Governing Council, November 2014

1.1 The Girth of Greenspan's Briefcase

Until the 1990s, central banks were opaque; they operated as if they had little need to explain their actions to the mass public or to markets. Monetary policy functioned through changing interest rates.

In the United States, the Federal Open Market Committee (FOMC) is the monetary policy decision-making body responsible for changing interest rates. In the FOMC, as with most central banks around the world, monetary policy decisions are entrusted to a *monetary policy committee* (MPC) rather than delegated to a single individual. Through the FOMC, a group of nineteen individuals makes collective economic policy decisions on behalf of the US government and its

Crafting Consensus: Why Central Bankers Change Their Speech and How Speech Changes the Economy. Nicole Rae Baerg, Oxford University Press (2020). © Oxford University Press.
DOI: 10.1093/oso/9780190499488.001.0001

citizens. The authority to do so comes from an early act of Congress, the Federal Reserve Act, enacted on December 23, 1913.[1]

When the FOMC meets, which it does approximately eight times yearly, committee members make two policy decisions. The first policy decision concerns whether, and by how much, to change interest rates.[2] In addition to a decision on interest rates, FOMC members vote on and edit an *official monetary policy statement*. Taken together, these two monetary policy decisions constitute monetary policy making by the US central bank.

Historically, policy makers have orchestrated changes to the economy by changing the interest rates charged to commercial banks and by creating monetary policy surprises. To make monetary policy surprises surprising, policy makers couched their future actions and communicated opaquely. In practical terms, this meant that central bankers generated very few public policy statements and issued limited official communications—and those communications they did offer were delivered infrequently and kept obtuse and unintelligible. One delightful example of the opacity of monetary policy communication during this period is known as the "briefcase measure."[3]

Alan Greenspan was chairman of the US Federal Reserve Bank, or the "Fed," from 1987 until 2006. The media paid significant attention to the size of Greenspan's briefcase before the start of every FOMC meeting—CNN in particular would televise Chairman Greenspan walking through the front door of the Federal Reserve Board building, briefcase in tow. News commentators would debate the relative girth of the briefcase, which analysis was then reported publicly during CNN's news program *Eyes on the Fed*.

Why the media's infatuation with the size of Chairman Greenspan's briefcase? First, in a policy environment with little official news about the future path of policy making, grasping at the straw of the size of Greenspan's briefcase could relieve the public of its anxieties about future interest rate changes. A "heads-up" might prove lucrative for

[1] U.S. Code, Title 12, Chapter 3, Subchapter II.

[2] The *fed funds rate* is the interest rate that depository institutions, such as banks, savings and loans, and credit unions, charge each other for overnight loans.

[3] What's in Greenspan's Briefcase? Federal Reserve Bank of St. Louis, October 1, 2000.

investors and might help shape the public's understanding of the future economy, as the Fed's changes to interest rates helped move other interest rates in the economy, such as for mortgages and car loans. Second, it was Chairman Greenspan, and not any other member of the FOMC, who mattered—the media gave little heed to the girth of other members' briefcases, or even to their existence. In other words, policy communication was more or less vague, and the chairman of the Federal Reserve commanded almost unlimited importance. By way of illustration, consider the following 1990 post on the blog *CNN Money*, titled "Fed Chief Briefcase: A Sign":[4]

> NEW YORK (CNNfn)—Economists say Alan Greenspan has all but announced his intention to rise interest rates this week. But while some point to the Fed chief's words about the need to "preempt" inflation, others look to his briefcase. The briefcase theory, as it's whimsically known, holds that the size of Greenspan's briefcase determines whether the nation's top banker wants to raise rates, lower them or leave them unchanged. If Greenspan wants to alter the direction of interest rates, he will need a briefcase full of documentation to make his case to the Federal Open Market Committee. If he wants to keep interest rates steady, the briefcase will be light. Recent history supports this hypothesis. The Fed has not moved on rates this year. At the same time, Greenspan's briefcase has been on the light side.

On the basis of the importance placed on the girth his briefcase, one might think that it was the chairman alone who made monetary policy decisions. If the chairman carried a large briefcase, then policy rates would change. Alternatively, if the chairman carried only a small briefcase, then the chairman had only a small number of supporting documents, which suggested the status quo. Unfortunately, and perhaps unsurprisingly in hindsight, the size of Greenspan's briefcase was a terrible predictor of Fed policy changes. More crucially, however, it was equally a terrible representation of how policy on the FOMC was

[4] Fed chief briefcase: a sign. CNN Money, June 29, 1999.

made. One report by Gavin and Mandal (2000) showed that during the May, 2000 FOMC meeting, Greenspan's briefcase was unusually thin, but despite this, the FOMC raised its interest rate target by half a percentage point, the largest increase the Fed had made to interest rates in more than five years. While some held on to the briefcase measure as a silly and fun gimmick, Gavin and Mandal soberly concluded in their study that it was "not the size of the briefcase that matters, but the information found inside" (2000, p.11).

As it turned out, the size of Alan Greenspan's briefcase was a misleading guide to monetary policy making during the Greenspan era. Greenspan revealed in his autobiography that "the fatness of my briefcase was solely a function of whether I had packed my lunch" (Greenspan, 2008, p. 198). Such a scenario—a central banker's homemade lunch (or not) acting as an important signal of the economy—can occur only when the information and policy environment is obscure. In an environment where policy makers announce their future policy intentions using much more precise language, now referred to as *forward guidance*, and when the public knows that it is a committee rather than a single individual that makes policy, the mass public and the market are better informed.

Central bank communications can affect the global economy in both positive and negative ways, and variation in how monetary policy information is presented by central bankers to the mass public matters (Ehrmann and Fratzscher, 2007, 2010). Increasingly, the signals or anchors that market participants and households use to understand the policy-making activities of central banks are the actual words, or *natural language*, that policy makers use to express their vision of the future economy.

Yet even the strategy of using natural language can backfire. Chairman Ben Bernanke was appointed to replace Alan Greenspan starting in February 2006. Unlike Greenspan, Bernanke hoped to use more natural language to communicate monetary policy to the public, but, he said, this was not as easy as it sounded:

> I found out that completely natural language just doesn't quite work, because the markets are so intently focused on every decision and every action that the Fed takes, that they're going to overreact. You

> know, if you use a verb a different way the second time, they're going to say oh, my gosh, they're going to do this, that or the other thing, and you're going to create unnecessary volatility. So [instead of speaking freely,] you have to become somewhat constrained in the way you speak.[5]

Financial markets are increasingly interconnected, and in such a world, the risk of exporting (or importing) others' communication mistakes, or of over- or underemphasizing certain language features, is grave in its repercussions on policy making and international financial stability (IFS) (Alesina and Cukierman, 1990; Morris and Shin, 2002). One oft-cited example of a communication mistake is the so-called taper tantrum of 2013. According to Bernanke,

> in May and June of that year, in my capacity as Fed chair, I publicly raised the possibility that the central bank could begin "later this year" to slow the pace of its asset purchases, initiated in the round of quantitative easing known as [quantitative easing 3—or] "QE3." Although I was careful to say that short-term interest rates would remain low for a long time even after the "tapering" of asset purchases had begun, some market participants evidently interpreted statements by me and others at the Fed as signaling a possibly imminent rise in rates. The market volatility resulting from this shift of expectations—the "tantrum"—was felt particularly strongly by emerging-market economies.[6]

Thus central bankers have motivations to be vague some of the time and more precise other times.

1.2 Central Bankers as Wordsmiths

In terms of monetary practice, throughout the 2000s, central banks issued a much larger number of policy communications. While the

[5] Radio Interview: Hugh Hewitt, On the Courage to Act. October 15, 2015.
[6] Tantrums and hot money. January 6, 2016.

great recession (2007–2010) and the European debt crisis (2009–2015), coupled with low to negative interest rates in many developed countries, may have increased the pace at which central banks adopted public communication strategies, the trend toward a larger number of announcements began even earlier. Thus, if central bankers were historically thought of as apolitical and skillful technocrats who spoke in vague and obtuse terms, today the modern central banker is now best thought of as a wordsmith: a skilled user of words and one that is expected to communicate with and reassure markets and the mass public.

This volume is about central bankers as "wordsmiths," or actors who carefully construct and deploy policy communications with an intention to guide the economy. However, rather than assuming that these wordsmiths work alone, I consider how the institutions where central bankers work and in which they deliberate policy, that is, central bank committees, play an important role in determining the things that central bankers can and cannot say. The crux of my argument is that a combination of central bankers' interests and institutional rules governs how they make policy and together determine the level of vagueness in official policy communications.

Economists and political scientists have long examined the way that central bankers make decisions and how committee members vote on changes to interest rates. Central bankers express their preferences over changes to the interest rate at the end of FOMC meetings in a "roll-call" vote. Following the political science literature, researchers have used committee members' voting behavior as important data to compute central bankers' policy preferences (see, e.g., Adolph, 2013; Ainsley, 2016; Chang, 2003; Chappell, Havrilesky, and Roy McGregor, 2000; Eijffinger, Mahieu, and Raes, 2017; Gerlach-Kristen, Meade, et al., 2010; Hix, Høyland, and Vivyan, 2010). Yet, while we see ample research explaining central bankers' interest rate decisions, significantly less studied is the content of the policy statement. This gap in the literature is likely present for two reasons: first, historically, what mattered was changes in interest rates, and communication policy, with its associated opacity, was strategically suppressed and therefore less important to markets and the mass public and subsequently also less important to researchers. Second, individual votes "aye" and "nay" are relatively easy to count, whereas analyzing words and natural language was computationally more challenging.

Importantly, however, both of these things have changed. First, central bank communication is of growing prevalence and importance. For example, the Federal Reserve itself is so concerned with monopolizing monetary policy communication that, prior to the release of the official policy statement, Federal Reserve staff members are restricted from speaking publicly about the US economy. The purpose of this blackout period, which begins a week prior to the Saturday preceding a FOMC meeting and the Thursday following that meeting, is to manufacture silence. Thus, the official monetary policy statement is expected to operate as an uncluttered market signal about the future economy. In the words of the Fed, the purpose of the blackout period is to "facilitate the effectiveness of the Committee's policy deliberations and the clarity of its communications." After this period of radio silence, the official policy announcement is released.[7]

Second, the number and availability of tools that researchers can use to study textual data has grown immensely. The explosion of "text as data" applications in central banking includes studying preferences, sentiment, topics, and networks, to name only a few features (Acosta and Meade, 2015; Baerg and Lowe, 2018; Oshima, Matsubayashi, et al., 2018; Schonhardt-Bailey, 2013). Applied to the official policy statement, this volume uses these exciting new tools both to measure and to explain the origins and effects of variation in the language of official central bank communications.

1.3 The Statement-Writing Process

Just because central bankers come to a consensus does not mean that they want the same things. For example, if we look at votes on the FOMC over time and under successive chairs, we see that there was on average one dissenting vote per meeting during Paul Volker's tenure and fewer than one dissenting vote per meeting during Greenspan's

[7] External Communication Staff. June 22, 2011.

and Bernanke's tenures (Thornton and Wheelock, 2014). Assuming that the MPC meets approximately eight times yearly and that, at every meeting, twelve people cast a vote, over the course of the year, this means that dissent occurs only 10 percent of the time, whereas agreement occurs 90 percent of the time.[8] Thus, more often than not, we observe central bank agreement, where a diverse set of policy makers, thrust together into two-day meetings approximately every four to six weeks, come together to make policies through a process of crafting consensus. And yet, while official voting behavior may be unanimous, the way that central bankers present information about the economy varies significantly. Sometimes the way that central bankers present information about the economy is vague, whereas other times, it is precise. For example, in summer 2012, the FOMC stated that future interest rates would remain low until "mid-2015." However, a more precise statement is where the FOMC declares an actual policy target. Interestingly, the FOMC declared not just one but two targets in December 2012, providing more precise information to the mass public. At this time, the committee declared a 6.5 percent unemployment target and a 2.5 percent inflation target, making it easier for households to understand the goals and objectives of the Fed's future policy. The adoption of a numerical target is generally considered more precise. For example, in January 2013, the Bank of Japan adopted a "two percent inflation target," replacing its earlier "price stability in the medium to short run" goal (Shirai, 2014). Yet, if central bankers tend toward public agreement and prefer precise communications, why do we see variation in the way that they present economic information in the first place?

While it might seem far-fetched to think that central bankers care so much about words that they sit around a meeting table and carefully craft statements for the public, in fact, that is what happens during central bank committee meetings. In the following passage, for example, three members of the FOMC talk about the communication strategy. Of importance is that we can see the members taking positions and bargaining over the public statement. We also see that committee

[8] While the FOMC is made up of nineteen people, only twelve of them cast an official vote at any given meeting.

members are concerned with the exact signal that their communication will send to the public. The following is a verbatim conversation between then San Francisco Bank president Janet Yellen and board member Randall Kroszner. They are discussing Philadelphia Bank president Plosser's suggested changes to the public statement.

MR. KROSZNER: That means we have to think a lot about what we want to say in the statement [. . .] if I could just for a moment get clarification from President Yellen. My understanding was that what she suggested about the change to the fourth paragraph and the assessment of risk was to change only the last sentence back to the December 11 statement.

MS. YELLEN: [Mr. Plosser] proposed, as I recall, changing two sentences, eliminating the one that referred to downside risks and also changing the last sentence. I would not want to see the downside risk sentence eliminated; I would change only the very last sentence.

MR. KROSZNER: Yes, I would agree that I would not want to see that sentence changed. I'm open to the possibility of simply changing the last sentence to go back to December 11. Now, that clearly would be taken by the market as a signal that we were moving back.

As this conversation shows, we see variation in central bank speech because central bankers negotiate public statements just as they negotiate changes in interest rates. Committee members form coalitions to bargain over official communications. Just as working on any team has implications for how team members act, working on a committee affects how committee members are willing to negotiate. In particular, the fact that others on the committee may (or may not) share views and interests means that the official policy statement is not a random sample of words. Instead, its content is a policy output that results from a process of selecting words, embedded with aims and objectives, long and short term, that the speakers themselves want to pursue.

This strategic speechmaking behavior is what makes central bankers wordsmiths. Many political pundits, newspapers, and commentators have suggested over the last few years that words matter for market outcomes. While this is true, in this book, I explain how committee member bargaining, and the politics that it entails, is the first stage in the policy-making process of central bank communication. The politics of wordsmithing and speechmaking happens in the central bank committee as members huddle together and fine-tune announcements destined for public consumption.

Consider as another example the December 2014 statement of the European Central Bank (ECB) on *quantitative easing* (QE), or large-scale asset purchases. In tough negotiations over whether the ECB would expand the central bank's balance sheet, then ECB President Mario Draghi and his colleagues spent time bargaining over whether the ECB "intended" to pursue QE or whether instead the ECB "expected" to pursue QE. The debate over the choice of words was noteable, and even the *Financial Times* (FT) joked about whether there was a monetary policy dictionary in the new ECB headquarters that could help to translate central bank speak. The FT called the ECB's choice of words "disappointing" and said that they made "a failure to impress" (Mackintosh, 2014), leaving one to wonder what "shock and awe" lexicon the financial news was after and what type of central bank committee would produce it.

Finally, I am not only interested in explaining speechmaking. In addition to explaining those conditions that enhance or constrain public information flows, I am also interested in linking changes in words—their precision and vagueness—with changes in the economy, and I examine how changes in information shape inflation outcomes by tailoring expectations.

1.4 The Importance of Committee Composition

The premise of this book is that policy makers can use monetary policy communication to move markets, especially (but not only) when markets are distressed. This book is different from previous research on central bank communication in that I argue that the content of central bank policy communication is jointly determined by central bankers' interests or preferences and the political institutional environment where central bank committee members decide on policy. By "political institutional environment," I do not mean how independent the central bank is from the government (a long and active research agenda considers this very important line of reasoning; see, e.g., Barro, 1977; Kydland and Prescott, 1977; Rogoff, 1985). Similarly, I do not mean the political appointment process or those factors that influence presidents to appoint some committee members rather than others, in the hope that they might better enact preferred policies (a similarly active and important research agenda examines this dimension of monetary policy making; see, e.g., Chang, 2003). Instead, my argument focuses on the intercommittee politics of bargaining over communication policy on a political committee comprising experts who, at the end of two days of meetings, must reach an agreement about what to say and to release that official announcement in the media.

While previous political economy literature has uncovered a number of important insights into the role and effects of central banks in the global economy, the politics of the central bank appointment process, or the individual career aspirations of central bankers themselves, much less attention has been paid to the political roles of the MPC and its effect on public communications. While the economics discipline has, to a large extent, generated many, if not most, of the important models of monetary policy making on committees reviewed in the next chapter, often missing from these models is the understanding that policy announcements by the central bank represent the transmission of public communications by political actors, which result from policy bargaining between actors with different policy preferences. An important omission in the previous literature, therefore, and one that I focus on throughout this book, is that rather than being dispassionate experts, MPC members are strategic actors with policy preferences and natural allies and foes, and that alliances (or their lack) help explain the content of public communications by the MPC. My aim, therefore, is to present a new political economy explanation of central bank communication, one that uncovers some important regularities in central bank decision-making on committees and that is currently unaccounted for in the literature.

The main argument is that differences in the composition of committee members' preferences, such as whether everyone in the room wants the same outcome or different outcomes, help predict the level of vagueness in the official monetary policy announcements. For the moment, I define *vagueness* as whether the statement produces some level of uncertainty about the conjectures, factuality of information, or uncertainty about likely outcomes. As a second step, I argue that changes in vagueness have real consequences for the economy. Namely, I argue that increases in policy vagueness make it harder for central banks to manage households' inflation expectations and, consequently, for policy makers to command the economy in ways that they intend.

Central bank communications vary in their level of vagueness both across countries and over time. According to the argument that I advance, variation that we observe in vagueness contained in central bank communications is determined by the composition of members' bargaining over policy communication. In addition to members' interests, I also argue that committee rules, and especially who gets to vote as well as the key roles played by the committee chair and the median committee member, matter for communicated vagueness. One key hypothesis is that central bank committees with more diverse policy preferences, or *opposing biases*, communicate more precisely than homogeneous central bank committees, or those with *alike biases*. Theoretically, this is because committee members with opposing biases have greater incentive to enact internal checks and balances against those members on the committee who hold different views. Alternatively, those committees with more homogeneity face fewer internal checks. In other words, more homogeneous committees have greater room to communicate opaquely for their own benefit—what I call *strategic vagueness*. Consequently, when committee members have similar preferences, or have alike biases, members have less incentive to constrain their fellow committee members, because they prefer similar outcomes and are therefore more likely to support the strategic use of vagueness when other, similar members support it.

By highlighting how committees fluctuate in their incentives for internal self-monitoring, my argument is different from previous explanations of monetary policy making on MPCs. Previous arguments mainly focus on the benefits of committee decision-making for information sharing, processing, and policy stability (Blinder et al., 2008; Gerlach-Kristen, 2006, 2008; Sibert, 2009). While some recent studies have looked at the effects of heterogeneity on interest rate setting (Riboni and Ruge-Murcia, 2010, 2008), I make a novel contribution to the literature by highlighting how, under some conditions, but not all, internal bargaining leads to greater central bank transparency.

My argument is that diverse committees more easily provide self-reinforcing mechanisms of oversight and horizontal accountability, whereas more homogeneous committees have greater difficulty in providing these things, and that the presence of self-disciplining mechanisms (or a lack there of) influences the degree of vagueness in public information dissemination. Furthermore, if more precise public information offers a better tool to guide the future economy in directions that policy makers intend, then committee composition matters for economic performance. Such a proposition, that a diverse and heterogeneous MPC distributes better information and yields self-enforcing mechanisms of oversight and transparency as well as better macroeconomic performance, places my argument in the literature on institutional design and political economy. Furthermore, my argument brings to the fore the politics of central bank decision-making among actors with real policy motivations and strategies to achieve them, yet who are also constrained by the institutions in which they work. Such an approach is different from previous research that depicts the central bank as solving credible-commitment problems, as a representative agent of political appointments, or as comprising self-interested bureaucrats (see, e.g., Adolph, 2013; Alesina, Roubini, and Cohen, 1997; Barro and Gordon, 1983; Chang, 2003; Kydland and Prescott, 1977; Rogoff, 1985). While all of these theories go a long way toward helping us understand central bankers, they offer little insight into how public information is produced, nor do they predict its content. Instead, I suggest that something as routine as intercommittee politics among a group of anywhere from two to twenty-one actors is one possible explanation for why we observe variation in central bank communication styles across countries as well as differences in macroeconomic performance in these same countries over time.

In addition to contributing a new approach in studying central banking, the manuscript speaks to a larger literature on transparency and accountability. Delegating policy-making responsibility to any committee or subcommittee, whether comprising election observers, legislatures, courts, or central banks, may result in accountability problems, where the agent may not do exactly what the principal wants. If the principal is concerned with monitoring the agent, according to my model, the principal can better his chances of overseeing the agent if he delegates authority to a diverse committee rather than either a single agent or a committee with homogeneous interests. Additionally, appointing more diverse committees rather than packing committees with similarly biased agents not only helps the principal monitor those actors inside the institution but also produces higher-quality public information. Such possible transparency gains from delegating to heterogeneous committees has, to my knowledge, henceforth been ignored, both theoretically and empirically.

Another contribution of this book is that I show how consensual public speechmaking is a product of monetary policy making in an institutional setting. This is in direct contrast to research arguing that central bankers share the same preferences and that these preferences result from membership in an epistemic community, their mandated policy objectives, or learning and persuasion (Helleiner, 1994, 2014; Kaplan, 2013; Meseguer, 2010). According to my argument, central bankers do not want the same policy outcomes; rather, they want different things. Instead, it is the institutional environment in which they work, and in particular, the committee structure in which they negotiate policy, that drives them toward consensus.

In summary, I show how diverse committees generate two previously unknown types of political "goods" in addition to one economic "good," and by "goods," I mean a good or service that has utility to society. First, diverse committees generate an internal, self-reinforcing mechanism that leads to greater transparency and less distortion in central bank information. One prediction from this is that in societies with heterogeneous central bank committees, public information quality is expected to be higher. Second, higher information quality makes it easier for the government to monitor the central bank. This means that the ability for the central bank to shirk its responsibility to its principal, usually thought to be the government, is lower. Thus another prediction is that the government's monitoring costs of the central bank will vary with the level of diversity on the MPC. This latter prediction is especially important, as central bankers are unelected officials, insulated from direct political control, and are therefore not directly accountable. One way that governments can make central banks more accountable, therefore, is to ensure that members on the MPC are diverse. Third, I also predict that higher information quality narrows the public's economic expectations closer around the truth, which leads to better macroeconomic performance. This means that the ability for the central bank to conduct effective monetary policy is enhanced when the central bank committee is more diverse. These three assertions highlight how the composition of the MPC can influence a wide set of political and economic outcomes, including transparency, accountability, and economic performance.

Taken together, I present evidence that central bank information varies due to differences in the institutions in which central bankers work. In chapters 2, 3, and 4, I show how not all central bank committees are alike; some committees can more easily negotiate precise information, while other committees have a harder time doing so. I show how those committees that have members with diverse preferences and opinions are more likely to speak clearly, whereas those committees with greater homogeneity are more likely to communicate with greater vagueness. In chapters 5, and 6, I show how variation in communicated precision changes household and market expectations about the future economy. I also show how information flows shape household inflation expectations and inflation outcomes, and my focus is on inflation, as central bankers' control of inflation is at the heart of what central bankers do.

As a result of these findings, I also predict what type of central bank committees are more likely to produce more precise information and, as a result, can transmit more precise information to the public, resulting in a better informed public. I derive propositions for optimal central bank design from a model that starts with individual actors with known preferences and self-interest in policy outcomes. I show how, when these self-interested actors bargain for policy outcomes in a political space with adversaries and allies, the information that they transmit to the public will vary in precision. This, then, provides some explanation for why information precision varies across different central banks despite similar levels of central bank independence and mandated objectives.

I test my theory with measures from primary textual reports – central bank committee meetings and official press releases. I use contemporary data science techniques from machine learning and computational social science to extract and construct new measures of central bank preferences and that capture the precision and vagueness of central bank pronouncements. In addition to developing these new measures from text, I also present evidence from an experimental survey, which shows that variation in information precision changes the public's expectations of the future economy. The approach—from collecting and analyzing thousands of textual documents to using survey experiments on real people to gauge how they change their expectations when confronted with central bank pronouncements–suggests that central bank information varies due to institutional differences and that variation in communicated precision helps explain differences in inflation and expectations thereof.

1.5 What Comes Next?

The next chapter outlines previous explanations for the role of central bank committee decision-making and contrasts these explanations to the approach here. In summary, previous models have generally focused on the benefits of committee decision-making from the perspective of information aggregation, information processing, and providing insurance (Blinder and Morgan, 2005; Maier, 2010). Complementary to these models, my approach argues that some types of committees offer additional political benefits of public accountability and greater transparency. I then relate this finding to broader debates in political science about principal agent models, delegation, and institutional design. I also review the influence of information on the economy and present possible alternatives and competing hypotheses.

In chapter 3, I introduce a simple theoretical model of how central bank messages are bargained over in the committees where central bank policies are made. I pay particular attention to the committee chair and the median committee member and assume that each of these two actors wants to get as close to his or her preferred policy outcome as possible. I show how different underlying preferences cause each central banker to pursue a strategic outcome that is different from the strategy he or she would pursue if the central banker worked alone. I highlight the factors that affect the precision of information released to the mass public: the preference heterogeneity of the median members relative to the preferences of the committee chair. Using this theory, I present expected relationships derived from the theoretical model, and I transform these expected relationships into testable implications that are useful for distinguishing supportive and contradictory evidence.

The remaining empirical chapters offer such tests. Chapter 4 tests the hypothesis that variation in central bank preferences leads to variation in information precision. I offer statistical analyses using textual data from the FOMC and estimates of committee member preferences based on how much members emphasize inflation during the committee meetings. To determine information precision, I measure how clear or vague the FOMC's public statement is over the same period. I then evaluate whether differences in central bankers' preferences help explain differences in the precision of information presented in the statements. I also evaluate whether differences in members' preferences are associated with the number of changes to policy statement. I also examine whether or not being on schedule to vote officially in the roll-call matters.

To ensure that the causal mechanism is correctly specified, chapter 5 presents evidence from a survey experiment administered to German households. In this survey experiment, I vary the level of information precision presented to survey respondents to see whether their inflation expectations are altered in a significant way. As suggested by the theory, I find that more precise information causes better-anchored (to the ECB's target) household inflation expectations and lowers the variance around these expectations.

Building on the evidence provided in the previous chapters, and to ensure that the theory travels across space and time, in chapter 6 I present more evidence that information precision helps attenuate inflation expectations and lowers inflation, only this time using a sample of six Latin American countries from 1993 to 2010. The importance of this particular sample of countries is that these countries and years demonstrate much larger variation in inflation outcomes and therefore help test the generalizability of the research findings. Using a new measure of information precision from Reuters news articles, I find evidence that an increase in the preciseness of the information environment lowers inflation expectations and reduces inflation in this sample. Moreover, I find that this relationship holds even when I account for alternative explanations such as the level of a country's monetary policy credibility.

The concluding chapter returns to the broad themes of delegation, institutional design, and macroeconomic performance. Common wisdom is that central bank independence solves the time-inconsistent problem of monetary policy. In this view, central bank independence means that an optimal central bank design is one that is independent from the government. Shifting the attention to the MPC and relaxing the unitary actor assumption, I find that committee design matters for central bank transparency and effective oversight of the central bank: a more diverse set of committee members provides better information to the mass public, which has beneficial outcomes for the economy while simultaneously allowing for better monitoring of the central bank by the government. In summary, this book brings to the forefront the role of central bank committees as political institutions, staffed by members with preferences and interests who behave strategically and are motivated to convince the public to act in ways they desire. The evidence suggests that committee composition is important for explaining transparency and governance. As central banks increasingly depend on communication to help guide the economy, it is vital that we better understand how the rules and decision-making structures of the institutions where they work shape how and why they can communicate and when they are constrained. Furthermore, as central banks have expanded their mandates and policy-making toolkits, it is important that we better understand those factors that work to guarantee checks and balances.

2

Monetary Policy Committees and Central Bank Communication

2.1 Introduction

This chapter provides a short review of the literature on central bank committees and central bank communication to situate my argument within the context of previous research. Theorizing about central bank decision-making and central bank communication policy is a relatively new area of research. In this chapter, I organize previous research into two topics. The first topic considers how differences in institutional design matter for central bank decision-making. In particular, I review theories of and empirical evidence on the roles of committee size, composition, and decision-making rules. I also provide descriptive statistics about how central banks around the globe vary across these features. The second topic focuses on central bank communication: I examine previous arguments estimating the impact of central bank communication policy on market and private-sector expectations and on macroeconomic outcomes. I also highlight observable changes in central bank communication over the last twenty years.

As shown in Figures 2.1 and 2.3, some of the world's most powerful central banks, such as the Federal Reserve and the Bank of Japan, have taken numerous steps toward improving their public communications and transparency over the last twenty years. We can observe three trends in changes to central bank transparency. First, an increase in transparency likely changed voting behavior on MPCs. Starting in March 1993, the FOMC began publicly releasing minutes of policy meetings, and in November of the same year, it began releasing full transcripts. Meade and Stasavage (2008) show how the publication of the meeting minutes made it less easy for members to dissent, and

Crafting Consensus: Why Central Bankers Change Their Speech and How Speech Changes the Economy. Nicole Rae Baerg, Oxford University Press (2020). © Oxford University Press.
DOI: 10.1093/oso/9780190499488.001.0001

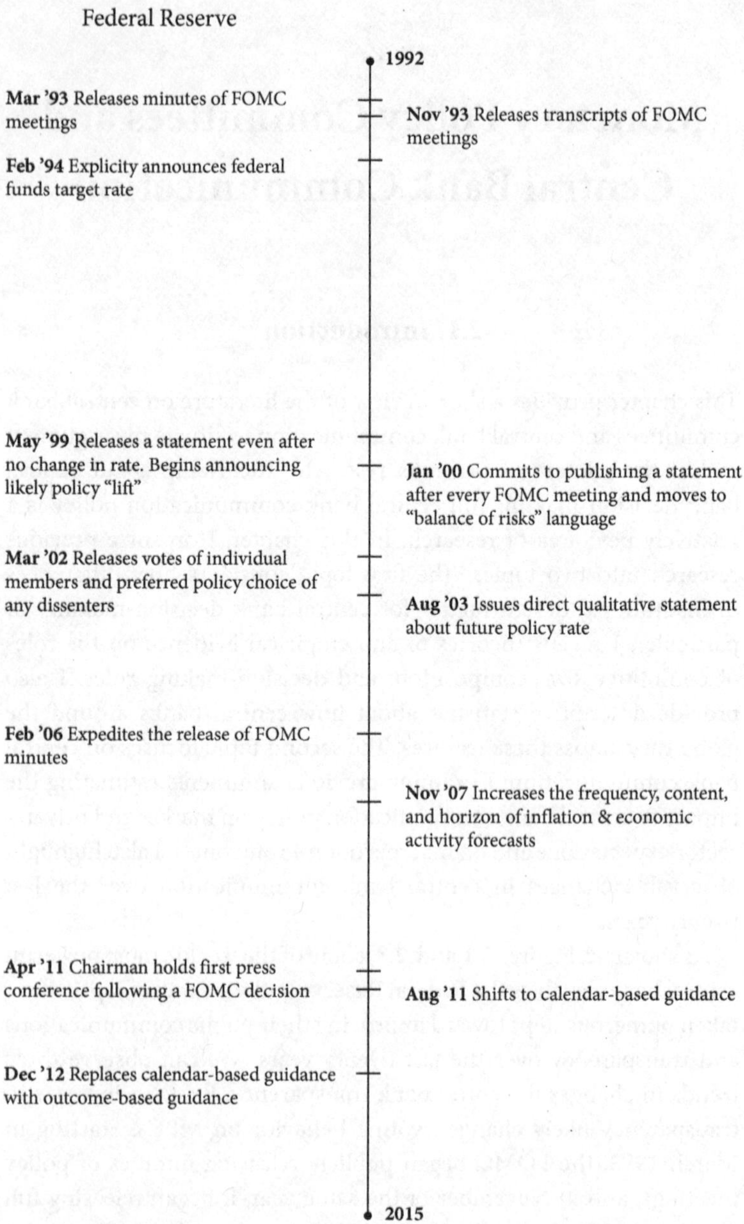

Fig. 2.1 Policy changes in central bank communications and transparency from 1993 to 2015 for the US Federal Reserve.

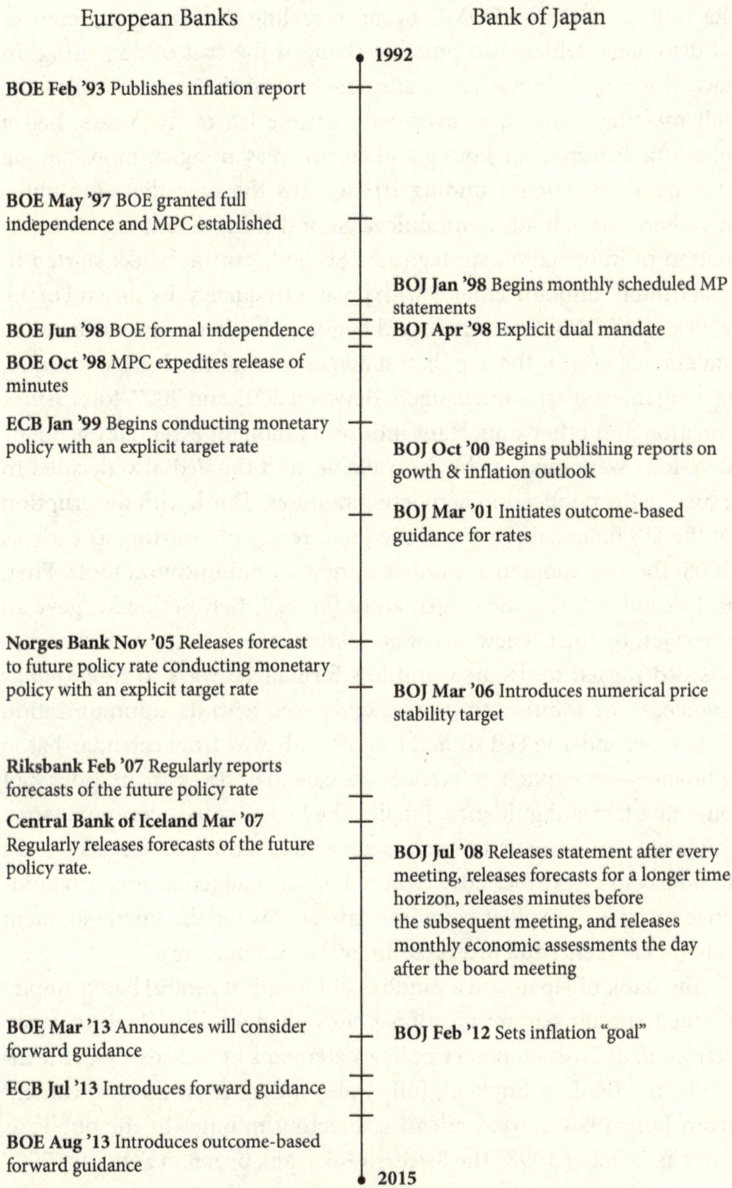

Fig. 2.2 Policy changes in central bank communications and transparency from 1993 to 2015 for a subsection of other national and supranational central banks, including the Bank of England (BOE), the European Central Bank (ECB), and the Bank of Japan (BOJ).

starting in 2002, the FOMC began revealing the voting preferences of dissenters, which also possibly changed the cost of dissenting. In fact, this study shows how transparency and the publication of the full meeting transcripts, even with a time lag of five years, had a measurable impact on voting and voicing dissenting opinions among the members. Such a finding strengthens the case that committee members care about communication and think about the dissemination of information strategically. Second, central banks started to make public announcements with greater frequency. By the end of the 2000s, the FOMC committee had begun publicly to announce policy statements even if those policy statements confirmed the status quo, leaving interest rates unchanged. Between 2003 and 2007, forecasts of inflation and other important indicators thought essential for policy decisions were made publicly available, and the Fed also decided to expedite the publication of meeting minutes. Third, with the eruption of the US financial crisis and the great recession, starting as early as 2008, the Fed adopted a number of new communication tools. First, in December 2010, the chairman of the Fed, Ben Bernanke, gave an interview on the US news show *60 Minutes*; this is noteworthy because the Fed started to use new and less formalized ways to reach *public audiences*, in addition to *market audiences*, with its communication policy. Second, the Fed shifted toward and away from calendar-based guidance—or explicit references to calendar dates in its policy of pursuing forward guidance. Finally, the Fed adopted economic target guidance—or explicit references to actual economic targets—most famously in December 2012, when the Fed changed its forward guidance to refer to explicit economic thresholds for the unemployment rate (6.5 percent) and projected inflation (2.5 percent).

The Bank of Japan and a number of European central banks implemented similar communication policy changes. The Bank of Japan started to publish monetary policy statements as early as 1998. Meanwhile, the Bank of England, fully independent from the government from June 1998, started releasing meeting minutes to the public as early as October 1998. The Swedish Riksbank began in February 2007 to report forecasts of the expected policy path of interest rates, and the Bank of Ireland followed suit the next month. In March 2006, the Bank of Japan used economic target guidance by publishing a numerical price stability target. Finally, as late as May 2013, the ECB introduced forward guidance as a policy instrument, a year after Mario Draghi, head of the ECB, announced, "Within our mandate, the ECB is ready to do whatever it takes to preserve the euro. And believe me, it will be enough."[1]

We observe similar patterns when we look at changes in central bank transparency in emerging and frontier (less advanced) markets. Figure 2.3 demonstrates changes in central bank transparency for these types of economies using an index of transparency by Dincer and Eichengreen (2014). The country categories are from the Dow Jones and are classified according to capital restrictions and foreign direct investment (FDI) access. Developed markets are the most accessible and supportive of foreign investors; emerging markets have generally less accessibility but demonstrate some openness; and frontier markets exhibit notable limitations in their regulatory and operational environments and support much smaller levels of investment.[2]

As the plot in Figure 2.3 illustrates, central bank transparency has increased quite rapidly over the last fifteen years and across all three country groupings. Furthermore, emerging markets are adopting greater central bank transparency at a rate similar to developed markets. Despite similar adoption rates, however, emerging markets continue to have lower average levels of transparency when compared against their developed-country counterparts. One striking feature is the rate of central bank transparency policy adoption by the frontier markets. The Dow Jones category for frontier includes relatively advanced countries, such as Argentina, Latvia, and Jordan, as well as others. Frontier countries increased their average level of central bank transparency to 5 (on a scale of 0 to 15), or about half as much as for developed markets; however, the adoption levels peaked in 2006 and stabilized thereafter.

On a pessimistic note, despite the march toward greater transparency, as seen in the previous chapter, communication disasters can and do occur. The fact that political communications demonstrate both risks and rewards to policy makers and the economy highlights

[1] Whatever It Takes.

[2] Dow's Country Classification, July 26, 2012.

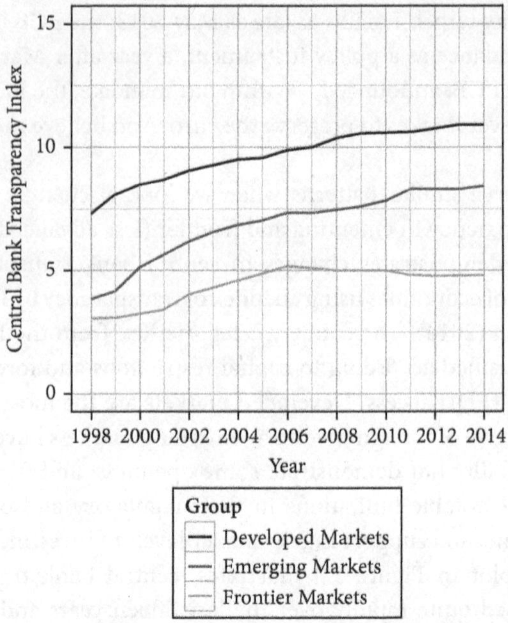

Fig. 2.3 Changes in central bank transparency from 1998 to 2014 for select countries around the world by level of market development.

the tough choices that committee members must make. Do MPC members say nothing at all and risk market incomprehension, or do they say too much, communicate unskillfully, and ultimately risk market overreaction?

Interestingly, previous studies have often focused on the things that those at the helm of the central bank—its chairperson, say. However, the official policy communication strategy adopted by central banks results from political deliberations among committee members. In other words, it is the committee members' collective decision over the policy statement that matters. In the case of the FOMC, for example, committee members deliberate specifically about the official policy statement and then vote on both changes to the federal funds rate and changes to the policy statement. Because of this deliberative process, it is important to examine those institutional features that enhance and constrain how policy makers choose information and ultimately, the type of information they decide to transmit. The next section examines variation in the composition and design of central banks around the world, pointing to theories and evidence of how variation in central bank design is related to differences in MPC communication strategies.

2.2 Central Bank Committees and Institutional Design

How central bank committees are designed matters for how they work and for the kinds of outputs they produce. Because decision-making in MPCs is increasingly the norm, it is essential that we understand the benefits, costs, and trade-offs that may result from variations in MPC design features. In what follows, I review previous theoretical and empirical research, taking a closer look at the effects of MPC size, composition, and decision-making protocols.

2.2.1 Committee Size

Much of the previous literature argues that it is better to have more than one person making monetary policy because more people will bring to the table a richer set of information (Blinder, 2007). If multiple policy makers have varying theoretical models of how the economy works or, alternatively, different information about the economy, pooling information across a larger number of individuals will lead to better (less biased) forecasts of the future economy. As central bankers are expected to predict future movements in macroeconomic variables, better estimates of the future are indispensable.[3] Relatedly, if, as in the case of the Fed's FOMC, nineteen committee members and their army of staff generate different estimates of future macroeconomic

[3] This logic is similar to the idea of "pooling the polls" in forecast models common in political science, such as in election forecasting. Pooling information from a variety of different election polls provides less biased and more accurate estimates than any one poll alone (Jackman, 2005; Linzer, 2013).

outcomes using different data and wide theoretical approaches, a larger set of forecasts will yield more reliable estimates of the economy. Thus, from the perspective of information aggregation, delegating monetary policy to a committee is likely to produce higher-quality information and, consequently, more informed decision-making.

Scholars have tested this argument a number of ways using both experimental and observational methods. Two early and important experiments by Blinder and Morgan (2005) and Lombardelli, Proudman, and Talbot (2005) confirm that policy making by committees outperforms individual decision-making. Observational research by Aksoy, De Grauwe, and Dewachter (2002) also finds that policy makers indeed bring different data sources and methods of analysis to committee meetings, which enriches available information. Furthermore, staff members in research departments across different regional banks collect microlevel information about their local economies, passing this along in committee meetings (Chappell, McGregor, and Vermilyea, 2008). Such evidence, while limited to the US case, lends some support to the idea that group decision-making is likely to provide a more accurate picture of both national and local economic conditions.

In addition to differences in modeling strategies or data inputs, committee members may vary in their capabilities. This implies that some committee members are better "skilled" than others either in their efforts or their expertise. One article by Gerlach-Kristen (2006) finds that larger committees will lead to smaller decision errors when committee members have different skills. Alternatively, however, research by Gersbach and Hahn (2008) finds that transparency in decision-making may motivate lower-aptitude committee members to vote alongside those of higher ability, causing policy overcoordination. Using a formal theoretical model, Sibert (2003) shows that when policy makers apply different levels of effort, monetary policy committees produce more stable-over-time inflation rates and higher expected welfare. In summary, like information, skill heterogeneity may be good for MPCs, with the one caveat that when roll-call votes are made public, policy making may end up too consensual.

The previous findings have a limitation, though: they assume that members always behave cooperatively rather than competitively. Sibert (2006) relaxes this assumption and finds that when policy makers have a strategic incentive to raise their own individual profiles on the committee, committees comprising members with differing abilities may in fact generate suboptimal outcomes. Relatedly, committees with competitive members may be more likely to discount alternative explanations and hypotheses, engendering more consensus-prone decision-making and free-riding problems as well as jockeying for prestige (Sibert, 2006).

In sum, theoretical and empirical claims for what constitutes optimal MPC size are mixed. Theoretically, understanding what constitutes optimal MPC size is made more difficult if we consider the possibility for strategic behavior among members. On one hand, larger committees may be better at collecting and aggregating information, yet, on the other hand, too large a committee, or committees that incentivize competition, may generate extreme decision-making and reduce policy debate. These findings warn that despite the possible benefits of greater information, committees can produce both negative and positive outcomes.

What do we see when we look at the data? Empirically, we observe significant variation in central bank committee size across countries. The central bank governor of New Zealand, for example, was the sole official decision maker until 2019, whereas in the ECB system, voting is conducted by the six members of the executive board, plus the governors of the national central banks of the nineteen euro area countries. Using survey data collected by Erhart and Vasquez-Paz (2007), Figure 2.4 shows the distribution of MPC size for a sample of central banks around the world.[4] Size varies significantly, ranging from one to twenty-one members (former ECB), with a median of seven members. Furthermore, the right-skewness in the distribution also implies that many central banks have well above the five "optimal" number of members as suggested by Sibert (2006). Despite across-

[4] Note that the data collected is from before the ECB expanded its size.

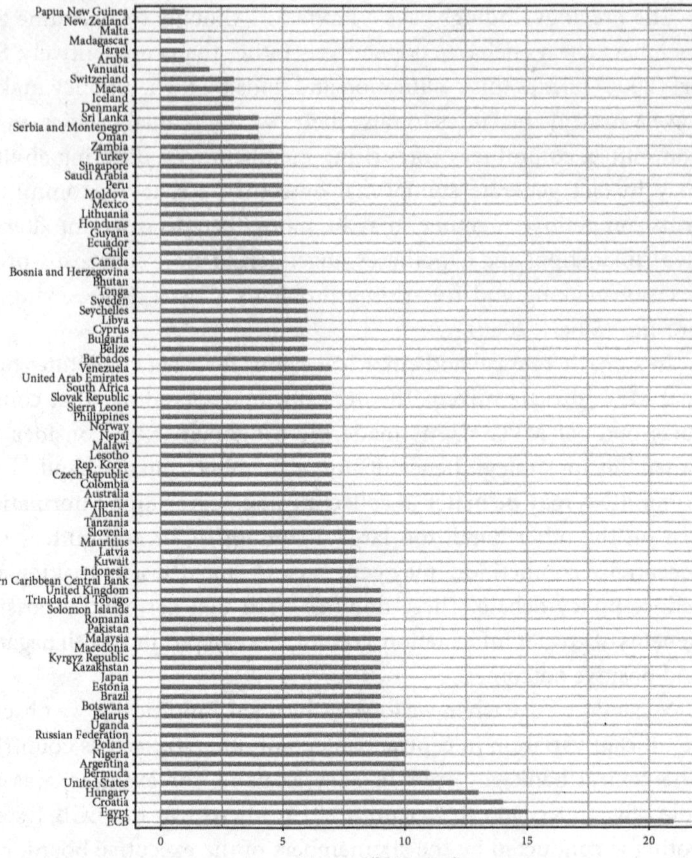

Fig. 2.4 De facto MPC size.

country variation in MPC size, we have few theoretical explanations that help us understand why, nor do we have theory that evaluates the economic and governance consequences that may (or may not) result from such wide differences in committee size. One possible area of future research, therefore, would be to offer an explanation for the origins of variation in MPC size. Other possible future research might link the size and diversity of the MPC with political and economic outputs that we are interested in such as central bank independence, central bank transparency, and governance and accountability.

2.2.2 Committee Composition

In addition to committee size, the composition of central bankers sitting on the committee matters. Researchers have examined a number of individual characteristics, including gender, vocational and education background, length of tenure, and political versus technocratic motivations. Further to individual-level explanations, the literature has examined differences in representation and constituencies, such as the size of a district or the economic preferences of the public in that district. Third, the appointment process also matters. In some central banks, such as the Fed, only a proportion of members are appointed directly by the government, whereas other members are elected by their district banks. Thus the appointment mechanism itself may play a role in casting who represents whom. Finally, one convenient way to group central bankers is by policy preferences or ideal points. By comparing members based on how much inflation aversion they have, researchers are able to locate committee members' positions on a single common dimension and evaluate how their policy positions and preferences change over time.

Committee size is expected to improve decision-making because of benefits associated with information gathering. Alternatively, heterogeneity on a committee provides benefits because individuals are more likely to adopt different decision-making *heuristics*, or ways in coming to a solution, which leads to better information processing. As discussed earlier, one possible cost associated with multiple strategic actors on central bank committees is that competitive behavior among members may lead to groupthink or the discounting of alternative explanations. This is especially so if members solve problems using the same approach. As a way to combat this, diverse membership can lead to a greater set of experiences and insure against consensus opinion. Furthermore, and as I will show in the next chapter, in a strategic model of communication, diverse committees are more likely to engage in intercommittee disciplining than homogeneous committees. Thus an additional by-product of committee diversity is greater monitoring and accountability.

Similar to understanding committee size, not much political economy research has examined central bank performance and ascriptive diversity, such as gender diversity, on central bank boards, with the exception of recent research by Bodea (2017). Much of the observational evidence for the effects of gender diversity and decision-making thus comes from studies on board diversity in corporate finance. Recently, Dhir (2015) interviewed corporate board directors in Norway to explore whether gender quotas on corporate board membership matter. These authors find that heterogeneity brought about by gender quotas enhanced the quality of boardroom deliberations and overall corporate governance in Norway. In an early study on group decision-making behaviors, Hong and Page (2004) find in laboratory experiments that a diverse set of individuals is much more likely to use different problem-solving techniques, leading them to outperform more homogeneous groups that get stuck at earlier stages in the problem.

Better studied than gender is the effect of occupational diversity in training. In his survey of central banks, Maier (2010) finds that some central banks have committees staffed primarily by those with finance, economics, and central bank backgrounds, whereas other committees have more diverse memberships and include politically appointed governors, academics, members from the business community, and parliamentary ministers. Recently, scholars have emphasized the role of central bankers as bureaucrats trying to advance their own careers. In an important book that explains China's remarkable inflation stability, Shih (2008) shows how self-interested technocrats use economic crises as an opportunity to push for the centralization of monetary policy into their own hands so as to expand their powers. Similarly, Adolph (2013) finds that "shadow principals" can induce central bank behavior through the promise of career advancements, especially for those interested in advancing their careers in the private sector. Thus the likelihood of regulatory capture of the central bank is related to who manages to sit on the MPCs, with mandated board diversity being one possible way to protect against such capture.

Figure 2.5 shows a subsample of vocational backgrounds of central bank committee members for those central banks that have diversity on their committees. The data are from 2010. As we can observe, central bankers clearly make up the largest proportion of committee members, followed by members from the business world and

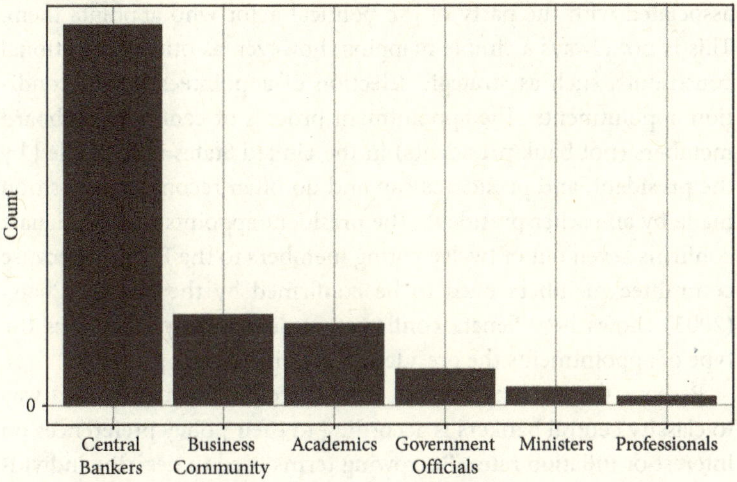

Fig. 2.5 MPC composition for diverse central banks.

academics. Despite these advancements, however, very little research has explored the role of diversity on central bank boards, nor have researchers linked diversity on MPCs with macroeconomic performance. This is another possible area for future research.

Because in some countries central bankers represent geographical districts and communities, the literature also examines constituency effects. Meade and Sheets (2005) and Chappell, McGregor, and Vermilyea (2008) find that Fed policy makers take into account both national and regional developments when casting votes on monetary policy. Similarly, in his study of Organisation for Economic Co-operation and Development (OECD) countries, Scheve (2004) finds that central banks reflect the public's preferences. Other literature, however, finds that the willingness to dissent to policy may not apply equally to all geographical areas. In her paper on district size, Meade (2010) finds that larger Federal Reserve districts are more likely to consent during roll-call votes. Importantly, this finding counters arguments about distance and separate staffs and budgets helping to generate positive competition over ideas and policy proposals (Goodfriend, 1999).

Another way that researchers have explored central bank preferences is by predicting that central banker behaviors will be positively associated with the party of the political actor who appoints them. This is not always a simple mapping, however, as other institutional constraints, such as strategic selection of appointees, might condition appointments. The appointment process of central bank board members (not bank presidents) in the United States is controlled by the president, and presidents can and do often reconfirm a position made by an earlier president. The president appoints and the Senate confirms seven out of twelve voting members to the FOMC. Because committee members need to be confirmed by the Senate, Chang (2003) shows how Senate confirmation strategically influences the type of appointments the president makes in the first place.

Perhaps the most convenient (and therefore most common) way to classify central bankers is according to their policy preferences on interest or inflation rates. Borrowing terms used to describe individuals' appetites for war, central bankers who worry about inflation risks more than output risks are called *hawks*, whereas central bankers who worry less about inflation risks and more about unemployment and output risks are called *doves*. Ranking individual central bank committee members according to their preferences along a single common dimension—"how much do I care about inflation risks relative to output and unemployment risks?"—is important, as it allows researchers to compare preferences across actors and over time on a stable, unidimensional policy space. While these preferences are unobserved, researchers have used the way that committee members vote and the things that members say in meetings as a way to appraise individual-level preferences (Adolph, 2013; Baerg and Lowe, 2018; Chang, 2003; Chappell, Havrilesky, and Roy McGregor, 2000; Gerlach-Kristen, Meade, et al., 2010; Hix, Høyland, and Vivyan, 2010).

Also important is that differences in inflation aversion are thought to map nicely onto programmatic left and right party positions, especially in Western democracies. Central bankers thought to be tough on inflation are thought to be right-leaning in their partisanship.

2.2.3 Decision-Making Protocol

Last, the voting procedure or decision-making protocol that aggregates members' preferences also matters. Like size and composition, the threshold for committees to reach de facto agreement varies significantly across countries.[5] For example, the FOMC has twelve voting members, seven of whom are members of the Board of Governors and hold permanent voting rights. The president of the New York Fed has a permanent voting right, the presidents of the Federal Reserve Banks of Chicago and Cleveland vote every other year, and the presidents of the other nine Federal Reserve Districts vote every third year. Decision-making requires a simple majority to pass, but official dissent on the FOMC is restricted to a relatively small subsection of votes and members (see, e.g., Baerg and Lowe, 2018; Thornton and Wheelock, 2014).

Similar to the FOMC system, the Governing Council of the ECB makes decisions as a committee, consisting of six executive board members and nineteen representatives of national central banks that share the euro as their common currency. With the introduction of Lithuania into the Eurozone in 2015, the European Governing Council moved from a one-member, one-vote system to a system in which national members vote in rotation, modeled after the Federal Reserve. Unlike the Fed's yearly rotation, the voting rights for the members of the ECB's Governing Council rotate every month, for a total voting block of the six members of the Executive Board, plus the governors of the national central banks of the nineteen euro area countries.

Figure 2.6 shows country variation in the number of votes needed for a central bank to reach a quorum. Rules here also vary, ranging from the governor casting the only and deciding vote (New Zealand) to consensus voting (Swiss National Banks) to two-thirds majority voting (ECB). In one study, Riboni and Ruge-Murcia (2010) consider differences across voting rules, including supermajority, chair agenda setting, single decision makers, and majority rule. These authors find that MPCs that follow either two-thirds majority or agenda-setting rules are associated with smaller changes in the policy rate, that is, more moderate policies, than MPCs with simple-majority rules.

The authors then empirically test this prediction using a sample of five countries and estimating inflation and output functions. Importantly, irrespective of the de jure decision rule, de facto, most

[5] I distinguish between de facto and de jure agreement because often decisions are made by supermajority or consensus, despite different official rules.

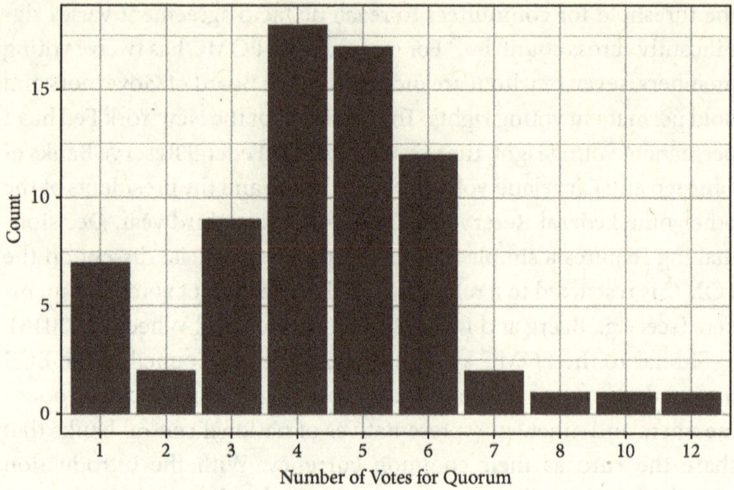

Fig. 2.6 MPC decision-making.

of the time, central bank committees make decisions by consensus opinion. This is because public consensus outcomes are at least partly determined by actors' desire to minimize apparent differences to quell any uncertainty and stabilize market expectations (Rosa and Verga, 2007; Woodford, 2005). Similarly, members' willingness to cooperate often depends on group hierarchy, and especially on whether the committee chairperson will allow for public dissent in the first place (Crawford and Haller, 1990; Shapiro and Varian, 2013).

In summary, previous research on MPCs helps us understand the possible benefits, and costs, of deciding monetary policy on a committee. Some of the known benefits include greater information retrieval, diversity in processing information, representation of geographical districts and nations, partisan positions, moderation in policy making, and consensus decision-making. MPCs can also have negative effects, however. Some of the costs uncovered by previous literature include more extreme policy making, gridlock, competitive jockeying, free riding, and groupthink.

A significant drawback of the previous literature is that, with few exceptions, most abstracts from any possible strategic behavior among committee members, nor are members usually depicted as invested in their own career trajectories, which we know from previous literature exerts a significant effect (Adolph, 2013). This is especially problematic because the literature also shows that central bankers express different preferences about monetary policy, which can then lead to within-committee coalition politics. For example, if central bankers have different policy goals, whether based on career or constituency motivations, and if members select themselves into subgroups, such as "hawks" and "doves," then committee members may engage in strategic behavior that can, under certain conditions, negate some of the advantages of committee decision-making highlighted earlier. On the other hand, competitive behavior may also lead to greater internal checks and balances, inducing self-reinforcing behaviors of monitoring and disciplining. The next chapter offers a formal theoretical model that helps us tease out those conditions that make intercommittee competition useful in inducing greater transparency and accountability.

2.3 Central Bank Communication

2.3.1 How to Communicate?

A growing body of research also explores the influence of central bank communication on the economy. In an excellent overview of the literature, Blinder and Morgan (2005) outline two main functions of central bank communication: to broadcast news and to reduce noise. Importantly, the news channel and the noise channel work through independent, though overlapping, mechanisms. In the case of the news channel, the central bank broadcasts public pronouncements, and these pronouncements in turn shape expectations about future economic variables. If the news alters individuals' expectations, and if expectations are an essential driver of prices, then changes in expectations can lead to changes in asset prices as well as other measures of the economy. In contrast to the news channel, the noise channel works by changing the predictability of the future, in particular, by making the information environment more reliable and less surprising. An increase in reliability is expected to reduce the variance in individuals' expectations and therefore to reduce the volatility of future outcomes. Like movements in expectations, a reduction in volatility is predicted to be positively associated with improved economic performance.

Results from both empirical and theoretical work on this topic suggest that central bank communication policy is indeed effective at steering the economy (see, e.g., Ehrmann and Fratzscher, 2007, 2009). Yet, some authors remain cautious. Seminal work in economics finds that too much public talk can lead to the crowding out of the private information market (Morris and Shin, 2002). Given a choice between free publicly provided information by the central bank and having to search for and process information from private sources, such as mortgage rates or union contracting, a rational member of the public will gravitate toward public information supplies, substituting private for public sources. In the aggregate, if everyone relies on public information, information diversity will decline, and a reduction in information diversity can have unintended consequences.

A lack of diverse information about the economy is a double-edged sword for central bank communication policy. On one hand, if all or most households coordinate on official information, this makes central bank communication especially effective. On the other hand, the absence of alternative sources of information can cause overcorrelation in market enthusiasm and market skepticism, which can increase volatility, exacerbate panics, and dampen economic recovery (Bloom, 2009). From the development economics literature, we know that overreliance on public information, and corresponding underuse of private information, may lead to herding behavior (Bowles, Durlauf, and Hoff, 2006; Hoff and Stiglitz, 2001; Murphy, Shleifer, and Vishny, 1989; Ray, 1998; Rodriguez-Clare, 1996). Furthermore, too much information can drive market outcomes toward those with unsophisticated rather than sophisticated knowledge about the economy, which again may lead to suboptimal outcomes (Morris and Shin, 2007).

Yet, not only how much central banks talk but also how they talk matters for the economy. For example, during a time of heightened financial turbulence and economic crisis, Brazil's central bank chief, Alexandre Tombini, was cited as "moving away from his typically convoluted, cryptic language of monetary authorities and opting for a new approach: speaking simply" (Soto, 2013). That central bankers shift their strategies toward and away from clarity in their communications raises two important questions. First, what type of central bank news is most effective in shaping expectations of the future economy? Second, do differences in the way that central banks are designed help predict variations in the ways that content is constructed?

To answer these questions, recent research examines different dimensions of communications and statements issued by central banks. Thus far, the literature has considered textual complexity, length, frequency, authorship, sentiment, and the level of surprise in central bank pronouncements. In one paper, Bulíř, Čihák, and Jansen (2014) use the ease or readability of central bank communications to assess whether central bank speech communicated with more simplicity has stronger economic effects. Fracasso, Genberg, and Wyplosz (2003) show that well-written inflation reports are associated with more predictable economic outcomes. Similarly, Jansen (2011) finds that not only the clarity of public statements but also the way that central banks present information to other branches of the government matters for the economy. In examining the Humphrey–Hawkins testimonies in the United States, where the governor of the Federal Reserve has to give a report to members of Congress, Jansen finds that more clearly articulated speeches are associated with lower levels of market volatility.

Perhaps unsurprisingly, as MPCs are increasingly the norm, researchers have also started to examine the effects of institutional design features of the MPC and the quality of central bank communication, most commonly by considering the number of individual bankers speaking and whether group size matters here too. Some have argued that when members on a committee say different things, whether intentionally or unintentionally, confusion can result, leading to a "cacophony of voices" that may have "no voice at all" (Blinder, 2007). Yet, the empirical evidence is mixed; some countries, such as the United States, demonstrate a negative relationship between individual committee members speaking and predictability, whereas other countries, such as the Czech Republic, demonstrate a positive relationship (Ehrmann and Fratzscher, 2007; Rozkrut et al., 2007).

2.3.2 Formal Models of Political Communication

While much of the aforementioned work is empirical, many formal theoretical models of communication can be helpful in thinking about how central bank communication works. Cheap talk models, for example, represent a class of strategic sender–receiver games. In these models, an expert (or experts) disseminates information to a strategic receiver (Crawford and Sobel, 1982; Minozzi, 2011; Stein, 1989). In one paper, Minozzi (2011) organizes previous models according to two dimensions: whether the senders' preferences are known or unknown and whether there are multiple senders or only a single sender (see, e.g., Crawford and Sobel, 1982; Gilligan and Krehbiel, 1987, 1989; Krishna and Morgan, 2001; Minozzi, 2011; Morris and Shin, 2002). In this way, the formal literature mirrors some of the earlier work on MPCs with attention to committee size.

Cheap talk models have some important limitations when it comes to depicting central bank communication, however. One problem is that cheap talk models generally assume that both the receiver and the sender behave strategically with one another. This behavior seems especially unlikely in the case of central bank communication, where the receiver is a representative member of the mass public, likely to be relatively uninformed about how to engage strategically with the central bank. Moreover, as understanding complex monetary policy decisions is difficult, the public is likely to apply simple heuristics rather than complex decision strategies and inference techniques in the wake of central bank news.[6] Another benefit of nonstrategic receivers is that they can account for several important features of central bank communication. Such features include the possibility that the sender exaggerates, the receiver remains skeptical despite truth-telling, and messages cluster (see, e.g., Chen, 2011).

[6] For the receiver to behave strategically, she must think that her actions are consequential for the sender (formally, enter into the utility function of the sender). While the sender is likely to consider individuals' actions, it is less clear why any one individual would think of his own actions as pivotal. A much more realistic assumption, therefore, is to have senders acting as strategic players, whereas the receiver is assumed to be naively unaware of the senders' incentives.

Another and perhaps more serious problem is that in multisender cheap talk models, experts compete with one another in terms of the messages that they send. In the case of Krishna and Morgan (2001), for example, two experts compete to have their expert advice adopted by a less informed principal. Alternatively, in central bank MPCs, multiple experts coordinate their message and bargain over the text prior to the public announcement. In other words, committee members bargain over the text and then send a coordinated rather than competitive message. Thus, at least for the depiction of understanding official proclamations by MPCs, game-theoretic models that allow experts to coordinate their actions before sending public messages are likely better depictions of how communication policy is crafted. Despite these criticisms, research interested in how individual central bankers communication outside of formal committee meetings may find the cheap talk literature particularly useful. In the next chapter, I present a simple spatial bargaining model based on Romer and Rosenthal (1978) to predict variation in central bank communication.

2.3.3 Communication and Expectations

Finally, there is also a burgeoning literature on the role of information and inflation expectations and the impact that such a relationship has on macroeconomic outcomes. The current literature assumes that central banks, or other government agencies, provide economic information to the mass public to reduce information imperfections and asymmetries. In a world with perfectly integrated and competitive markets, prices should give consumers sufficient information about past and contemporary prices. Empirically, however, we find that public information about the economy and privately held beliefs are often inconsistent. Overcoming this information gap is one way that central bank information coordinates public expectations; coordination can strengthen the economy and steer it away from suboptimal equilibrium outcomes (Carrillo and Shahe Emran, 2012).

But how much do households actually use public as opposed to private information in formulating their beliefs? To answer this question, Carrillo and Shahe Emran (2012) leveraged a unique natural experiment in Ecuador. Over the course of fifteen months, the national statistics agency in Ecuador published erroneous inflation statistics as a result of a glitch in its computer software. Using survey data on household inflation expectations, the authors then tested whether households' expectations were formed based on the publicly available (but incorrect) information about past inflation rather than on the prices that households encountered daily on local markets. The study found that households did indeed base their aggregate inflation expectations more on the public information, even though it was incorrect. This is corroborated by evidence in Armantier et al. (2016). Using a survey experiment, these authors found that people indeed incorporate new information into their inflation expectations and that by doing so, their estimates of future inflation show less variance.

In addition to understanding whether public information matters for inflation expectations, researchers study who public information affects the most. Interestingly, not everyone responds to information in the same way. Armantier et al. (2016) found furthermore that the impact of public information is stronger for women and those with lower levels of education. The rationale here is that women and the less educated have weaker (more diffuse) inflation priors, and are more likely to overestimate current and future price aggregates, in the first place. New information can then shift these individuals' expectations more. In the aggregate, the population's beliefs about inflation also tend to be right-skewed, meaning that they systematically overestimate inflation.

Individuals' errors, however, also vary according to what type of prices they are estimating. Two types of prices on which individuals have been tested are their own consumer price basket (such as food costs, gas prices, or service costs) and estimates for aggregate inflation statistics (e.g., core inflation, headline inflation). In these studies, researchers find that older people and those with lower income levels update more strongly on information for items they regularly buy, for example, food, as opposed to aggregate statistics. This is interesting, as on one hand, older and poorer people are more likely to have fixed incomes, meaning that purchases of items like food represent a significant and thus important share of their expenditures. Yet, on the other hand, fixed income recipients should also worry about aggregate inflation, as aggregate inflation erodes the purchasing power of their income, unless it is indexed. Future research might aim to examine whether such variation in information is prevalent in countries where indexing varies across recipients or aggregate inflation rates are more volatile.

Finally, the public's ability to update their inflation beliefs also depends on the context of the information. Using an experimental design, Armantier et al. (2016) administered different information treatments—official information on past food price inflation and experts' forecasts for overall inflation. They found that, by and large, respondents update inflation expectations when presented with new information that is directly relevant to the type of inflation they are asked to predict. This means that it is difficult for respondents to infer national price changes from product price changes. A notable exception regards people with higher education; such respondents are able to make a connection between different drivers of inflation. This might imply that public information is more relevant and effective when tailored to cater to all sorts of social groups. This is all the more important since the authors conclude that new information is incorporated into respondents' beliefs very consciously rather than through unconscious "anchoring" (Armantier et al., 2016).

Of course, the public's inflation beliefs are inconsequential to the economy unless changes in beliefs also change behaviors. The link between inflation expectations and behavior has been tested using an incentivized investment experiment (Armantier et al., 2015). In this experiment, respondents' payoffs depended on future inflation. The study found that respondents' investment behaviors are consistent with both reported inflation expectations and predictions from standard economic theory. Respondents' investment decisions are sensitive to changing inflation expectations over time. Yet, as we observe in the aforementioned studies, results are heterogeneous across social groups. Two groups stand out. First, individuals with less education do less well linking changes in inflation to changes in returns on investments. Second, there is a positive relationship between expressed uncertainty in inflation expectations and respondents' risk profiles. The former is important because it points out that one key way to make central bank communication more effective is to increase the financial literacy of those with lower education. An important consequence of the latter finding is that if central bank communication reduces uncertainty and lowers individuals' risk appetite, central bank communication can again help prevent suboptimal equilibrium outcomes by reducing excessive risk taking, helping to stabilize the economy. Complementary to studies that examine how households form and update inflation expectations, Mirkov and Natvik (2016) surveyed professional economists about their medium-term expectations for US headline inflation. Like what was found with surveys conducted on households, even experts held significantly heterogeneous views, with the midpoint inflation expectations reported to be 1.97 percent, very close to actual reported inflation, which hovered between 1.7 and 1.9 percent. Also important is that, similar to findings from respondents in consumer surveys, the distribution of experts' expectations were, on aggregate, right-skewed, although the level of skew is significantly less than was found in those surveys conducted on average households.

2.4 Conclusion

Previous literature has examined both the effects of variation in central bank committee design and also the role that public communications has on inflation expectations and on the economy. To date, however, most of this literature has considered these two topics in isolation. New to this volume is that I consider how internal deliberations on the MPC conditions how policy makers communicate to the mass public in the first place. The content of a central bank committee's official monetary decision is bound up in who speaks for the MPC. For this reason, one of the most important stages in the decision-making process is the collective bargaining over the public statement.

In addition to who is on the committee, interests and institutions also matter. As we will see in the next chapter, the committee chair plays a special role in that he has proposal power over the policy statement. However, rather than always being able to pursue his own goals unconditionally, the ability for the chairman to pursue his own policy objectives depends on the prevailing preferences of the other members on the committee, especially the median member. Adding to this, the institutional context, such as whether the median member can cast a publicly recorded dissenting vote, also matters. My claim is that central bankers' decisions, and the policy statement that ensues, results from the pursuit of their policy preferences within constraints that stem from the sometimes collegiate and sometimes conflicting nature of the MPC.

3
A Model of Central Bank Communication

3.1 Introduction

In this chapter, I present a formal model of central bank communication that draws on bargaining models that depict monetary policy changes from the status quo. Bargaining models are useful for examining the adoption or amendment of economic policies among diverse committee members. Researchers have applied models of bargaining to understand policy making under closed or open rules in legislatures and to explain the costly delay of economic reforms (Alesina and Drazen, 1991; Baron and Ferejohn, 1989; Frechette, Kagel, and Lehrer, 2003; Gilligan and Krehbiel, 1989). The bargaining model in this chapter is an application of an earlier bargaining model by Romer and Rosenthal (1978), augmented to illustrate negotiations over monetary policy and especially central bank communication policy. Monetary policy committees decide not only on whether and how much to change policy interest rates but also on the content of official policy anouncements. In most central banks, the final published official policy text is agreed on by a committee of members and only after deliberating over its content. To model this process abstractly, the theory highlights two important features of official monetary communications. First, the theory allows policy makers to bargain over the exact content of the message, in particular, the level or degree of vagueness contained in the statement. Second, the theory assumes that bargaining occurs under conditions such that policy makers are mindful of the aggregate influence of the policy statement once it is publicly released. In sum, the theory presented in this chapter illustrates policy bargaining over official monetary policy statements,

Crafting Consensus: Why Central Bankers Change Their Speech and How Speech Changes the Economy. Nicole Rae Baerg, Oxford University Press (2020). © Oxford University Press.
DOI: 10.1093/oso/9780190499488.001.0001

asking under what conditions policy makers will send more or less vague policy proclamations.

To model the crafting of central bank communications, the theory is tailored such that it includes features of central banking that, I argue, are essential for understanding communication policy. First, I assume that the central bank committee has multiple committee members (rather than a single decision maker). Second, I assume that the committee members have heterogeneous interests (i.e., actors differ based on the outcomes they want rather than the information they know). Third, I assume that some committee members hold different roles that grant them special privileges. The committee chair is especially important, as in this theory the chair makes the initial policy offer or policy proposal.

Committee members do indeed bargain over the exact content (i.e., words and phrases) of official announcements in policy meetings; however, because we cannot model bargaining over every possible word and phrase, as a simplifying assumption, I assume that policy makers bargain over the level of distortion or vagueness in any given official policy message. Importantly, in this model, strategic or distortionary vagueness is different from not telling the truth. Consider the following two statements:

> *Annual inflation will likely be higher, well above the target rate.*
> *Average inflation is expected to be between 2 and 3 percent, well above the target rate of 2 percent.*

The first statement is more vague, that is, less precise, despite being as truthful as the second statement. Finally, to disallow policy makers from straying too far, committee members are assumed to have an aversion to higher levels of vagueness such that, given a choice between two policy statements of equal utility, the committee members always prefer the less vague (i.e., more precise) statement.

To isolate the effects of strategically using vagueness as distinct from lying, committee members can only communicate truthfully about the economy in the model. As a result, information is assumed to be credible. The degree to which members attempt to obfuscate the truth to further their own preferred policy outcomes varies, however.

Members obfuscate the truth by strategically increasing the level of vagueness. A member may try to create a misleading impression by playing with words and using language that obscures meaning. Thus the theory depicts important features of central bank communication policy. The model attempts to emulate general features of central bank decision-making over monetary policy communications, hoping to generate an explanation for central bank communication policy that is more general than a single central bank, such as the Federal Reserve Bank.

The model is generalizable enough and could apply to the official monetary policy communications of central banks around the world. In the case of the Israeli central bank, for example, MPC members convene to edit public statements over the course of two days, again with the aim to manufacture a consensual policy statement. Similarly, at the Bank of England, the governor puts to the meeting the policy he believes will command a majority, and members of the MPC vote on that proposal. The preceding model assumptions help construct a theoretical model of central bank deliberations. Such a model is then used to help us understand how policy deliberations on a central bank committee shape the level of strategic vagueness contained in policy statements released to the public.

Until now, I have used the term "information precision" to mean "the act of defining, or of making something definite, distinct, or clear." Information precision has a more technical definition in the model and refers to "the degree of granularity, or variance, in the state space that is revealed." The state space is an abstract representation of the true state of the economy. As in previous models, I assume that the state of the economy is perfectly known by the committee members and is predetermined at the beginning of the committee meeting (Riboni and Ruge-Murcia, 2010). To keep it simple, I also assume that the state of the economy can be represented by a single, unidimensional line, θ, and that the true state of the economy θ is private information observable by MPC members but not by the general public. Access to such private information about the economy is what makes the members of the MPC policy experts.

According to the technical definition of information precision, more precise information means that senders "carve up" or "partition" the state space into increasingly finer intervals. Alternatively, vague information implies a lower number of partitions and a lower level of granularity in the state space. This means that as the level of granularity increases, policy makers communicate with greater precision (lower vagueness) about the state of the economy, whereas as the level of granularity decreases, policy makers communicate with less precision (greater vagueness) about the economy.

The actors in the model include two central bank committee members and an information receiver.[1] Policy makers differ in two important ways: first, by their institutional roles, and second, by their preferences. In the model, one policy maker is assumed to be the committee chair (hereinafter the "Chair"). As the Chair, this policy maker has proposal power. The second policy maker is the median committee member (hereinafter the "Member"). As the Member, she is pivotal on the committee and has the deciding vote for the policy. The Chair and the Member are assumed to have differences in their preferred policy outcomes or biases, which means that the Chair and the Member hold different desires for the economy. For example, sometimes the Chair is more inflation "hawkish" than the Member, whereas at other times, both the Chair and the Member are relatively inflation "hawkish."

While the Chair and the Member have different policy preferences, I assume that they have the same expertise or "true" information. By drawing the distinction between preferences as opposed to information, the important dynamics of the model revolve around intermember policy competition rather than efficient information gathering, which has generally been the focus among economic models of monetary policy committees. In fact, at its core, by using a bargaining model where members have different desires or policy goals, the theory illustrates that intermember politics is essential for understanding the dissemination of central bank communication and, more broadly, the politics of central banking on committees.

Finally, the message receiver is assumed to be a representative household who is the recipient of the announced public policy statement sent by the Member and the Chair after they choose a message,

[1] For a more generic version of the model that accounts for *N* players, see Baerg and Krainin (2016); however, similar to this model, even in a model with *N* players, the median member is the pivotal actor. Readers interested in seeing the proofs of the propositions can also find them in the appendix of the aforementioned paper.

which, in the model, is denoted by m_i. Unlike in previous cheap talk games, the representative household does not enter the game as a strategic actor and is instead assumed to be naive (see also, e.g., Chen, 2011). Despite the receiver's naivety, however, the household sets expectations given the information contained in the policy statement, and the household's expectations are essential for the model's equilibrium outcomes. In fact, both the Chair's and Member's utility depends on the degree to which the representative household forms expectations upon receiving the public announcement.

The game follows a predefined sequence and lasts only one period. First, the Chair sets the agenda and offers an official policy statement with a given level of strategic vagueness, v, to the Member with median bias, who is assumed to be pivotal. Observing v and θ, the Member can either accept or reject the Chair's proposal. If the proposed statement is accepted, then the proposed policy statement is implemented with the equilibrium level of vagueness v. If the proposal is rejected, then the statement is amended through a supplemental stage of deliberation, which, while unmodeled, is assumed to result in a higher level of information precision for reasons I will explain in the next section. This means the outcome level of vagueness is v'. Thus the Member accepts a proposal whenever the expected utility from the proposal is larger than or equal to the expected utility from the amended statement, and the Chair picks the policy closest to his ideal point given his expectation of what the Member will do. Equilibrium, then, refers to those conditions that set out what types of strategies result from this game. In particular, we examine the influence of different configurations of the Chair's and the Member's policy preferences, such as when they hold either opposing or similar policy preferences. The next section presents the model as well as the equilibrium conditions.

3.2 The Model

3.2.1 Strategic Vagueness

Unlike previous bargaining models, which often depict policy makers bargaining over policy positions, the model here depicts committee members bargaining over a given level of strategic vagueness (as distinct from untruthfulness) in a policy statement, which I denote as v. As in previous bargaining models, I assume a finite number of equilibrium actions. I also depict the state of the economy as a unidimensional state space bounded between 0 and 1. We then talk about message precision as the number of partitions, or n intervals, into which the state space can be carved, for example, $(0, a_1), (a_1, a_2), \ldots, (a_{n-1}, 1)$. For illustrative purposes, Figure 3.1 shows two hypothetical outcomes, one where the state space is partitioned into five intervals, or $n = 4$, and another where the state space is divided into two intervals, or $n = 1$. In this example, an equilibrium outcome where $n = 1$ is more vague than an equilibrium outcome where $n = 4$. We can then say that the equilibrium outcome where $n = 4$ has lower *strategic vagueness* or higher *information precision* than the equilibrium outcome where $n = 1$.

Thinking about information precision as levels of granularity, or alternatively, as the variance of the expected state variable, is a useful way to think about expressions of uncertainty. For example, consider central bankers sending informative messages about their expectations of future inflation. On one hand, they could say something very precise, such as that inflation will be "very low" out of a potential list of options "very low," "low," "average," "high," and "very high." As in the preceding example, here, $n = 4$. Alternatively, when central

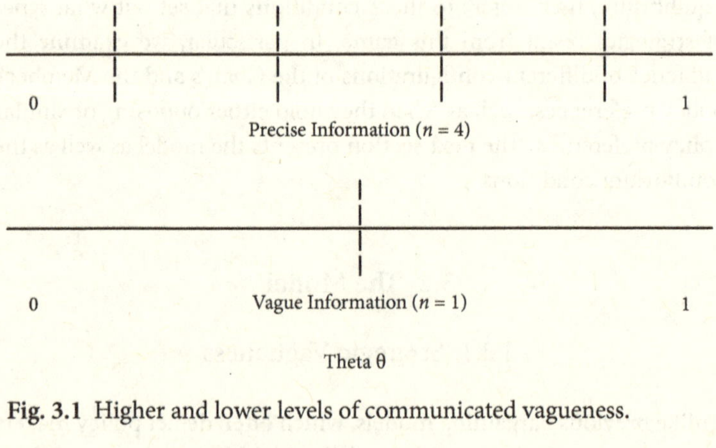

Fig. 3.1 Higher and lower levels of communicated vagueness.

bankers are more opaque, they may say that inflation will be "maybe low" out of a potential list of options "maybe low" and "maybe high," or $n = 1$. The higher n is, the lower strategic vagueness is, and the more precisely central bankers are communicating. In the limit, full or perfect information revelation refers to senders identifying a partition for every value of the state variable in the state space.

Although what I have described is abstract, consider how we might observe variation in strategic vagueness in the real world. In the United States, when deliberating over monetary policy communication, the Chair always speaks first. As in the model, this provides him with proposal power over the message content and its level of vagueness. In the case of the FOMC, for example, the Chair makes his offer by indicating which proposal he prefers out of a set of predrafted options. Second, the Chair and the members deliberate over this offer in a policy process called "taking the rounds." Committee members can agree with the Chair's proposed statement, select another one, or try to amend the one proposed. Collectively, committee members voice their preferences in an official roll-call, and the decision is governed by majority rule. Following is a record of the rounds from a typical meeting of the FOMC in 2007, provided to illustrate how the process unfolds. Ben Bernanke (Federal Reserve Bank chair) starts the rounds by making a policy proposal, and committee members Timothy Geithner (Federal Reserve Bank of New York) and Thomas Hoenig (Federal Reserve Bank of Kansas City) express their positions:

BERNANKE (CHAIR): If the choice were between 0 and 50 basis points, I would be very tempted to do 50 basis points. That said, I think there are some risks going with 50 basis points. I recommend 25 basis points and the [policy statement] alternative B.

GEITHNER: I support the reduction in the fed funds rate or basis points and the language in alternative B.

HOENIG: I would support maintaining the rate. I can accept the 25 basis point cut, if that is the Committee's preferred action. I would be very uneasy with a 50 basis point cut at this time. I think the language in alternative B is the right language, regardless of whether A, B, or C options that we choose.

This passage shows the Chair making an offer of a policy statement containing a certain predetermined level of strategic vagueness and the members agreeing to the Chair's proposal.

3.2.2 Model Departures

As I suggested at the outset of this chapter, my model relates to previous bargaining models of economic policy making, especially those of Romer and Rosenthal (1978) and Riboni and Ruge-Murcia (2010). To determine the level of strategic vagueness disseminated, the Member and Chair bargain over the content of the policy announcement, in particular, over its level of precision or vagueness. The representative household then uses whatever information is provided to it from this bargaining to update its beliefs about the economy, in particular, about inflation.[2]

The theory I provide departs from previous literature in three important ways. First, I assume that the receiver is a nonstrategic actor. This means that the representative household sets its own expectations in light of the information it is given, mechanistically, rather than strategically anticipating how her? expectations matter for the choices that policy makers make. While in this model, the household does not behave strategically, we know from previous models those conditions that must be met for there to be informative equilibria, even if the household were to behave strategically. First, from previous models, we know that information can only be credibly transmitted to the receiver if each sender confirms the other sender's message, that is, if they send consensual messages (Krishna and Morgan, 2001; Minozzi, 2011). Second, we know that to be informative, senders cannot have policy preferences too far away from the receiver (Crawford and Sobel, 1982; Krishna and Morgan, 2001). This is similar to other models in the literature. Morris and Shin (2002), for example, argue that while the behavior of any one individual independently is noninfluential, collectively, the decisions of many households matter for policy

[2] The committee's private information is θ, which is distinct from the committee's publicized information, which is m_1, m_2.

makers. As a result, each individual actor rationally discounts the importance of his own behavior despite being critical in the aggregate. Crucially, this is not true, however, for the average committee member, who knows that on a MPC, the probability of being influential is much larger and as a result, acts strategically.

Second, I assume that the household responds bluntly to information sent by the central bank. For example, if the central bank sends a message that future inflation "will increase between 1.09 and 2.06 percent," the household sets its inflation expectations to the mean of the revealed interval 1 and 2 percent, which is 1.5 and not 1.575. In a similar vein, I also assume that the senders can only partition the state space into equal-length partitions such that they cannot disport the information by making unequal tranches or intervals.

Third, if the Chair makes a proposal and the Chair and the Member do not agree, I assume that this leads to an unmodeled bargaining phase in which the actors amend the statement. When amending occurs, the Member is assumed to take an outside offer with a known value determined by the outside game. Instead of including this game directly in the model, for simplicity, I merely assume that the known value of this game has higher associated levels of information precision than the value initially proposed by the Chair. An assumed value such as this is consistent with previous literature. For example, Riboni and Ruge-Murcia (2010) explicitly model bargaining over changes to interest rates. In their model, committee members bargain over changing the interest rate from an assumed status quo interest rate where the disagreement or "breakdown" value is the status quo interest rate set at the previous meeting. Similarly, in my model, committee members bargain over information, specifically the precision of information contained in the policy statements. Instead of being the status quo policy statement from the previous meeting, the disagreement or "breakdown" value is an assumed level of information precision that is higher than the value of precision if members agreed at the outset.

Why is information precision higher if members come to a consensus only after they have initially disagreed? The logic is that there are differences in the risks of withholding information when more precise information was initially proposed than there is supplying information when more vague information was initially proposed.

One easy way to see why this is likely to be true has to do with possible public scrutiny. Because minutes, and in some central banks, even verbatim records, of committee meetings are published, even with a lag, there is the possibility of future scrutiny of today's actions. Under these conditions, committee members may be held accountable for their behavior during policy deliberations. Furthermore, it is likely to be more costly for the Chair and the Member to collude to withhold information after a more precise statement was initially proposed than it is for the Chair and the Member to agree to provide more information after a vague statement was proposed. In other words, it is harder to take a precise position at the outset and then add strategic vagueness than it is to adopt a vague position at the outset and reduce strategic vagueness.

More technically, for any given meeting, a Chair proposes a public statement, $m_{1,p}$, where p is the proposal. The other committee members, represented by the Member, can either accept or reject the Chair's initial proposal. If the Member accepts, then the issued policy statement is $m_1 = m_2$. The associated level of information n, in this case, is denoted by n_a, because it comes from a game where the Chair and the Member agree at the outset. If the Chair's initial proposal, $m_{1,p}$, is rejected, however, the Chair and the Member play an unmodeled outside game in which they deliberate about the language of the statement. The outcome of this game is a new consensus, $m_1' = m_2'$, where, again, the Chair and the Member agree after bargaining. The associated level of information n after disagreement is n_d.

There are three possible configurations of n_a and n_d, $n_a > n_d$, $n_a = n_d$, and $n_a > n_d$, and I treat each case in turn. Assume first that $n_a > n_d$. For n_a to be greater than n_d, the Member and the Chair must collude to withhold some of the information that the Chair initially proposed. For example, the Chair might propose, "Inflation is improving and moving closer toward our objective of 2 percent." If the Member tries to amend the statement such that it is more vague, for example, "Inflation is moving closer to target," the Member must convince the Chair that it is in the Chair's best interest to adopt something less precise. Furthermore, she must convince the Chair to adopt a more vague statement despite that the Chair is already on record as providing more precise information in his proposal.

Assuming that agreeing to withhold information is potentially risky to the Chair's reputation, colluding to withhold information opens up the opportunity for future scrutiny. Schonhardt-Bailey (2014), for example, argues that "importantly, . . . actors are fully aware that the publicised hearings are further scrutinized by audiences outside the committee meeting rooms." If both the Member and the Chair are held accountable by actors who value transparency, withholding public information is likely to introduce reputation risks.

In the next case, assume that $n_a = n_d$. In this case, the precision outcomes from playing the disagreement game and the agreement game are equal. There are no additional benefits to playing the disagreement game, as the players construct equivalent statements from playing either game.

Now assume, as I do, that $n_a < n_d$. For example, the Chair might propose the statement "Inflation is moving closer to target." If the Member were to select the disagreement game and try to make the statement more precise, such as "Inflation is improving and moving closer toward our objective of 2 percent," the Member would have to convince the Chair that it is in the Chair's best interest to increase the information precision (decrease strategic vagueness) in the statement. The Chair, on record as initially supporting something more vague, would then have to agree to the inclusion of additional information. Assuming again that it is less risky to add rather than to subtract information once the initial proposal is on record, the addition of precise information is less worrisome for the Chair in terms of his reputation. If both the Member and the Chair are held accountable by actors who value transparency, then being on record as supplying public information is likely to be less of a problem.

In sum, because monetary policy making is subject to external scrutiny and oversight, and given that members have real reputation concerns, it follows that it is more risky to withhold information from the public statement after a more precise statement was proposed than it is to add more precision to an already proposed vague statement. Importantly, empirical evidence also supports this view. Meade and Stasavage (2008), for example, found a decline in the levels of disagreement in FOMC meetings once the members were made aware, in 1993, that the verbatim meeting transcripts would be published. They also found that committee members were less likely to disagree with the Chair, strengthening his proposal power. If committee members are concerned about future reputation costs of their choices today, they will likely be more reluctant to remove already proposed information than they will be to add new information to the textual statement. Such a mechanism suggests that the information precision from the breakdown value that represents consensus after deliberation is likely to be greater than the precision of information after initial agreement.

This, then, brings up another related point: if it is more costly to disagree than it is to agree, do we ever observe disagreement over the policy statement? We do. Consider again a discussion among Bernanke, Geithner, and Hoenig during a policy meeting in 2007. In this particular meeting, six members of the FOMC dissented to the *language of policy statement B* (as distinct from dissenting to changes to the interest rate), with the majority of members preferring alternative C:

BERNANKE (CHAIR): [I propose to] take no action and to maintain a bias toward further tightening. [I also propose to] take alternative B as written. Alternative B, section 2 does, I believe, clearly signal that we have seen a change from December, but, there's a risk that there would be a perception of a significant policy shift, which is not intended. We do need to think hard about this language.

GEITHNER: I'm very comfortable with the language in alternative B. Of course, all the alternatives are flawed. Alternative B seems the least flawed among the alternatives.

HOENIG: I'm very comfortable with alternative B as far as the rate goes, on language, however, I feel that we would be better served with sections 2 and 3 of alternative C.

The next section shows who the actors are and what they want, and it presents the equilibrium conditions and propositions as well as testable predictions following from them. The final section of the chapter introduces a mechanism that shows one way that changes in vagueness can influence the economy through the channel of households' inflation expectations.[3]

[3] Because many of the propositions build from formal models already published, I refer those interested in the formal proofs to the more general version of the model

3.2.3 Actors

The Household

In this model, the central bank targets its communication to a representative household. The household acts as an important economic decision maker whose generic actions influence the real economy. Furthermore, the actions that the household takes depend on its own expectations of future economic conditions and thus can be influenced by policy makers' announcements. Some examples of everyday decisions that depend on households' expectations of the future economy include purchasing new consumer products; making saving and investment decisions; buying a car or a home; and negotiating salaries or other contracts, such as mortgages.

Like the committee Chair and the committee Member, the representative household has its own preference, or ideal point, over policy outcomes. The underlying reason why preferences may differ between central bankers and households, as well as over time and across countries, may include differences in preferences based on levels of personal debt (Frieden, 1991), differences in aversion to unemployment (Scheve, 2004), and distributional concerns (Alesina and Drazen, 1991). In this model, we can include the household's preferences but make them not the focus by normalizing the policy preferences of the Chair and the Member to the household's preferred outcome or bias, such that $b_{hh} = 0$. As previous models show, in a strategic model, experts cannot have preferences that are too different from those of receivers, or else they are not persuasive.[4]

The household's objective is to guess the true state of the economy using publicly disseminated central bank communications. I also assume that public information is less costly than private information for everyone, and so the household has the incentive to coordinate on public information rather than private information. This is because public information is nonrival and nonexcludable. Because public

available in Baerg and Krainin (2016) and in other articles, such as Krishna and Morgan (2008), Crawford and Sobel (1982), and Riboni and Ruge-Murcia (2010).

[4] For a formal proof of the relationship between extreme preferences and credible communication, see Krishna and Morgan (2008).

information is less costly, the household has an incentive to collect public information over private information. As a result, public information "crowds out" private information (Morris and Shin, 2002). As outlined earlier, however, public information can vary in its level of strategic vagueness, v, and this variation is assumed to be independent from variation in the true state of the world, θ.

The household's objective, therefore, is to choose an optimal action for a given θ when θ is unknown to the household but perfectly known to all members of the MPC. In receiving the message, the household updates its inflation expectations. For example, if the household receives perfect information about θ, the household will update its inflation expectations exactly to θ. At the other extreme, if the household receives no information, and if all θs are assumed to be equally likely between 0 and 1, the household's best guess is the average of the entire interval, or $\frac{1}{2}[0 + 1] = 1/2$. The household, upon receiving messages, can use information disseminated by the MPC to determine its best action. For example, if, in equilibrium, the Chair and the Member reveal that $0.25 < \theta < 0.5$, then the household's best guess is the average of this interval, or $\frac{1}{2}[0.25 + 0.5]$. In between the two extremes of perfect information, where θ is perfectly revealed, and no information, central bankers try to influence the household's action by sending messages about θ.

The Chair and the Member

In contrast to the household, central bankers are assumed to know the true state of the world, θ, and they also have varying preferences, or biases, about policy outcomes. Such biases, while exogenous to the model, may reflect partisanship or class differences (Frieden, 1991), differences in career objectives (Adolph, 2013; Hallerberg and Wehner, 2018), differences in constituencies (Meade and Sheets, 2005), or distributional interests (Alesina and Drazen, 1991).

Central bankers care about the household's actions because households' inflation expectations help drive actual inflation outcomes (Sargent and Wallace, 1982). For example, in 2014, Minneapolis bank president Narayana Kocherlakota strongly advocated that the Federal Reserve Bank purchase bonds as part of its monetary policy strategy. Kocherlakota cited lower household and business inflation expectations as evidence for "doubts in households and businesses about whether the FOMC is truly aiming for 2 percent inflation." Further monetary stimulus was needed, he argued, to get household expectations up and therefore inflation higher.[5]

Committee members, therefore, have a strategic incentive to communicate their private information publicly if they think that their information can be influential. Because of their policy biases, however, they also have an incentive to obfuscate information such that they get outcomes to shift toward their preferred outcomes. For example, if an MPC can dissuade the mass public from thinking that aggregate prices will rise tomorrow, households will not demand higher wages today, and consequently, inflation will not rise as quickly. Alternatively, if MPCs believe that inflation is too low, if they can change expectations such that the mass public believes that aggregate prices will rise, households will be more likely to demand higher wages, to spend instead of save, and consequently, inflation will be more likely to rise as well.

How precisely the MPC communicates about θ in equilibrium, however, depends on internal bargaining between the Chair and the members. As shown previously, the greater the number of partitions that the Chair and the Member identify, or n, the more precisely information is transmitted to the household. As I show in the following pages, there are four different equilibrium outcomes, and the important variables that drive differences across the equilibrium cases are the *distance* and the *biases* of the median committee Member and the committee Chair.

Because distance and bias are the key variables that matter to understanding the propositions, it is important to discuss them more fully. First, consider policy preferences over inflation: if the Chair and the Member have like preferences, such that both are inflation "hawks" or inflation "doves," then we say that the Chair and the Member are of *like bias*. By contrast, if the Chair and the Member have opposite biases, such that one is a "hawk" (relative to the household) and the other is a "dove" (relative to the household), then we say they are of *opposed bias*. Distance refers to how far away they are from one

[5] http://www.minneapolisfed.org

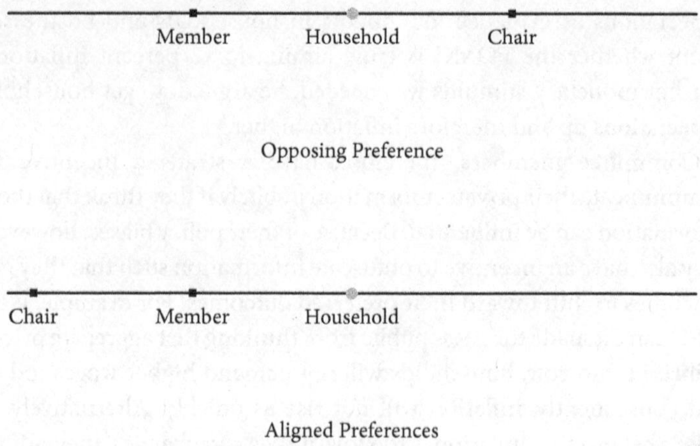

Fig. 3.2 Differences in actors' preferences.

Table 3.1 Notation

Symbol	Meaning
π^e	Household's expectations
π^{e*}	Household's optimal expectations (best response)
b_C	Preferences of Chair
b_M	Preferences of Member
b_{hh}	Ex ante preferences of household, normalized to 0
$m_{1,2}$	Message sent at time 1 or time 2
v^*	Equilibrium level of strategic vagueness
v_C	Level of strategic vagueness if Chair were only actor
v_M	Level of strategic vagueness if Member were only actor

another. Figure 3.2 shows the different configurations of preferences where sometimes central bankers' biases are opposed and at other times central bankers' biases are alike.

As we will see, the ability of the Chair and the Member to transmit precise or vague information about the economy depends not only on their biases (or the configuration of the actors' positions) but also on the distance between the Member's and the Chair's preferred policy outcomes. Figure 3.3 illustrates the difference between bias and distance. Finally, Table 3.1 presents further notation presented in the chapter.

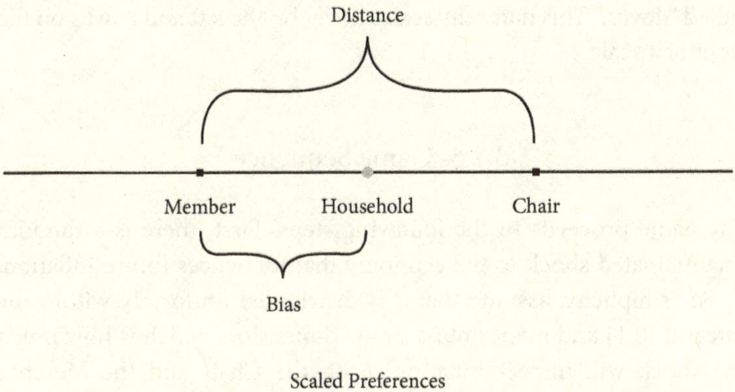

Fig. 3.3 Preference differences according to bias and distance.

3.2.4 Utility Functions

As is standard in the literature, the average household's objective function can be represented by the quadratic loss function shown in equation (3.1). The household's utility is at a maximum when its expectations are exactly equal to θ:

$$U_{hh}(\pi^e, \theta) = -(\pi^e - \theta)^2. \tag{3.1}$$

Like the average household, the Chair and the Member have preferences. The objectives of the Chair and the Member are represented by the quadratic loss functions shown in equations (3.2) and (3.3). The Chair and the Member's objective is to get the household to hold expectations equal to the true state of the world, θ, offset by the committee member's own bias, b_i:

$$U_C(\pi^e, \theta, b_C) = -(\pi^e - (\theta + b_C))^2 \tag{3.2}$$
$$U_M(\pi^e, \theta, b_M) = -(\pi^e - (\theta + b_M))^2, \tag{3.3}$$

where b_C and b_M denote the bias of the Member and the Chair, respectively. If we consider the labels inflation "hawks" and "doves," inflation biases ≥ 0 are called "hawks" and inflation biases ≤ 0 are called "doves." This naturally scales doves on the left and hawks on the right of a scale.

3.2.5 Game Sequence

The game proceeds in the following steps. First, there is a random unanticipated shock to the economy that influences future inflation, θ. For simplicity, assume that θ is distributed uniformly within the interval [0,1] and maps onto a single dimension, which is how much the shock will impact inflation. Both the Chair and the Member perfectly observe θ.

Knowing θ, the Chair makes a pronouncement, sending a message, m_1. This message includes a certain amount of distortion or vagueness, implying that θ is within an interval $[\underline{\theta}, \overline{\theta}]$. The choice that the Chair makes is how much distortion or vagueness is included in the interval. Recall that I assume that there are sufficient reputation incentives that this interval must be accurate in the sense that it must include the truth, and that the Chair can only segment the state space into equal partitions. The Member observes θ and the message that the Chair sends, m_1, and either agrees or disagrees with the Chair's proposal. Once an agreement is reached, the Member sends m_2. If the Member agrees, the committee successfully transmits to the representative household that $\theta \in [\underline{\theta}, \overline{\theta}]$. If the Chair and the Member do not agree, the representative household learns that $\theta \in [\underline{\theta}', \overline{\theta}']$, where this interval represents the consensus breakdown value from playing the disagreement game. The breakdown value, as discussed earlier, is assumed to be a known outcome of a disagreement game where the Chair and the Member edit the message together but without initial cooperation. The representative household then takes an action given these messages $\pi^e(m_1, m_2)$, which, in this case, means that the household updates its inflation expectations conditional on the information and makes economic decisions based on its expectations. The Chair and the Member speak once. Pronouncements are free and sequential. The household always integrates the public information because public information is less costly than a search for private information, and as we have assumed that the biases are not too far away, the assumption is that the household always listens to the MPC's advice.

3.2.6 Equilibrium

The benefit of the model is that it generates important hypotheses about the effects of institutional design and committee composition on the strategic use of vagueness in monetary policy announcements. Solving for equilibrium outcomes—(equilibrium involves solving the strategic bargaining problem between the Chair and the Member, meanwhile anticipating the household's response). The model is solved by backward induction. Importantly, it generates four different cases.

Proposition 3.2.1. *The following statements characterize equilibrium message vagueness, $v*$:*

- *Median Chair: $b_C = b_M$, then $v_C = v_M = v*$*
- *Dominant Chair: $b_C < |b_M|$ and $0 < b_c < b_M$ or $b_M > b_C > 0$, then $v_C > v_M = v*$*
- *Constrained Chair: $b_C > |b_M|$ and $b_C < 0 < b_M$ or $b_M < 0 < b_C$, then $v_C > v* > v_M$*
- *Constrained Committee: $b_C < |b_M|$ and $b_C < 0 < b_M$ or $b_M < 0 < b_C$, then $v_M > v* > v_C$ and $v*_a = v*_d$*

Example A. Median Chair: *When there is no preference difference between the Chair and the Member, such that $b_C = b_M$, the Chair proposes the level of precision ideal to him, and the Member accepts. Equilibrium level vagueness is the same as if the Chair were a unitary actor.*

If the Chair and the Member are exactly alike, then the Chair always proposes a level of vagueness to which the Member will consent. Because of this, in equilibrium, the level of vagueness is equally preferred by the Member and the Chair, and there is no need to amend the statement. Similarly, there is no additional transparency gain for decision-making by committee rather than by a single actor.

Example B. Dominant Chair: *When a preference difference between the Chair and the Member exists but is such that they have like bias,* $0 < b_C < b_M$ *or* $0 > b_C > b_M$, *and* $b_C < |b_M|$, *the Chair always gets the level of precision that he proposes. As in the Median Chair case, equilibrium vagueness is the same as if the Chair were a unitary actor.*

In addition to the case where the Chair and the Member have exactly the same preferences, there is another case where the Member has similar bias as the Chair. As in the preceding example, this case results in the Chair proposing his ideal policy statement with a given level of vagueness and the Member accepting the proposal without exerting any influence over the policy statement.

Because the Chair is less extreme, the Chair proposes a message that is closer to his own preference, and the Member is better off agreeing. The Member could refuse to send a confirmatory message, but because the Member's preference is alike and more extreme, she is not made better off by doing so. Similarly, the Chair is not made better off by shifting his message closer to the ideal point of the Member. Thus the equilibrium outcome is one where the Chair proposes his own ideal level of precision and the Member agrees. The Chair is dominant in this case and is unconstrained by the Member's bias, despite the Member being more extreme. As in the first example, from the perspective of the associated level of transparency, the predicted level of strategic vagueness is the same as if the Chair made policy alone.

Consider a numerical example. Assume that there is an economic shock to inflation that can be characterized as $\theta = 0.25$. The household maximizes its utility (minimizes its loss function) if it guesses that θ is 0.25. Without any information such that the shock could be anywhere in the state space, the household's best guess is $\theta = 0.50$, the midpoint of the state space. If the Chair has lower preferences than the household (is dovish), with an inflation bias of -0.17, for example, and if the Member is even more dovish than the Chair, at -0.20, then the equilibrium outcome is one where the Chair will maximize his utility by revealing information that induces the household to guess a θ slightly below its true value. The Chair, in this example, selects a message with a level of information precision equivalent to $n = 4$ partitions. Recall that the number of partitions of the state space represents the precision of the signal. The Member agrees. Then both the Chair and the Member send a consensual and true message that θ is in the interval $\theta \in [0.0, 0.25]$. The household optimizes by guessing the midpoint of the revealed interval, $\theta = 0.12$. Thinking backward, the Member agrees to this because the Member prefers to induce the household to guess a lower value than the true value, as does the Chair; the Member is better off if the household guesses 0.12 instead of 0.25. Similarly, the Chair is better off. Finally, from the perspective of the household, it is also better off compared to if it had received no information. With no MPC communication, the household's utility would be $-(0.5-0.25)^2 = -0.0625$. With MPC communication such that $n = 4$, its utility is -0.0169. This is because, given the assumption of a quadratic loss function, the household's utility is maximized when the loss function is minimized.

Such a finding suggests a new consequence of delegating monetary policy communication to an MPC. If one of the policy goals of delegating responsibility to a central bank is to increase the level of transparency (reduce the level of vagueness), then from an institutional design perspective, delegating authority to a monetary policy committee with members of like bias will, according to this model, not lead to an increase in transparency in public communication. According to the model, if all committee members are alike, the Chair will propose and get his ideal level of distortion, and the committee members will exert little influence on communication policy independently.

Importantly, other configurations lead to more transparent and thus more optimal outcomes. In these cases, committee members can (and do) exert pressure on the Chair to implement a policy statement with more precise content. For example, consider the situation in which the Member and the Chair have opposing preferences and the Chair has preferences that are more extreme than the Member's in terms of distance. In this case, the Chair makes a proposal for a level of precision, and again, the Member can agree or disagree.

Example C. Constrained Chair: *When the preference difference between the Chair and the Member exists, such that $b_C < 0 < b_M$ or $b_M < 0 < b_C$, and the Chair is more extreme than the Member, $b_C > |b_M|$, and where $n_d > n_a$, the Chair makes an initial offer, the Member rejects, and the Chair and the Member agree to amend the statement.*

Under these conditions, the Chair and the Member have such differences in their biases that anything that the Chair proposes the Member will reject. This is similar to legislative bargaining when members of the legislature enact the status quo policy because no policy compromise can be made. Recall that rejection in this model means that the Member and the Chair play a different game where amending the announcement occurs. As mentioned previously, when the Chair and the Member play the amending game, I assume that the negotiated precision of the information sent in equilibrium is higher than it is in the game where the Chair makes a proposal and the Member agrees. I test whether this is true empirically in the following chapter.[6]

Consider the same numerical example from before, only now the Member has opposite preferences from the Chair and is an inflation "hawk." As before, assume that the shock is 0.25. The household maximizes its utility if it guesses 0.25. Assume also that the Chair is still an inflation "dove," with an inflation bias of −0.17. Assume also that the hawkish Member has an inflation bias of 0.10. In this example, the equilibrium outcome is that the Member will choose to play the disagreement game, forcing a renegotiation of the statement. Once the Chair and the Member come to an agreement, they select $n = 5$, which is 1 higher than if they had aligned preferences. They then reveal that θ is slightly higher than the true value of θ, or $\theta \in [0.2, 0.4]$.

With this information, the household's best response is to set its beliefs at 0.30, which is again the midpoint of the revealed interval. Under this scenario, the household's utility is −0.0025, which implies

[6] One can also think of this process as reverting to the status quo rate of precision rather than a breakdown value. In this interpretation, as the status quo precision rate converges toward zero, perfectly precise information is transmitted in equilibrium.

additional benefits for the household compared to the previous scenario, where her utility was −0.0169.[7]

As the preceding example shows, the value of equilibrium levels of information precision depends on the preference configurations, or biases, of the Chair and the Member. When the Chair and the Member have aligned preferences, strategic vagueness in equilibrium is higher than it is when they have opposing preferences or biases.

Another parameter that matters is the breakdown value. As discussed previously, owing to asymmetrical risks of withholding versus adding information after a certain policy announcement has been proposed, the theory assumes that the equilibrium information from breakdown is more precise than the equilibrium information from initial agreement.

Finally, there is a fourth equilibrium in which the Chair makes an offer with lower levels of strategic vagueness than he would if he made policy alone and the Member accepts without making amendments. This occurs when the Member has an opposing bias that is close or equal to the breakdown value. This case is called the "Constrained Committee":

Example D. Constrained Committee: *When a preference difference between the Chair and the Member exists such that* $b_C < |b_M|$, *and the preferences are opposing, and the bias of the Member is close or equal to the breakdown value* n_d, *the Chair will propose a level of vagueness, and the Member will accept. The level of strategic vagueness in equilibrium is between what the Member and Chair would choose if they were to act alone.*

To understand this case, consider another example. Assume that $b_C = 0.1$ and $b_M = -0.2$. Also assume that $\theta = 0.50$. The Chair's most preferred message space is $\in [0.5, 0.7]$. Alternatively, the Member's most preferred message space is $\in [0.5, 0.9]$. If there were no Chair and the Member set the proposed vagueness, then the Member would send the message $\in [0.5, 0.9]$, and the household would set its beliefs

[7] This means that, for this example, in order for this condition to hold, the breakdown value must be > 4.

to $\frac{1}{2}[0.5, 0.9] = 0.7$. Alternatively, if there were no Member, then the Chair would send the message $\in [0.5, 0.7]$, and the household would set its beliefs to $\frac{1}{2}[0.5, 0.7] = 0.6$. In this example, the Member would prefer more vagueness than the Chair, and so the Member can choose to try to amend the statement by playing the amendment game. If the resulting level of precision from playing the amendment game is higher than what the Chair wants, it is in the interest of the Chair to make an offer that is up to and/or equals the level of precision that would result if such a game were played. If he would offer more, then the Member would reject, and therefore this would not be a credible offer. Thus the Member's position constrains the Chair's offer under these conditions, which is unlike that which occurs in the case where the preferences of the Member and the Chair are of like bias.

What can we deduce from these equilibrium cases? A number of theoretically interesting and empirically relevant hypotheses can be tested from the model. The first and already discussed claim is that delegating communication policy to central bank committees with like biases leads to no informational improvements when compared with communication policy dictated by a unitary actor. This is because there are no political pressures from divergent policy interests to generate concessions. This is an important qualifier to previous literature that considers the relationship between the central bank and the government. For example, in a canonical model, Rogoff (1985) suggests that by appointing a conservative central banker, the central bank can minimize any inflationary bias induced by the public's inflation expectations. According to my model, the composition of the committee also matters. My findings suggest that if public transparency is a public policy goal, it is better to delegate to a heterogeneous committee rather than a committee of like-minded actors so that the intercommittee politics naturally keeps in check any personal incentives to be vague.

A second important empirical implication of the model is that bargaining breakdown and amendments to the policy statement are likely to occur more frequently when the Chair and the Member have opposing biases than when they have like biases. This, among other things, suggests that we will be more likely to observe textual editing and disagreement over policy wording and phrasing when committee members have divergent preferences and when the Member is more extreme.

Finally, a third implication is that as the bias of the Member approaches the outcome if the amendment game was to be played, the Chair is likely to concede to a reduction in the strategic use of vagueness at the outset and incorporate the Member's preferred level of vagueness into his proposed policy statement. As the concession is similar to what the Member would want through the process of amendment, the Member will agree without dispute and the initial proposal will pass. What is interesting about this point is that the credible threat of policy rejection generates incentives for the Chair to behave in a way that is different than he would if he were alone or if everyone were on his "side." Again, as in the first point, this suggests that committee member diversity has an effect on the informative content of public policy. As a second and perhaps less obvious consequence, it also suggests that policy consensus by committee members may be generated by very different mechanisms despite being observationally equivalent. In the first case, policy consensus occurs because the Chair, leveraging his proposal power, gets what he wants. In the latter case, however, the Chair, anticipating the possibility of future conflict with the Member, makes a concession beforehand, in the policy proposal stage, to manufacture the Member's agreement.

3.3 Disseminating Economic Information

So far, we have examined those conditions that predict when committee members will select precise central bank communication and those conditions when committee members will select vague central bank communication. In addition to explaining the sources of variation in information, also important is specifying a mechanism for how public dissemination of central bank communication changes the economy. How does the dissemination of more precise or more vague central bank communication influence macroeconomic outcomes? This section offers one possible mechanism.

To develop a simple explanation for the economic consequences of public news, I first assume that the public's inflation expectations are positively correlated with actual inflation outcomes. This is relatively uncontroversial, as it implies simply that as individuals' inflation expectations go up, inflation also goes up in the next period. I also assume that this process is symmetrical in that when expectations go down, inflation also goes down. We can write this as $\pi_t = f(\pi^e_{t-1})$, where π is inflation and π^e_{t-1} is expected inflation in the previous period.

As a second step, I assume that the population within a country has inflation expectations that are distributed according to a positively skewed, skewed normal distribution. This means that, different from a normal distribution with symmetrical variance, the skewed normal distribution allows for nonzero skewness (i.e., a fatter and/or longer right or left tail).

To characterize how much skew the skewed normal distribution has, a parameter, α, governs its skew. In the case of a normal distribution, $\alpha = 0$. When there is a thick left tail, $\alpha > 0$, and for a thick right tail, $\alpha < 0$. Following the empirical survey literature in the previous chapter, I assume that inflation expectations have $\alpha > 0$ skew. Practically, this means that inflation expectations are distributed with a relatively longer and/or fatter left side, stretching over higher levels of expected inflation. In other words, I assume that inflation expectations are asymmetrical around the mean, lengthening with more density and hence positive skew.

Importantly, both of my assumptions are supported by empirical research. In chapter 5, for example, I show how, using a sample of German household survey respondents, their inflation expectations are both positively associated with inflation and also, in the aggregate, are described as positively skewed.

To isolate the effect of central bank communication on actual inflation outcomes, I assume that the representative household considers the information that is disseminated by the MPC, in particular, the variance of information around θ, or v. Recall that the Chair and the Member can reveal, for example, in the case of $n = 4$, four intervals, "Very High," "High," "Low," and "Very Low," which is more precise than $n = 2$, or two intervals of "High" and "Low."[8] Thus MPCs, by disseminating more precise public communication, can shift the public's estimate of the variance of the distribution of inflation. Furthermore, if everyone adjusts her expectations similarly, this will shift the expectation of the variance among the population. As a result, as the precision of information increases, the variance of households' inflation expectations decreases, and the variance of the distribution of inflation also decreases.

This mechanism implies that relationship inflation can be written as before, where inflation is positively associated with inflation expectations, but now I include a further condition where expectations themselves are conditional on public information, or $\pi_t = f(\pi_{t-1}^e | I_t)$. Building on the model in the previous section, I denote I_t as the equilibrium level of public information disseminated by the monetary policy committee at time *t*. If inflation is positively skewed normal, then this means that as the precision of communication increases, average inflation expectations will attenuate. As average inflation expectations attenuate, aggregate average inflation is expected to go down.

Proposition 3.3.1. *If inflation is positively correlated with inflation expectations, $\pi_t = f(\pi_{t-1}^e)$, and if inflation expectations are distributed according to a positively skewed, skewed normal distribution, $\alpha > 0$, then as the average precision of central bank communication increases (vagueness decreases), inflation expectations will attenuate, and actual average inflation will decline.*

While simple, this mechanism suggests one possible channel by which information from the MPC is expected to change the aggregate economy. As a result of this mechanism, we can go from a simple game-theoretic understanding of how intercommittee politics shapes the dissemination of information to an expectation for how changes in information may shape the aggregate economy.

[8] The numerical equivalents for "Very High" and "High" are $\theta \in [0, 0.25]$ and $\theta \in [0, 0.50]$.

3.4 Empirical Implications

The theoretical model and the inflation expectations channel presented in the previous sections generate several testable empirical predictions. First, the model helps to predict those conditions where we would expect to see more precise speech and those conditions where we would expect to see central bankers communicate with greater levels of vagueness. The main conditioning variable is whether the Chair and the Member have like or opposing preferences.

Second, we should see an increase in precision in central bank communication when the Member and the Chair disagree with each other in the rounds and choose to amend the statement. These two empirical implications of the theoretical model suggest the following empirically testable hypotheses:

Hypothesis 3.4.1. Committee Composition: *When the Chair and the Member have opposing preferences, policy statements will be more likely to be precise than when the Chair and the Member have like preferences.*

Hypothesis 3.4.2. Dissents and Amendments: *When the Chair and the Member have opposing preferences, as the Member and the Chair get farther apart in terms of preferences, we are likely to observe more dissent and greater edits to the policy statements.*

In addition to predicting those conditions that explain variation in the content of central bank communications, I am interested in predicting the consequences of varying types of communication on the aggregate economy. Thus the final empirical prediction from the theory is that, given that inflation expectations are positively associated with inflation, and given that inflation expectations are assumed to be distributed positively skewed, skewed normal, an increase in information precision should have a conditioning effect on inflation expectations such that an increase in precision should attenuate the effects of inflation expectations on actual average inflation outcomes.

Hypothesis 3.4.3. Information and Inflation: *More precise (vague) economic information is more (less) likely to attenuate the public's inflation expectations, reducing aggregate inflation.*

3.5 Conclusion

In summary, this chapter presents a comprehensive explanation for why we observe variation in monetary policy statements in terms of their level of vagueness and precision. According to our model, we expect to observe precise communication when central bank committees comprise heterogeneous actors each with individual interests. The mechanism at work here is that differences among actors exert pressures on their colleagues not to misconstrue the truth. Furthermore, the model suggests that, left to their own devices, some types of MPCs are better suited for transparent public dissemination of information than other types of MPCs.

The theory also contributes a new understanding of the benefits of committee policy making by a group of experts. For example, previous literature mostly examines how committees more efficiently process diverse sources of information so as to get better estimates of what is happening in the real economy. Alternatively, in my theory, rather than paying attention to what policy makers know, I highlight how interelite politics can shape central bank communication. As a final step, I then demonstrate how communication policy exerts its own anticipated independent effect on the economy by shaping the expectations of the mass public.

Both for convenience and to make the model parsimonious, the theory relies on a number of simplifying assumptions. The model has only two actors struggling over policy decision-making instead of more than two. The model also assumes that, once amendments to a policy statement have been made, the level of precision is higher than it would have been had amendments not occurred. Importantly, however, such a simple model in the spirit of the Romer and Rosenthal (1978) "setter model" sheds new light on features of central bank policy making, including transparency and accountability, previously unexplored in the literature. Similarly, the idea that policy makers bargain over vagueness as they do other kinds of policy leads to a number of important and novel theoretical predictions.

This, then, brings us to the next pillar of the book. Naturally, a theoretical expectations need to be evaluated empirically. This task is taken up in the remaining chapters. Importantly, the empirical tests use a number of sources and methodologies, including econometric analysis of observational data, textual analysis, and information gathered from survey data and survey experiments. The goal is not to provide a single conclusive test but rather to consider a number of possible avenues where evidence for and against the theory might be found.

4

Central Bank Committees and Political Communication

I wouldn't worry about the statement being stale. It has been stale for a very long time.

—Chair Alan Greenspan speaking in the FOMC,
November 2005

4.1 Introduction

In this chapter, I test whether differences in the inflation preferences of central bank committee members predict the content of official central bank statements. Different from normative theories about whether a central bank *should* be more diverse, my theory highlights how diversity in members' policy preferences as well as institutional constraints shape the way that policy makers craft official statements about the economy. Importantly, my argument stresses that more precise language arises from the strategic choices and actions of individual committee members who bargain with one another over their policy goals in the committees where they make policy.

To evaluate the argument, I consider data from unstructured textual information produced by the Federal Open Market Committee (FOMC), which is the committee tasked with making monetary policy in the United States. Using historical documents, including full committee meeting transcripts and the official FOMC policy statement released to the public at the close of the meeting, I develop a number of new measures from textual information released by the FOMC. I then use these new measures as input variables in the statistical analyses I conduct in the chapter. As a preview of the results, I find

Crafting Consensus: Why Central Bankers Change Their Speech and How Speech Changes the Economy. Nicole Rae Baerg, Oxford University Press (2020). © Oxford University Press.
DOI: 10.1093/oso/9780190499488.001.0001

some evidence in support of my argument. In particular, I find that when the median committee member and the committee chair have dissimilar inflation preferences, the committee is more likely to issue more precise monetary policy statements. As an interesting condition, however, I find evidence of this when I consider the median committee member's and the committee chair's preferences using a sample of committee members *on schedule to vote*. When I calculate the median committee member's and the chair's preferences using all committee members, including those not on schedule to vote, I do not find evidence consistent with my theory. I also find evidence of a positive relationship between the absolute distance between the median committee member's and the committee chair's policy preferences and the number of amendments made to the official policy statement. Taken together, these results provide new evidence on how the policy preferences of central banker committee composition affect the content of central bank communication and highlights the importance of institutional constraints, especially policy voting rights, on the FOMC.

This chapter is organized as follows. In the next section, I discuss the research design and the construction of the dependent and independent variables using computational tools and textual data. Section 4.3 introduces the empirical model and presents the statistical results. The final section concludes.

4.2 Research Design

The FOMC of the US central bank meets approximately eight times a year. During these meetings, policy makers are tasked with deciding on US monetary policy. Importantly, verbatim FOMC meeting transcripts are recorded and are made publicly available making them the most detailed accounts of FOMC meeting proceedings. Starting in 1994, the FOMC Secretariat compiled meeting transcripts of members' policy deliberations during the entirety of the meeting. Publication of the meeting transcripts is time restricted, with meeting reports made public after a five-year lag or moratorium.[1] The purpose

[1] Transcripts and other historical materials.

of the five-year moratorium is to encourage committee members to speak sincerely and truthfully during deliberations without concern for immediate market effects that may arise with the immediate publication of the verbatim transcripts. While meeting participants are allowed to review the transcripts for accuracy, the transcripts are only (if ever) lightly edited. In addition to small changes that can be requested by the members, some information in the transcripts, either confidential information or names of people and entities, is redacted for privacy reasons. And while previous research shows that publication of transcripts can stifle or suppress speech among the members (Meade and Stasavage, 2008), the meeting transcripts offer the closest thing to a record of what members say they want during the course of policy deliberations.

4.2.1 The Sample

The sample that I use for empirical testing covers twenty-four, two-day FOMC policy meetings held between January 2005 and December 2007. These twenty-four meetings have a number of important features that make them particularly useful for theory testing. First, the time period itself represents the end of an economic period known as the Great Moderation. The Great Moderation was a historical period between 1984 and 2007 when the United States enjoyed relative macroeconomic stability. Averageinflation during this period was relatively low, hovering around 3 to 4 percent, and interest rates were more or less stable. For example, the yield curve for US Treasury securities, which represents the cost of borrowing US government bonds at different rates of maturity, was relatively flat during this time, suggesting that markets saw little risk. Taken together, all of these indicators suggest a somewhat stable national economic outlook for the conduct of monetary policy.[2]

If the period of the Great Moderation is characterized by its economic stability, then the period is bookended by two distinct periods

[2] FRB: 93rd Annual Report, 2006.

of economic crisis: inflation volatility leading up to 1984, sometimes called the Great Inflation, and the Great Recession, which was a period of economic and unemployment instability following the US financial crisis (2007–2008). The sample that I use for theory testing in this chapter therefore best reflects "normal economic times." By analyzing central bank policy making between, but not including, the two crisis periods surrounding this period, the empirical model is fit to data that reflect a stable economic outlook and therefore conventional monetary policy making.

The sample period also ensures that the measures used for the analyses are comparable both across actors and over time. In particular, by ending the analysis in 2008, the sample avoids unexpected shifts in policy makers' preferences that occurred as a consequence of the US financial crisis. This is important because the US financial crisis makes it much more challenging to compare policy makers' preferences, both among each other and over time. As one example, starting in 2007, the United States faced a steep decline in the housing sector. As early as the last quarter of 2007, growing financial fragility prompted policy makers to consider housing-related issues in their deliberations, despite that the real estate market is not part of the Fed's official dual mandate, which has twin aims of low inflation and maximum employment. In reading the transcripts from 2008, it is readily apparent that policy makers spoke more about housing-related topics in the meetings, which suggests that policy makers were concerned with topics outside of their normal roles of balancing inflation and unemployment/output concerns (see also Acosta and Meade, 2015). Even more important, as policy makers are expected to make decisions, governed by the twin arms of the Fed's dual mandate, censoring the time period before the financial crisis helps ensure that policy makers' concerns are firmly anchored in their everyday management of a stable economy.

Also important is that while I consider only twenty-four meetings occurring across three years, there are a number of important sources of exogenous variation to the committee during this period. First, there is important exogenous variation in the preferences of the committee members as a result of changes of membership on the committee rotation system. The FOMC committee rotation system enables only a subset of all committee members to vote at any given meeting. A maximum of twelve members vote out of a possible nineteen members. Importantly, members cannot self-select into official voting, and official voting is determined by a preset schedule and is therefore exogenous to members' inflation preferences. At the conclusion of the meeting, the committee chair takes a "roll call" of members' votes. Those members on schedule to vote have their votes recorded and made publicly available. Those members not on schedule to vote also report their votes *as if they could vote*, but importantly, these votes are not made public and are only released in the transcript data five years later.

A second important source of exogenous variation in the time period under study are important changes in committee composition as a result of new appointments made to the FOMC. In February 2006, in the middle of the sample, the committee chair changed, with chairman Ben Bernanke replacing chairman Alan Greenspan. Similarly, FOMC committee member Kohn (Federal Reserve Bank Board) took over the role of vice chairman during this period, and another three people were appointed to the FOMC: Warsh (Federal Reserve Bank of NY), Kroszner (Federal Reserve Bank of Richmond), and Mishkin (Federal Reserve Bank of Boston). These changes altered the preferences, or ideal points, of both the chair and the median committee member. This is important, as it helps ensure that any empirical model fit to the data is not fit to a specific committee; rather, the results hold for a more generic configuration of committee members, who can and do change over time.[3]

The sample also holds constant a number of important political variables that can act as codeterminants and that, consequently, might bias the model estimates if unaccounted for. First, in the United States, the president appoints and the Senate confirms all members representing the Board of Governors. Previous research finds that the preferences of the president and the Senate matter for who gets appointed to the FOMC in the first place (Chang, 2003), in a process similar to Supreme Court nominations. During the sample period covered in this study, the US president, George W. Bush, wielded

[3] FOMC Board Membership and Appointments.

official appointment powers to the FOMC across the entire sample, thus holding the partisan hue of the appointing president constant. Similarly, all new appointments to the FOMC that occurred in the sample happened before the 2006 Senate election in November. This again ensures that the politics of appointments, either due to the partisanship of the president or the partisanship of the Senate, is held constant across the sample period.

While there are significant benefits to holding economic and political variables constant, so as to control factors that may compromise the validity of the uncovered relationship between the variables, also important is an understanding of how well the results generalize to other conditions, where conditions might change. In chapters 5 and 6, I specifically relax these assumptions to test the generalizability of my argument in other places and times under different conditions. Using a survey experiment, chapter 5 tests whether households adjust their inflation expectations to central bank announcements when the economy is facing deflationary, rather than inflationary, economic conditions. Furthermore, chapter 6 tests the theory using a sample of countries in Latin America during the 1990s and 2000s. Across these two decades, a number of Latin American countries experienced both high and hyperinflation conditions. Both chapters therefore test the universality of the research findings in economic environments that are extraordinary rather than ordinary.

How FOMC Meetings Work

The FOMC members meet approximately eight times a year to decide on changes to interest rates and deliberate the content of an official monetary policy statement. Both decisions are made public directly after the close of the FOMC meeting. Importantly, FOMC meetings follow a uniform protocol. There are two policy deliberation rounds, one called the "economic go-round" and the other the "policy go-round." In the economic go-round, central bank district presidents report on local economic conditions "on the ground" in the geographical districts that they represent. To do this, they often read aloud preprepared speeches about conditions in their districts. These reports are unusually highly structured in terms of length, topics, and organization. Members first outline regional inflation developments in the first paragraph of the text and then regional output and unemployment developments in the second paragraph. During this part of the meeting, committee members also relay anecdotal information from local business owners in their regions and report findings from research conducted in their district branches by their research departments. Sometimes, but not always, the preprepared statements are sent to the FOMC chair one week in advance of the FOMC meeting; however, those members other than the chair hear the preprepared speeches for the first time at the meeting.

In the second round of policy deliberations, or the policy go-round, committee members verbally announce their preferred policies. Here they report how they want the federal fund rate to move, and they also vocalize their preferred official monetary policy statement. Importantly, members are asked to select their preferred policy statements from a set of possible alternative policy statements. Those members that are on schedule to vote are then asked for their votes in a formal roll call. The statements, including all of the statement alternatives, are given to the committee members, both to those on schedule and off schedule to vote, in advance of the FOMC meeting. The statements and their alternatives are issued in the *Report to the FOMC on Economic Conditions and Monetary Policy*. This is produced by staff members at the Board of Governors in Washington, DC. This report is distributed to members of the FOMC prior to each regularly scheduled FOMC meeting, approximately one week in advance of the meeting. This implies that members have the same information and, given this information, a week in the leadup to the meeting to determine their ideal statements in advance. Of course, some editing of the statements also occurs during meeting deliberations, but the initial structure and content of the statements are predetermined by the Board of Governors.

During most meetings, three to four draft policy statements are made available to the FOMC members. Sometimes the content of the statements vary as a consequence of different policy options or scenarios that policy makers might adopt that result from different choices made to the federal funds rate. For example, assume there is a status quo statement A, where the federal funds rate is 3 percent. If FOMC members decide to raise interest rates by 25 basis points, statement

B might report that change. Alternatively, if members decide to raise interest rates by 50 basis points, statement C might report that change instead. In addition to particular statements mapping to different changes in policy, different lexical features are deployed across the statements. Once they come together in the meeting and during the policy go-around, committee members lobby both for their preferred statements and to make linguistic changes to their preferred statements, and sometimes members take one section of one statement and export it to or replace it by another statement.

For example, in making changes to the official statement, members can either agree or disagree with the changes proposed by other members. One member might propose that the statement say "inflation is rising slowly," and a subsequent member might oppose the qualifier "slowly" and ask instead that the statement say "inflation is rising." Because all of the policy statements are drafted in advance of the FOMC meeting and all members receive these statements prior to the meeting, committee members use the time in the meeting to bargain over the text of the policy statement. In the final roll call at the close of the meeting, members ultimately vote on policy statements directly from a finite (or near-finite) number of known alternatives that are agreed on during deliberations.

The data used in the analyses, therefore, include the twenty-four *adopted*, not proposed, monetary policy statements. While a larger subset of statements is available if we include all of the statements, such as those not selected or debated, only twenty-four statements are ultimately distributed to the general public. I consider these and not the unadopted policy statements as the official communications of the FOMC. Importantly, those statements that are unchosen are, like the meeting transcripts, published with a five-year lag, and there is therefore little reason to believe that they affect either the market or the public. Future research, however, might be wise to examine what explains the adoption of a given statement in the first place.

In terms of the temporal structure of the statements, I call the adopted statement at the previous meeting the *status quo statement* (SQ) and the policy statement adopted at the current meeting the *new and revised statement* (NS). It is important to note that the official policy statements change slowly, a fact reflected in the epigraph to this chapter. It is common, for example, for entire paragraphs of the statement to be the same across multiple meetings, only being replaced years later.

In summary, the data used in the analysis come from unstructured textual data from twenty-four FOMC meeting transcripts and twenty-four adopted policy statements of FOMC meetings held between 2005 and 2008. The main dependent variables are the level of precision or vagueness in the adopted policy statement and the number of edits to the policy statement from the status quo statement (more on these later). The main independent variable is whether the committee chair and the median committee member have opposing or like biases when it comes to inflation. Finally, as a control variable, I include the number of dissents to the policy statement expressed by all members as reported in the transcripts, irrespective of whether they are on schedule to vote. The next section outlines how I construct and operationalize these variables from the textual information provided by the FOMC's historical archive.

4.2.2 Dependent Variables

Information Precision

To measure the precision of the content of any given FOMC policy statement, I count the relative number of uncertainty and certainty words and word phrases that are deployed in the policy statement from a curated dictionary. Dictionary approaches in machine learning are *supervised learning* approaches. To build context-specific uncertainty and certainty words and phrases, I developed a custom-made dictionary from human annotation of the FOMC transcripts. Once constructed, the certainty and uncertainty dictionary had 288 words and word phrases, or *keys*. Among these 290 words and word phrases are 136 uncertainty words and 154 certainty words. These 290 keys in my dictionary built from the relatively less structured text from FOMC verbatim transcript data are what I then apply to the policy statements.

The official policy statements adopted by the members are both relatively short, varying from seven to eleven sentences, and highly structured. The first part of the statement reports the decision, the second part of the statement discusses the policy rationale, and the final part of the statement expresses the committee's outlook. Applying a relatively large dictionary constructed using domain-specific language but out of sample texts helped protect against model overfitting.[4] The following section details the dictionary's construction, mentions alternative dictionaries, and presents a metric of the information precision in FOMC policy statements using the relative counts of certainty and uncertainty words.

To make the dictionary, I first randomly selected (without replacement) 200 individual speaker-meeting contributions from the full texts of the FOMC transcripts across the twenty-four meetings. For example, everything that Chairman Bernanke says at his first meeting in 2007 pasted together is a speaker-meeting contribution. From these randomly selected 200 speaker-meeting contributions, I then randomly selected 300 sentences (without replacement) from the speaker-meeting contributions. From these 300 sentences, I removed substantively unimportant sentences, such as "Thank you, Mr. Chairman" and sentences concerning meeting logistics, such as the introduction of lunches and breaks. After I removed these sentences, 292 sentences were left. I then split the 292 remaining sentences into a training set (132 sentences) and a test set (160 sentences). The training set of 132 sentences was given to three annotators for human annotation. Annotations were performed by two graduate students at the University of Mannheim and me using the annotation software Multipurpose Annotation Environment (MAE), which was created to annotate medical records (Stubbs, 2011).

The three annotators were instructed to annotate the 132 training sentences for two things. First, the annotators were asked to label a given sentence, in its entirety, according to whether it used speculative/hedging language or nonspeculative/nonhedging language. Annotators were instructed that speculative and hedging language refers to using language to "protect speech claims." Hedging is used "to soften what we say or write. . . . The most common forms of

[4] I also ran the analysis using a larger dictionary of 418 words split by 184 uncertainty words and 234 certainty words and found similar results to those reported here. These results are available in the Appendix.

hedging involve tense and aspect, modal expressions including modal verbs and adverbs, vague language such as sort of and kind of, and some verbs."[5] Second, in addition to coding the entire sentence, the annotators were instructed to highlight those words and word phrases that triggered sentence labeling. The dictionary, and the associated words, were then complied from the list of "trigger" words and word phrases that the annotators highlighted as indicating either hedging or decisive language. For example, the annotators often marked the phrases "I've become somewhat more" and "as suggesting" as speculative or hedging words and phrases, whereas the annotators marked "are consistent" and "continues to be" as nonspeculative or nonhedging words and phrases.[6] The dictionary was then populated with these 290 words and word phrases. importantly, the dictionary was relatively balanced, with 136 uncertainty words and phrase keys and 154 certainty words and phrases keys, and was generated naturally by the annotators in their responses to FOMC language.

To validate the dictionary, I considered context validity, sensitivity, and specificity. Context validity judges a dictionary based on whether the dictionary's category scheme, or the underlying dimension the dictionary keys are trying to represent, is appropriate for the data to which it is applied. By building the dictionary directly from language used by committee members on the FOMC in the transcripts, I could ensure that the dictionary would be likely to capture hedging/uncertainty and nonhedging/certainty words used by policy makers themselves and in the appropriate context. Application of a more generic uncertainty dictionary, such as off-the-shelf dictionaries, would not necessarily have captured nuances of economic uncertainty and certainty. For example, in preliminary analysis, I applied one commonly used off-the-shelf dictionary—the Linguistic Inquiry Word Count (LIWC) dictionary, which has a dimension used for certainty and uncertainty words. When applied to the policy statements, however, the LIWC dictionary reported 0 certainty words across the sample. Furthermore, research by Loughran and McDonald (2011) finds that

[5] Hedges: Emphasising and Downtoning.

[6] The full list of words and word phrases in the dictionary used in the analysis is made available in the Appendix.

generic sentiment dictionaries are not good at identifying uncertainty in finance-related contexts, as many finance words have negative terms despite not having negative meaning.[7,8]

Another way to assess dictionary quality is by thinking about the trade-off between specificity and sensitivity. A good dictionary properly identifies important concepts yet also protects against false positives and false negatives. The inclusion of word phrases (as opposed to just single-word unigrams) is particularly helpful in this regard. This is because many of the ways that FOMC members discuss uncertainty and certainty reference underlying economic theories and concepts with associated jargon, and these are likely to be phrases rather than just single worlds (Baerg and Lowe, 2018). The annotators were also not given limits on the length of word phrases they highlighted. The benefit of a custom-made dictionary, therefore, is that it is context specific, is populated on both the positive and negative dimensions of the concept of interest, and includes words and phrases of arbitrary length. Furthermore, because it is constructed on less structured data, it can achieve specificity without being overfit to the data.

Once I had constructed the dictionary, I applied it to the corpus of twenty-four adopted policy statements. I then counted the number of words and word phrases that were simultaneously present in the statement and present in the dictionary keys.[9] Uncertainty words were counted as (c_1), and certainty words were counted as (c_2). I did not normalize the counts, as there is little variation in the length of the official policy statements and the number of sentences is relatively small, varying from seven to eleven. Furthermore, one could expect that the length of the statement might be related to the level of uncertainty, and so normalizing might ignore important variation specifically on the dimension in which we are interested. Because I kept only those words

[7] For performance measures on different dictionaries, including this one for detecting speculative sentences, see Štajner et al. (2016). I also considered the finance dictionary by Loughran and McDonald (2011), which was specifically built for finance words, but it suffers the same problem as LIWC in that it accounts for positive words (uncertainty) but not negative words (certainty) and also only uses single words rather than words and word phrases, which are common across the statements.

[8] Results using these dictionaries are available in the Appendix.

[9] When applying the dictionary to the statement, I found that keeping all words and word phrases of length three or less was best for dictionary performance.

and word phrases that appeared in the dictionary, I did not preprocess the textual data with the exception of removing punctuation, meaning that I did not stem or lemmatize the words and word phrases. My measure of information vagueness, therefore, is the proportion of raw counts of (c_1) and (c_2), or $\frac{c_1}{(c_1+c_2)}$.

Amendments to the Policy Statement

I also used the official policy statements to construct a measure of the number of policy changes made to the statements—or edits—across statements over time. To do this, I counted the number of changes made to the policy statement at the current meeting (NS) compared with the status quo policy statement issued at the last meeting (SQ). Rather than calculating this by hand, I took a computational approach, using a measure called the *Levenshtein distance measure*. The Levenshtein distance measure computes the minimum number of single-word deletions, insertions, or substitutions required to match the new text (NS) to the old text (SQ).

As an example of Levenshtein distance, consider two different subsections of a FOMC policy statement. In this example, the first statement-pair has a distance metric of 1, and the second statement-pair has a distance metric of 14. Assuming these two sections make up the complete statement, summing together, the total number of changes to the new statement from the status quo statement is 15 for this example.

SQ_1: The Federal Open Market Committee decided today to raise its target for the federal funds rate by 25 basis points to 3 percent.

SQ_2: Pressures on inflation have picked up in recent months, and pricing power is more evident. Longer-term inflation expectations remain well contained.

NS_1: The Federal Open Market Committee decided today to raise its target for the federal funds rate by 25 basis points to 3-1/4 percent.

NS_2: Readings on inflation have been subdued in recent months, and longer-term inflation expectations have declined.

The Levenshtein distance measure is commonly used in linguistics, including in spelling algorithms and translation, and in statistical models to evaluate language similarity. In political science, Baerg and Hallerberg (2016) use it to measure deliberations over the recommended policy changes in European Union member statements. Applied to this sample of policy statements, the measure ranges from 2 to 185, with a median number of edits at 64 and the mean number of edits at 71.

4.2.3 Independent Variables

Committee Preference Diversity

To measure variation in committee members' inflation preferences, or ideal points, I use previously published measures of central bank preferences from Baerg and Lowe (2018). These authors measure FOMC members' inflation aversion by examining the emphasis members place on inflation versus output and unemployment topics at each meeting. This measure then ranks committee members according to their ideal points. Actors are scaled such that those members who talk the most about inflation are located to the right, or as inflation "hawks," and those actors who talk the most about output and unemployment are located to the left and called inflation "doves." Other actors are located in between.

Given the distribution in members' preferences at every meeting, I then compute the inflation preferences of the median member and the chair. From here I can then determine whether the median member and the chair have like or opposing inflation biases. I code the variable *Opposing Biases* as 1 when the chair and the median committee member have differently signed ideal points and 0 when they have similarly signed ideal points. In those cases where there are two median members, where one is positive and the other is negative, I code the median member who agrees with the chair as having a like bias. This is called *Opposing Biases (median A)*. In a second measure, for those cases where there are two median members, where one is positive and the other is negative, I code the median member who opposes the chair as 1 and call it *Opposing Biases (median O)*. For those cases where there is single median member, the measures *Opposing Biases (median A)* and *Opposing Biases (median B)* have the same value. As another measure, I also calculate the mean rather than the median member. When the mean member has oppositely signed ideal points to the chair, the variable *Opposing Biases (mean)* is coded 1, and 0 otherwise.

Next, I repeat the preceding procedure a second time, except this time, instead of using all members for the sample, I restrict the sample to include only those FOMC members who are *on schedule to vote at that particular meeting*. As before, I calculate three measures: *Opposing Biases (median A)*, *Opposing Biases (median O)*, and *Opposing Biases (mean)*.

Interestingly, Figures 4.1 and 4.2 show remarkable variation in the measure *Opposing Biases (median A)*, depending on whether we consider the sample of individuals who are on schedule to vote or all members. In the sample where all members are used, irrespective of their voting rights, we observe similarity in the chair and the median member's preferences at the start of the sample period. As the sample period progresses, however, we observe an uptick in meetings with opposing ideal points. Using the sample that computes the median member from those members with FOMC voting rights, however, we observe somewhat of a different pattern. Here we see a larger number of oppositely signed preferences to the chair at the start of the sample period and more congruence near the end of the sample. Because of

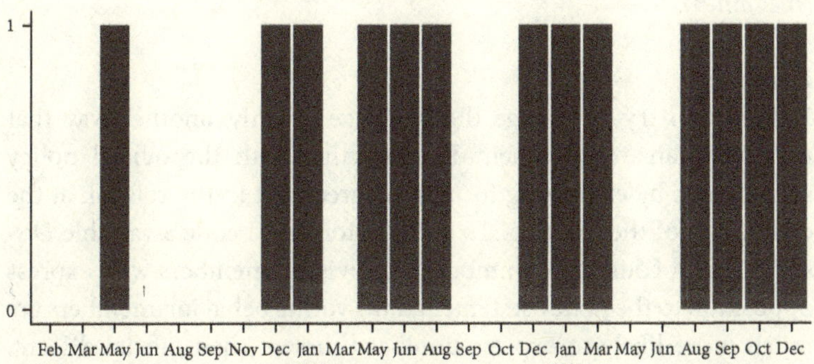

Fig. 4.1 Opposing bias of chair and median based on all members.

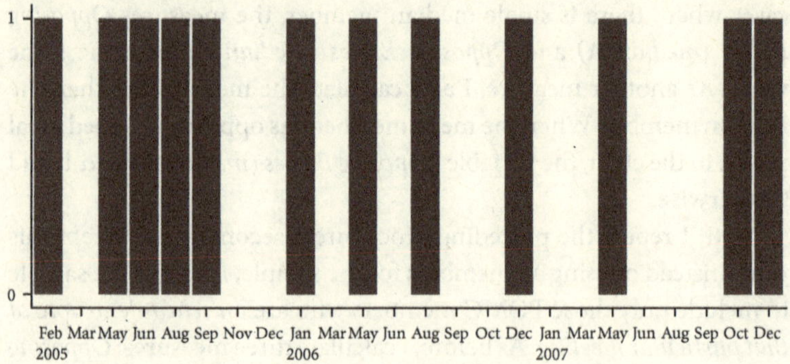

Fig. 4.2 Opposing bias of chair and median based on voting members.

the potential differences presented by the rotation voting system, the empirical analyses are conducted on both samples. Interestingly, I find evidence that the relationship between bias and information precision depends on from which sample I compute the median member's position.

Preference Distance

To measure the distance between the chair and the median member's preferences, I take the absolute difference in their estimated ideal points. As earlier, I calculate this using both in the full sample of FOMC members and the sample that includes only those on schedule to vote. These variables are called *Distance (median A)* and *Distance (median B)*.

Dissents

Rather than try to change the language directly, another way that members can express their dissatisfaction with the official policy statement is by expressing formal disagreement in the roll call at the conclusion of the meeting. To account for this, I code a variable *Dissents*, which counts the number of individual members who express opposition to the policy statement. Like voting behavior, members are much more likely to express unofficial dissent than official dissent. I include all members who made some verbal protest to the official policy statement. I collected these data by hand by reading and hand-coding members' opposition to the policy statement during the policy go-round as made available in the transcripts. This variable ranges from 0 to 8, and the series has a median of 2 and a mean of 2.4.

4.3 Empirical Model and Results

I focus on testing the following hypotheses:

Hypothesis 4.3.1. Committee Composition: *When the chair and the median member have opposing preferences, policy statements will be more likely to be precise than when the chair and the median member have like preferences.*

Hypothesis 4.3.2. Dissents and Amendments: *When the chair and the median member have opposing preferences, as the median member and the chair get farther apart in terms of preferences, we are likely to observe more dissent and greater edits to the policy statements.*

The statistical model used to test these predictions is a mixed-effects logistic regression model where the dependent variable is the proportion of the raw counts of uncertainty words and phrases over all uncertainty and certainty words and phrases contained in the policy statement. The independent variables, as discussed, are whether the chair and the mean or median member have opposing inflation bias and the absolute distance in the median and chair's preferences. I also include as a control variable the number of dissents to the policy statement expressed by members during the meeting. The model also includes year and chair random effects. These effects aim to account for changes to the economy across the three years and for possible variations in the chair styles of Chairman Greenspan and Chairman Bernanke, unaccounted for in their ideal points.[10]

[10] Specifically, I fit the model in R using glmer with a binomial link function, with the dependent variable specified as *cbind*(c_1, c_2) and year and chair name as random effects.

4.3.1 Results for Diversity on Policy Statement Uncertainty

Table 4.1 reports the estimates using the operationalization where all FOMC members (minus the chair) are used to compute the mean and median. Counter to the expectations of the first hypothesis, I find a positive relationship between opposing biases and the proportion of uncertainty words and word phrases expressed in the policy statement. The positive relationship is robust to a variety of specifications, including those models where I control for the number of dissents, which, also surprisingly, is unrelated to the level of uncertainty in the policy statement.

Rather than look at change in the log odds, Table 4.2 reports the fitted values on the scale of the linear predictor for all models.[11] Similar to the preceding findings, across all models, meetings where the median member holds oppositely biased preferences to the com-

Table 4.1 Effects of committee heterogeneity on uncertainty and certainty in FOMC statements: All members

	Model 1	Model 2	Model 3	Model 4	Model 5	Model 6
Opposing Biases (mean)	0.358			0.338		
	(0.254)			(0.274)		
Opposing Biases (median A)		0.441*			0.449	
		(0.254)			(0.284)	
Opposing Biases (median B)			0.270			0.232
			(0.274)			(0.288)
No. of dissent				0.012	-0.004	0.026
				(0.063)	(0.066)	(0.062)
Constant	0.253	0.230	0.258	0.235	0.236	0.223
	(0.185)	(0.176)	(0.230)	(0.207)	(0.199)	(0.243)
Chair and year effects	✓	✓	✓	✓	✓	✓
Observations	24	24	24	24	24	24
Log likelihood	−38.430	−37.912	−38.942	−38.410	−37.910	−38.852
Akaike inf. crit.	84.859	83.824	85.884	84.821	83.820	87.704
Bayesian inf. crit.	89.571	88.536	90.597	89.533	88.532	93.594

$^{*}p < 0.1$. $^{**}p < 0.05$. $^{***}p < 0.01$.

[11] Effects are calculated for glmer using the Effects package in R.

Table 4.2 Committee heterogeneity on uncertainty and certainty in FOMC statements: All members, fitted on the scale of the linear predictor

	Condition	Estimate	Lower	Upper
Model 1	Like bias	0.563	0.473	0.649
	Opposed bias	0.648	0.567	0.722
Model 2	Like bias	0.557	0.471	0.640
	Opposed bias	0.662	0.577	0.737
Model 3	Like bias	0.564	0.452	0.670
	Opposed bias	0.629	0.556	0.696
Model 4	Like bias	0.566	0.471	0.656
	Opposed bias	0.646	0.563	0.722
Model 5	Like bias	0.556	0.464	0.644
	Opposed bias	0.663	0.574	0.741
Model 6	Like bias	0.571	0.455	0.680
	Opposed bias	0.627	0.554	0.694

mittee chair are also those meetings where we see higher expressed uncertainty in the policy statement. Interpreting model 5, for example, we see that moving from like bias to opposing biases is associated with a predicted probability of 0.556 in the associated level of uncertainty to a 0.663 level of uncertainty.

Table 4.3 reports the estimates using the sample where the mean and median are calculated only from those members on schedule to vote rather than from the full sample. In contrast to the preceding results, I find some evidence in support of the first hypothesis, although as before, likely due to the low sample size, the results are not statistically significant at conventional levels. When the chair and the median (mean) member have opposing bias, we see a reduction in the level of uncertainty expressed in the policy statement. The negative relationship is also robust to a variety of different model specifications, including controlling for the number of dissents. The dissent variable continues to be unrelated, either substantively or statistically, to the level of uncertainty in the policy statement.

Again, I transform the estimates to their linear predictors. If we interpret model 5 for comparability with the preceding results, we see that for those members on the FOMC on schedule to vote, when

Table 4.3 Effects of committee heterogeneity on uncertainty and certainty in FOMC statements: Voting members only

	Model 1	Model 2	Model 3	Model 4	Model 5	Model 6
Opposing Biases (mean)	−0.131			−0.174		
	(0.259)			(0.264)		
Opposing Biases (median A)		−0.031			−0.104	
		(0.272)			(0.268)	
Opposing Biases (median B)			−0.041			−0.127
			(0.258)			(0.275)
Dissent				0.049	0.049	0.052
				(0.060)	(0.062)	(0.063)
Constant	0.526***	0.462**	0.469**	0.437*	0.383*	0.395*
	(0.202)	(0.185)	(0.192)	(0.229)	(0.205)	(0.210)
Chair and year effects	✓	✓	✓	✓	✓	✓
Observations	24	24	24	24	24	24
Log likelihood	−39.298	−39.419	−39.413	−38.959	−39.101	−39.069
Akaike inf. crit.	86.596	86.837	86.826	85.918	86.201	88.138
Bayesian inf. crit.	91.308	91.550	91.538	90.630	90.914	94.028

*$p < 0.1$. **$p < 0.05$. ***$p < 0.01$.

Table 4.4 Committee heterogeneity on uncertainty and certainty in FOMC statements: Voting members, fitted on the scale of the linear predictor

	Condition	Estimate	Lower	Upper
Model 1	Like bias	0.629	0.533	0.715
	Opposed bias	0.597	0.520	0.671
Model 2	Like bias	0.614	0.525	0.695
	Opposed bias	0.606	0.517	0.689
Model 3	Like bias	0.615	0.523	0.700
	Opposed bias	0.606	0.523	0.682
Model 4	Like bias	0.635	0.538	0.723
	Opposed bias	0.594	0.516	0.668
Model 5	Like bias	0.623	0.534	0.704
	Opposed bias	0.598	0.510	0.681
Model 6	Like bias	0.627	0.532	0.714
	Opposed bias	0.597	0.514	0.676

the committee and the median member have like biases, we see that predicted probability of changes in uncertainty is 0.623. Alternatively, when the committee and the median member have opposing biases, the predicted probability of changes in uncertainty is 0.598. Thus the difference in the predicted probability on the proportion of uncertainty words is approximately 3 percent lower for diverse committees if we consider only those with FOMC voting members and 10 percent higher for diverse committees if we consider all members, irrespective of their voting rights.

The foregoing analyses test the relationship between uncertainty and committee diversity, measured by differences in the inflation preferences between the chair and the median committee member. The empirical findings yield mixed support for the theory. When I estimate the relationship considering all members on the FOMC committee, I find a substantively large and positive relationship between the proportion of uncertainty words and word phrases when the chair and the median member have opposing biases (i.e., one is an inflation hawk and the other is a dove). This suggests that counter to the theoretical argument, when the chair and the median committee member have opposing bias, the policy statement is more vague. Alternatively, when I restrict the sample to calculate the median committee member only from those FOMC members who are on schedule to vote at that particular meeting, I find the opposite: a small and negative relationship between the proportion of uncertainty words and word phrases in the policy statement when the Chair and the Median member have opposing inflation bias.

One can speculate on why the results vary across the composition of the members. One possible reason might be the fit to the dictionary rather than any substantial differences as an effect of differences in the committees. For robustness, I rerun the analysis using the larger dictionary of uncertainty and certainty words. Doing so, I find similar results, suggesting that the model is unlikely being driven by specific words in the dictionary. A second theoretical interpretation may be that only those members with actual voting power, and therefore an outside option to publicly dissent, are the ones who count when it comes to constraining the chair from making more vague policy statements. According to this argument, a median member of the subcommittee with voting rights, not the full committee, having opposing preferences to the chair reduces vagueness in the policy statement. This interpretation suggests that only some members having an outside option to dissent publicly by expressing dissenting votes matters for communication policy. This interpretation fits into other evidence that finds that FOMC members act differently when they are on schedule to vote. For example, recent research shows that voting members dissent less both in speech and in votes when they are on schedule to vote, even if we account for their preferred policies (Baerg and Lowe, 2018; Meade and Stasavage, 2008). Finally, still another, more technical interpretation is that a larger group leads to higher likelihood that the median member is actually centered around the median. Consequently, what matters for communication policy is the combination of both the median position of the committee member and also whether the chair is similarly biased or more extreme than the median member. Further research might exploit ways in which this finding can be further tested, for example, by expanding the sample back to 1994, when members were first made aware that their meetings were being recorded.

4.3.2 Results for Diversity on Policy Editing

In this section, I examine the relationship between the number of edits to the policy statement and the amount of *Distance* between the ideal point of the chair and the median committee member. The number of edits to the policy statement is right skewed (recall that the minimum is 2 and the maximum is 185, with a median number of edits of 64 and a mean number of edits of 71). Owing to the skew and also the fact that there are no instances of zero edits to the statement, I take the log of the variable and use this as my dependent variable (this effectively down-weights cases where there are a large number of dissents and up-weights cases where only a small number of dissents are cast). In addition to the preference distance between the chair and the median member, I include the number of dissents expressed over the policy statement. As earlier, the model also includes the year and chair random effects.

Table 4.5 reports the findings for all members. According to this table, we find a positive relationship between the absolute distance

Table 4.5 Effects of distance on edits to the FOMC statements: All members

	Model 1		Model 2	
	Median 1	Median 2	Median 1	Median 2
Distance (median A)	0.244		0.269	
	(0.328)		(0.335)	
Distance (median B)		0.271		0.327
		(0.362)		(0.377)
No. of dissent			0.060	0.070
			(0.088)	(0.090)
Constant	3.644***	3.561***	3.469***	3.325***
	(0.450)	(0.546)	(0.523)	(0.637)
Chair and year effects	✓	✓	✓	✓
Observations	24	24	24	24
Log likelihood	−33.749	−33.660	−35.032	−34.858
Akaike inf. crit.	77.498	77.320	82.065	81.715
Bayesian inf. crit.	83.389	83.210	89.133	88.784

*$p < 0.1$. **$p < 0.05$. ***$p < 0.01$.

between the median member and the chair and the number of edits. Recall that the estimates are logged. If we interpret model 2, for example, a one-unit increase in distance between the chair and the median member, equivalent of moving them apart so that one is a "hawk" and the other a "strong hawk," is associated with approximately twenty-seven additional edits to the policy statement ($100 * 0.269$).

Table 4.6 reports the findings for only those voters with voting rights at the meeting. According to this table, we still show a positive relationship between the absolute distance between the median and the chair and the number of edits. Interpreting model 3 again, a one-unit increase in distance between the chair and the median member is associated with approximately eleven additional edits to the policy statement ($100 * 0.113$). As before, once we control for the number of dissents, we see the estimate rise slightly.

The foregoing analysis examines whether there is a statistical relationship between the number of edits to the official policy statement and the distance between the preferences of the chair and the median committee member. The results suggest that while there is a positive relationship between distance and the number of edits, the uncertainty

Table 4.6 Effects of distance on edits to the FOMC statements: Voting members

	Model 1	Model 2	Model 3	Model 4
Distance (median A)	0.074		0.113	
	(0.289)		(0.299)	
Distance (median B)		0.142		0.194
		(0.308)		(0.320)
No. of dissent			0.059	0.065
			(0.090)	(0.091)
Constant	3.859***	3.789***	3.673***	3.576***
	(0.382)	(0.389)	(0.481)	(0.493)
Chair and meeting effects	✓	✓	✓	✓
Observations	24	24	24	24
Log likelihood	−34.127	−33.988	−35.403	−35.219
Akaike inf. crit.	78.255	77.977	82.807	82.438
Bayesian inf. crit.	84.145	83.867	89.875	89.506

*$p < 0.1$. **$p < 0.05$. ***$p < 0.01$.

around the estimates is large, so the results are not statistically significant. Unlike the earlier analysis of the level of lexical uncertainty and certainty expressed in the policy statement, I find no differences across subsamples when calculating the median member from either a sample of all FOMC members or only those FOMC members on schedule to vote. I do, however, find a slightly lower estimated number of edits (eleven compared to twenty-seven) when I restrict the median members to only those members on schedule to vote. This again provides further evidence that those committee members on schedule to vote are less likely to demonstrate opposition to the status quo. Owing to the large uncertainty around the estimates, including overlapping estimates, such differences between those on schedule to vote and the full committee should be interpreted cautiously in this case.

4.4 Conclusion

The statistical analyses presented in this chapter indicate mixed results for my theory. On the one hand, evidence from the sample of all FOMC members suggests that there is a positive relationship between committee diversity and the level of expressed lexical uncertainty in the policy statement, and this finding is counter to the expected relationship. On the other hand, when I restrict the sample to only those FOMC members on schedule to vote, I find a negative relationship, as predicted by my theory. For voting members, I find some evidence that the proportion of uncertainty words expressed in the policy statement by committees with opposing biases is negatively related to preference diversity. One explanation, consistent with the theoretical model, is that only those members on schedule to vote have the "outside option" to dissent publicly. For those members not on schedule to vote, any opposition is published five years later, which makes their opposition significantly less meaningful. Consequently, one take-away from the analysis is that the rotation-voting system likely generates differences in members' behavior over crafting policy communications as it does other behaviors, such as voting to change interest rates. I also find a positive relationship between the absolute distance between the median member and the chair and the number of edits to the policy statement, as expected by the theory. Owing to the small sample size and the uncertainty of the estimates, however, the results are mostly indicative rather than definitive. Future research would do well to enlarge the sample and/or improve on the measures developed here.

By examining within-committee and across-time dynamics, the evidence in this chapter provides some, albeit inconclusive, evidence that diversity in committee members' inflation preferences likely matters for central bank communication policy. Much of the previous literature studying the role of committees examines the relationship between monetary policy committees across countries and institutions rather than exploring within-committee variation. For example, Ehrmann and Fratzscher (2007) find that there is no single approach to communication across monetary policy committees. Novel here is that by examining policy making within a single committee over time, exploiting variation in who is appointed as chairman and also who is a voting committee member, I uncover new patterns that were previously unknown.

The differences generated by the voting rotation system and the development of new techniques to uncover central bankers' policy preferences using computational textual analysis offer exciting new avenues for theory development and empirical testing. While this chapter focuses on committee diversity in terms of inflation preferences, other kinds of diversity, such as members' heterogeneity in regional affiliation, committee role, appointers, and even ascriptive diversity, may go some way in explaining central bank communication. Finally, length of tenure, reputation, and expertise might also be important factors that can help us explain why central bank committees choose the words they do for public consumption. In the models in this chapter, these individual-level nuances are swept aside. Future research therefore might do well to uncover additional individual and institutional characteristics that influence communication policy.

5
Central Bank Announcements and Inflation Expectations

5.1 Introduction

Central bank communication is an important tool in the tool kit of today's modern central bank. Increasingly, central banks are interested in communicating to a much larger audience than historically. Rather than only focusing on financial markets, central bank officials now give public speeches with an aim to educate industry groups and shape citizens' beliefs about the future. Official policy communications are drafted to guide public expectations about where the economy is going, especially, but not only, with an aim to anchor inflation expectations. In the words of German central bank president Jens Weidmann (2018),

> Speeches have become a vital means of communication for monetary policy decision-makers.... And speeches are just one means of communication. Other channels of central bank communication are interviews, press conferences, and regular publications of reports. Close attention is paid, in particular, to the ECB President's introductory statement at the beginning of the press conferences following ECB Governing Council monetary policy meetings. ECB watchers scrutinize every word. Changes in communication are very keenly noticed and analyzed. And it is not only what is said but also what is left unsaid that can send a message.

Because central bankers worry about how their messages are understood by the mass public, one goal is that "central banks should communicate as precisely as possible, because if their signals are not clear enough, the result can be unwanted volatility in the

Crafting Consensus: Why Central Bankers Change Their Speech and How Speech Changes the Economy. Nicole Rae Baerg, Oxford University Press (2020).
DOI: 10.1093/oso/9780190499488.001.0001

markets, which can also spread to developments in the real economy" (Weidmann, 2018). To study whether central bank communication shapes individuals' expectations of future inflation, I conducted a survey experiment that examines how variation in policy language affects citizens' inflation forecasts. The use of a survey experiment rather than observational data is important because with the experiment, I can estimate the direct effect of textual changes to central bank communications while holding other possible confounding variables across the groups constant. Furthermore, I can also directly manipulate changes in linguistic content and control for information exposure. Citizens collect numerous impressions of the economy from a wide range of sources, both public and private, each with its own level of detail. In empirically evaluating the influence of word changes in official communications on citizens' inflation expectations, it is important to be able to manipulate directly official monetary news while also accounting for other possible confounding sources of information individuals may have at hand.

The survey experiment presented in this chapter was conducted on a cross section of German survey respondents in 2014, during the European Debt Crisis. The European Debt Crisis was a period of economic and policy uncertainty between 2007 and 2015, with peak unemployment at 12 percent in the last quarter of 2013.[1] In 2012, as a response to the crisis, policy makers agreed to the Outright Monetary Transactions (OMT) program, which allowed the ECB to buy sovereign bonds of euro-area countries. The OMT program was not without its critics, especially in Germany.[2] Conducting the experiment during the European Debt Crisis, therefore, leverages the fact that the ECB was conducting unconventional monetary policy during this time. This makes the timing of the experiment of particular importance, as "precise communication is especially important in times of great uncertainty" (Weidmann, 2018). To preview the results, I find that more precise central bank communication attenuates households' average inflation expectations and reduces the variance in inflation expectations as well.

[1] Unemployment statistics and beyond.

[2] "Not a good day for democracy"—German Critics Attack ECB Court Ruling.

This chapter is organized as follows. In the next section, I discuss why inflation expectations vary across individuals in the economy. In section 5.3, I introduce the survey experiment and the research design. Section 5.4 presents the findings. The final section concludes.

5.2 Origins of Inflation Expectations

Where do citizens' inflation expectations come from? How do individuals evaluate the future economy? I organize previous studies into three categories: those that consider the link between inflation expectations and sociodemographic features; those that consider the link between expected inflation and economic sophistication and financial literacy; and finally, those that consider the role of politics in shaping what citizens know (or believe) about the future economy.

A substantial economics literature explores how demographic and experiential factors influence how households forecast the future economy. Much of the evidence suggests that younger people and women exhibit greater variation in their inflation expectations and also make more mistakes in forecasting future values. Why this so, however, remains puzzling. One possible explanation is that different demographics construct different consumer price baskets when they calculate changes in prices. When asked to forecast future inflation, for example, variation in what people put in their imaginary price baskets can lead to variation in how much these people think the items will cost in the future (Bryan and Venkatu, 2001*a*, 2001*b*). Some groups, such as younger people, purchase consumer items like technology, fuel, and food at different rates than older people. Furthermore, these items may be perceived to increase in price at a faster rate than other goods and services. Variation in how respondents imagine a representative consumer price basket, therefore, might cause wider variation across respondents' expected inflation despite all respondents being asked the same question.

A second literature considers financial literacy and education levels as possible explanations for differences in citizens' inflation expectations. The evidence here suggests that people with higher financial literacy and those with higher education levels are more sophisticated consumers of economic news and are therefore more likely to report future inflation with greater accuracy. On the other hand, other research, mainly from the psychology literature, finds that everyone, irrespective of financial sophistication, uses heuristics in forming financial opinions, which can lead to systematic mistakes or biases in how a person forecasts future variables (Tversky and Kahneman, 1974). In investigating inflation specifically, some authors find that individuals fail to incorporate all available information provided (Armantier et al., 2016; Mankiw, Reis, and Wolfers, 2003), while others suggest that individuals use inaccurate sources of information when forming their inflation expectations (De Bruin et al., 2011; Malmendier and Nagel, 2015). Whether the cause of variation in people's beliefs about inflation is rational inattention—such that individuals have a rational incentive not to pay attention—or whether the findings should be interpreted as evidence of cognitive biases is an active area of study.

Finally, a third literature considers whether political variables act as important mediators in public opinion formation about the economy. One particularly interesting study on eastern European countries transitioning to democracy finds that some people hold favorable views about future inflation despite the fact that actual inflation levels in their home countries are escalating. The fact that citizens expect inflation to be lower in the future even though the economy is worsening is puzzling, especially since inflation is cumulative, with higher rates most likely predicting even higher future values of inflation. This research shows evidence that citizens' economic forecasts depend on their political support for the incoming regime. Those citizens in support of the old communist regime are found more likely to hold negative economic assessments of the future economy, whereas those citizens in support of the new regime are more likely to have lower assessments of future inflation (Tverdova, 2012). In other words, respondents may see the economy with "political" rather than "cognitive" biases. Still other studies show that households' perceptions of the economy are driven by partisanship and media biases as well as the political opinions of copartisan elites (Carroll, 2003).

In addition to within-country variation, there is important across-country variation in financial knowledge. According to one OECD study on financial knowledge, only 53 percent of people living in

Group-of-Twenty (G-20) countries know what happens to the purchasing power of money if inflation stays at the same rate for one year (Atkinson and Messy, 2011). In emerging markets, inflation knowledge is even more spread out. In Brazil, a country that has experienced historically high periods of inflation and currency crises, 58 percent of respondents were unable to define "high inflation" when asked to do so. With regard to interest rates, on average, only half of respondents (51 percent) were able to calculate simple interest on savings. Furthermore, the proportion of respondents across countries who were able to do simple calculations dropped to less than half the population in Mexico (12 percent), Argentina (22 percent), India (42 percent), South Africa (42 percent), Saudi Arabia (46 percent), Italy (47 percent), and the Russian Federation (48 percent) (Atkinson and Messy, 2011). In other words, despite the relevance of future price movements to people's lives, financial literacy is relatively low, and this is true irrespective of where people live.

5.3 Research Design

The goal of the chapter is to investigate whether changes in the content of central bank communications change the public's beliefs about the future economy. To uncover a causal relationship, I administered a vignette survey experiment to a quota sample of German survey respondents. The experiment was administered to 120 participants in July 2014, using the GESIS Online Panel. First started in 2010, the GESIS Online Panel Pilot (GOPP) is an access panel based on a probability sample of nearly eighteen hundred German-speaking adults living in private households in Germany. The panel members were recruited through telephone interviews. Participants were asked to fill out an online questionnaire and received 5 euros for participating. To make the sample representative, the selection of the target population was based on age-group, education, and gender quotas. Importantly, the panel replicates many questions from other large panel studies, such as the European Social Survey and Eurobarometer, and includes a large set of demographic variables in addition to the survey question results reported herein, which I include as possible confounders.

The vignette experiment was conducted in three stages. In the first stage, I asked all respondents to consider a hypothetical person who currently pays €1500 per month for purchasing goods and services. Respondents are then asked to indicate how much they expect this same person to pay for exactly the same goods and services twelve months from now. To control for the fact that participants might imagine different price baskets if I asked them only about inflation, the respondents were given some items in the hypothetical basket, such as clothing and a haircut. I did this so as to anchor what respondents thought was in the basket, thereby minimizing any across-participant variation in the basket respondents imagined. After reading the information, respondents were given a drop-down list of possible future prices from which to choose, reporting different price categories with values ranging from less than €1500 (deflation) to €1650 and more (more than 10 percent inflation). Each category represents a 1 percent increase in inflation, although respondents were not told the mathematical conversion between price changes and annual inflation rates during this stage of the experiment.

In the second stage, the survey respondents were randomized into two groups: a treatment group and a control group.[3] The treatment group received a more precise central bank statement than the control group (shown later). For the statement to appear realistic, the content of the monetary statement was constructed from an actual ECB press release issued in July 2013. The two statements differed only in the way that the information was detailed. The following passage provides an English translation of the statements given to both groups (original in German). The bold font in the text emphasizes differences in the statements for ease of distinguishing the differences across the texts; this text was not emphasized in the text given to respondents during the experiment.

Control Group: The European Central Bank expects the key interest rates to remain at present or lower levels for **an extended period**

[3] Note that there is no real control group in the sense that there is no group of respondents who received irrelevant information. The reason for this was concerns about power given the small number of participants as well as being directly interested in explaining variation in content rather than whether or not information is present.

of time. This expectation is based on the overall subdued outlook for inflation and is firmly anchored in line with the ECB's aim of maintaining inflation rates at **a reasonable level.**

Treatment Group: The European Central Bank expects the key interest rates to remain at present or lower levels for the next **6 to 12 months.** This expectation is based on the overall subdued outlook for inflation, **currently at 1%**, and is firmly anchored in line with the ECB's aim of maintaining inflation rates **close to 2%.**

Finally, in the third stage, participants in both groups were presented with their answers from the first stage as a corresponding inflation rate in annual percentage terms. Respondents were then told to keep the information from the ECB in mind and were asked again to indicate how much they expected prices for the same goods and services to increase (or decrease) in the next twelve months. To find out whether respondents thought such information would matter in the medium and long term, participants were also asked to provide their five- and ten-year inflation expectations.

Respondents were then asked a number of other questions that acted as manipulation checks to ensure that the respondents internalized the central bank message (i.e., that they were treated with the information). Following this, participants completed a brief posttest survey about their knowledge of economic issues. In addition to level of education, economic knowledge was measured by the self-reported frequency participants said that they read financial news. Finally, information about the participants' gender and age was provided by the demographic questions of the GESIS Online Panel.

5.4 Data and Results

5.4.1 Dependent Variable: Posterior Inflation Expectations

Respondents' self-reported inflation expectations after treatment is the main dependent variable in the analysis. Inflation expectations are reported in one-year-ahead, five-years-ahead, and ten-years-ahead intervals. I refer to respondents' posttreated inflation expectations as their posterior expectations.

5.4.2 Independent Variables

I use participants' answers to the first hypothetical question about price changes as their prior beliefs or evaluations of future consumer price changes. Because of the 1 percent intervals, the variable is actually ordered categorically, ranging from less than 1 percent to greater than 10 percent; however, I treat this variable as if it were continuous. As a second main independent variable, I have the treatment condition: the level of information precision given to the respondent. This variable is an indicator variable that equals 1 if the respondent was given precise information, and 0 otherwise. Recall that this treatment indicator is randomized across participants. Finally, because I am interested in the conditional effect of the information given a respondent's prior beliefs, I also include in the model the interaction of an individual's prior inflation beliefs times their treatment condition. It is this interaction term that I am most interested in interpreting.

More formally, the hypothesis that I am testing follows:

Hypothesis 5.4.1. Information and Inflation: *More precise (vague) economic information is more (less) likely to attenuate the public's inflation expectations, reducing aggregate inflation.*

While I cannot test the second part of the hypothesis directly, I can test whether the public's inflation expectations are altered as a consequence of the way that central bank news is presented. The next chapter then links changes in inflation expectations with changes in inflation outcomes. The expectation is that those who receive more precise information will have a lower estimated weight on their prior inflation beliefs compared with those who receive more vague information.

In total, of the 120 participants, 107 individuals completed the questionnaire, with 55 people receiving the precise information treatment and 52 receiving the vague information control. Table 5.1 shows the demographic composition of the group of participants.

Table 5.1 Participant quotas

	Education	No. female	No. male	Total
Age (years)				
18–40	No high school	11	7	18
	High school	12	15	27
≥41	No high school	19	18	37
	High school	10	16	26
Total		52	56	108

5.4.3 Descriptive Statistics

Before presenting the statistical results, I first describe some of the features of the data as they pertain to previous literature discussed earlier. To see whether our respondents behave in ways consistent with previous research findings, I check for variation in prior inflation expectations across sex, financial literacy, and age categories. Figure 5.1 illustrates respondents' prior inflation expectations by self-reported binary sex responses. Similar to results in previous surveys, I find that women have larger variation in their inflation expectations than men (e.g., Lusardi and Mitchell, 2008). In addition to sex, we might also think that education or financial sophistication will produce differences in expectations. By splitting up the sample based on self-reported financial news consumption, we find that individuals who self-report higher financial literacy have considerably less dispersion in their inflation estimates than individuals with lower self-reported literacy rates (Lusardi and Mitchell, 2008). For example, Figure 5.3 shows that avid readers of financial news have inflation expectations much closer to the ECB target rate (i.e., they are more accurate) when compared to participants who self-report following financial news. Finally, also as expected, inflation expectations vary by age, with younger people (defined as aged <40 years) holding higher inflation expectations than older people (defined as aged 40 years or older), who also show less dispersion.

My theory predicts that those citizens who receive more precise central bank news will have lower and less variable inflation expectations compared with those who receive information that is more vague. Figure 5.4 illustrates the difference in inflation expectations

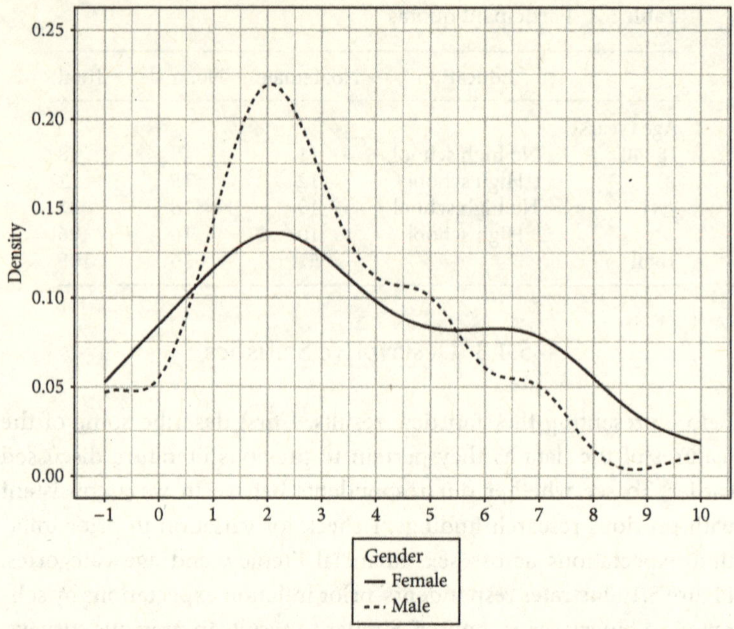

Fig. 5.1 Expected level of inflation (twelve months) by gender.

by experimental group assignment. In total, individuals in the precise treatment condition were more influenced by the central bank statement than those respondents in the control group ($t = 1.93, p = 0.06$). Individuals in the treatment group expected inflation to increase by approximately 2 percent ($\mu = 2.15$), while those in the control group expected inflation to increase by almost 3 percent ($\mu = 2.90$). Moreover, comparing both groups, answers by individuals in the treatment condition are less dispersed ($Var = 2.17, \sigma = 1.47$) compared to answers by those in the control group ($Var = 6.23, \sigma = 2.50$).[4]

Also important is examining whether differences in information impacted long-term as well as short-term and medium-term inflation expectations. Figure 5.5 shows participants' one-year, five-year, and ten-year inflation expectations after conditioning on treatment status.

[4] Tables listing respondents' prior and posterior answers are made available in the Appendix.

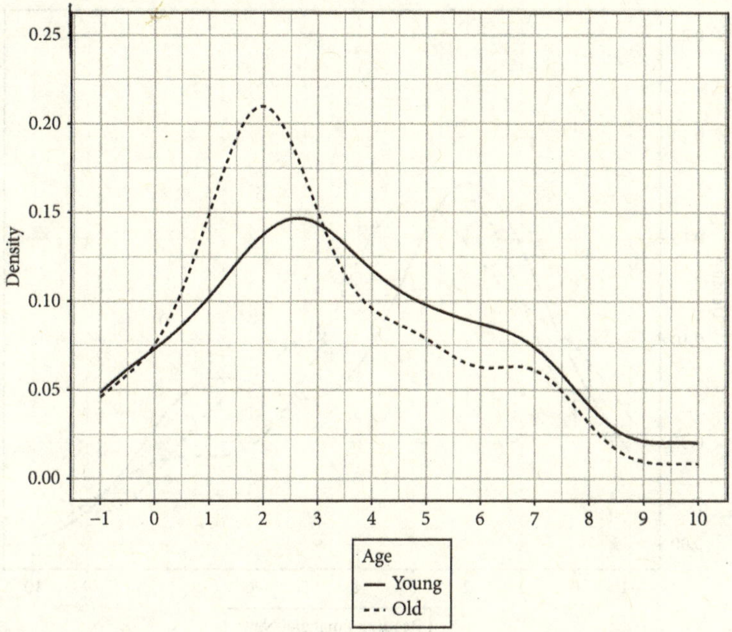

Fig. 5.2 Expected level of inflation (twelve months) by age cohort.

On average, answers by participants in the treatment group are closer to 2 percent and less dispersed compared with answers in the control group, even for medium-term inflation expectations. Mean inflation five years ahead is estimated at 3.07 percent for the treatment group and 3.94 percent for the control group. In addition to differences in the means, there are also differences in variance. The five-year-ahead forecasts of the treatment group are statistically significantly less dispersed than those of the control group (1.98 vs. 2.67 percent; $t = 1.91, p = 0.06$).

Moving from five years ahead to ten years ahead, however, respondents' answers in both the treatment and control groups converge with the control group, expecting ten-year inflation at 4.43, and the treatment group, at 3.82. The associated t-test statistic for the ten-year-ahead expectations across groups is $t = 1.10$, $p = 0.28$, implying that the differences are no longer statistically significant. This finding implies that central bank communication helps households adjust

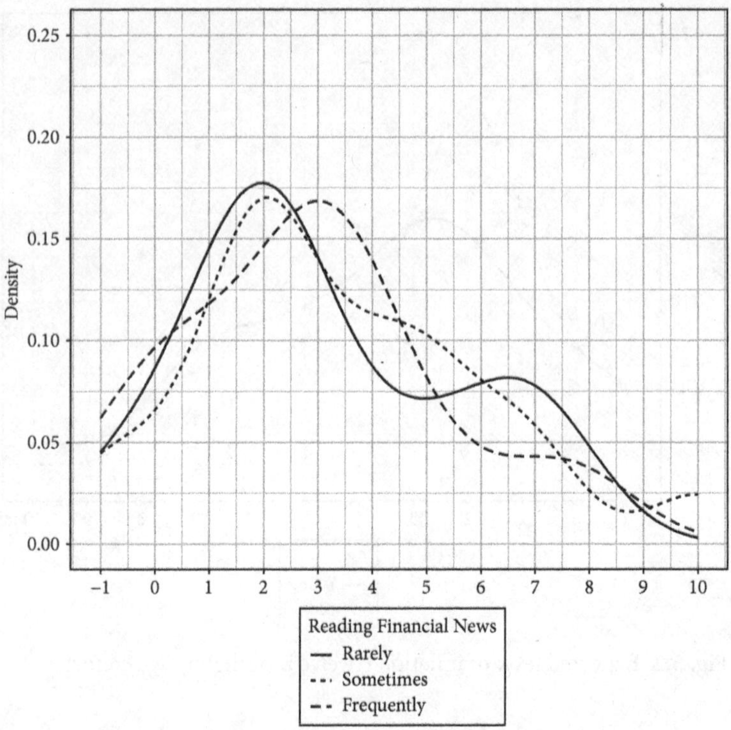

Fig. 5.3 Expected level of inflation (twelve months) by news readership.

short- and medium-term expectations but not long-term expectations. In other words, respondents who are treated with precise information about short- to medium-term inflation remain as uncertain about long-term inflation rates as those who receive vague information. Again, this helps to bolster the claim that not only does more precise central bank communication help to lower inflation expectations but also respondents are sophisticated enough to know that the information is time dependent.

Figure 5.5 shows these findings graphically. For the control (vague information) group, inflation expectations for one year ahead, five years ahead, and ten years ahead are all relatively uncertain, with relatively higher inflation expectations and longer tails in the distribution. Alternatively, for the control group, one-year-ahead and

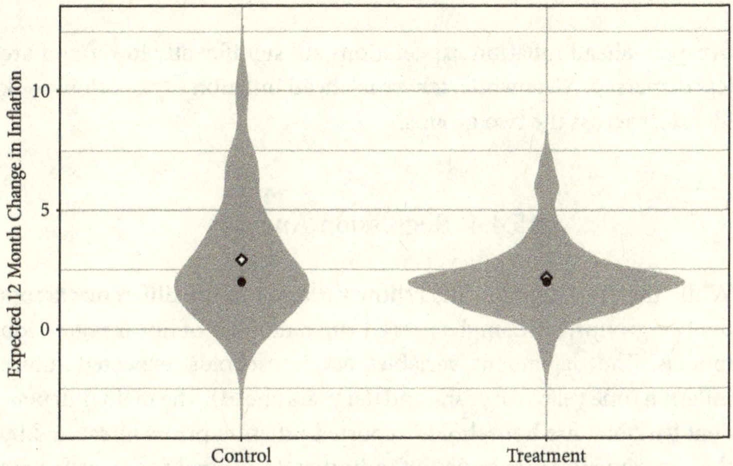

Fig. 5.4 Expected level of inflation by respondents in control and treatment groups. Group mean is indicated by the white diamond; the median is indicated by the black dot.

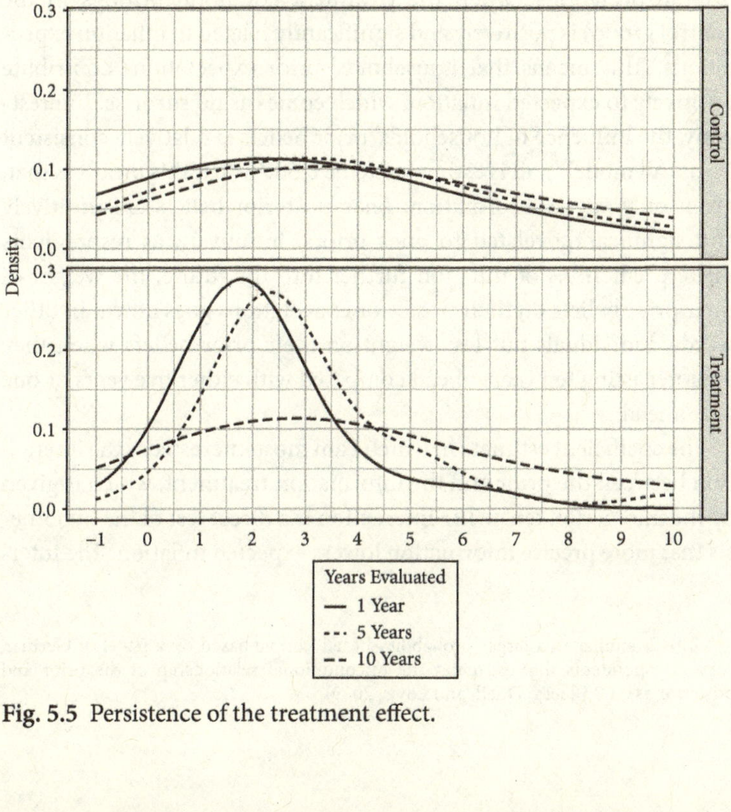

Fig. 5.5 Persistence of the treatment effect.

five-year-ahead inflation expectations are significantly lower and are less dispersed. Meanwhile, ten-year-ahead inflation expectations look identical across the two groups.

5.4.4 Regression Analysis

While the preceding findings show variation in the difference across the two groups, for completeness, I run a number of linear regression models. The dependent variables are households' expected future inflation (one year, five years, and ten years ahead). The main independent variables are households' reported inflation priors interacted by the experimental manipulation indicator. To control for other factors that may matter for expectations, I include demographic information as independent variables as well. Table 5.2 reports the results.

According to the results, the independent effect of households' prior expectations (when the treatment condition belongs to the control group) is positively and significantly related to inflation expectations. This means that households' prior expectations contribute positively to expected inflation, which comes as no surprise. Interestingly, the influence of households' prior beliefs is relatively consistent across all models and is estimated to be 0.50.[5] What this means is that, given only vague information, one's posterior beliefs are positively and significantly related to one's priors. Intuitively, as respondents make predictions of inflation further into the future, the weight of their prior beliefs on their posterior expectations goes down. In other words, individuals put less weight on their prior beliefs when they are forecasting ten years ahead compared with either five years or one year ahead.

The coefficient estimate in which I am most interested is the interaction between the prior and the information treatment, which is given by the interaction term. The interaction is a direct test of the hypothesis that more precise information lowers expected inflation. The inter-

[5] This is similar to a larger probability-based sample based on a panel of German survey respondents that estimates the unconditional relationship of the prior and posterior as 0.60 (Baerg, Duell, and Lowe, 2019).

Table 5.2 Effects of information on households' inflation expectations

	Expected inflation 1 year			
	Model 1	Model 2	Model 3: Expected inflation 5 years	Model 4: Expected inflation 10 years
Prior	0.590***	0.591***	0.554***	0.427***
	(0.091)	(0.092)	(0.121)	(0.158)
Precise	0.457	0.445	0.530	0.238
	(0.515)	(0.521)	(0.682)	(0.893)
Older (≥41 years)		−0.303	−0.330	−0.513
		(0.337)	(0.435)	(0.571)
Male		−0.045	−0.298	−0.621
		(0.319)	(0.412)	(0.541)
Prior × Precise	−0.252**	−0.272**	−0.346**	−0.208
	(0.124)	(0.128)	(0.165)	(0.217)
Constant	0.736*	0.968*	2.263***	3.521***
	(0.401)	(0.512)	(0.689)	(0.871)
Observations	107	107	106	106
R^2	0.385	0.390	0.249	0.129
Adjusted R^2	0.367	0.360	0.211	0.086
Residual std. error	1.615 (*df* = 103)	1.624 (*df* = 101)	2.077 (*df* = 100)	2.750 (*df* = 100)

***$p < 0.01$. **$p < 0.05$. *$p < 0.1$.

action term is negative, suggesting that the prior weight on inflation expectations when information is vague is larger than the prior weight on inflation expectations when information is precise. The point estimate is statistically significant at the 10 percent level. In examining the marginal effects plot, shown in Figure 5.6, it is easy to see that for the control group, the estimated weight on the prior is 0.590(0.768, 0.413), whereas for the treatment group, the estimated weight on the prior is 0.338(0.503, 0.173). The difference between these two estimates, −0.252, equals the regression coefficient in the first column (model 1). If we account for both age and sex, then the estimated difference is slightly larger, at −0.272. When we look at medium-term inflation, we see an even larger difference at −0.346. Once we move to ten years ahead, however, there is no statistically meaningful difference between forecasts of our treatment and control groups.

5.4.5 Sensitivity Analysis

In addition to age and gender, other things that might matter for inflation expectations are a respondent's level of financial knowledge and political biases. Because the experiment uses randomization, it is expected that these concerns are accounted for by the balance across the treatment groups. However, in conducting sensitivity tests, we want to examine whether there is any within rather than across variation among respondents.

To examine the effects of financial literacy, I use education levels. I transform respondents' education into a continuous variable, ranging from low to high levels of education. Because the sample is from Germany, I have to compare schooling under East and West Germany following the schema given in the appendix.[6] Table 5.3 shows the effect of including education (model 1) and self-reported financial news exposure (model 2) in the analysis.

When I include education in the analysis, the interaction variable is slightly higher than before. The demographic variables Age

[6] Thanks to Julia Partheymüller for help with this schema.

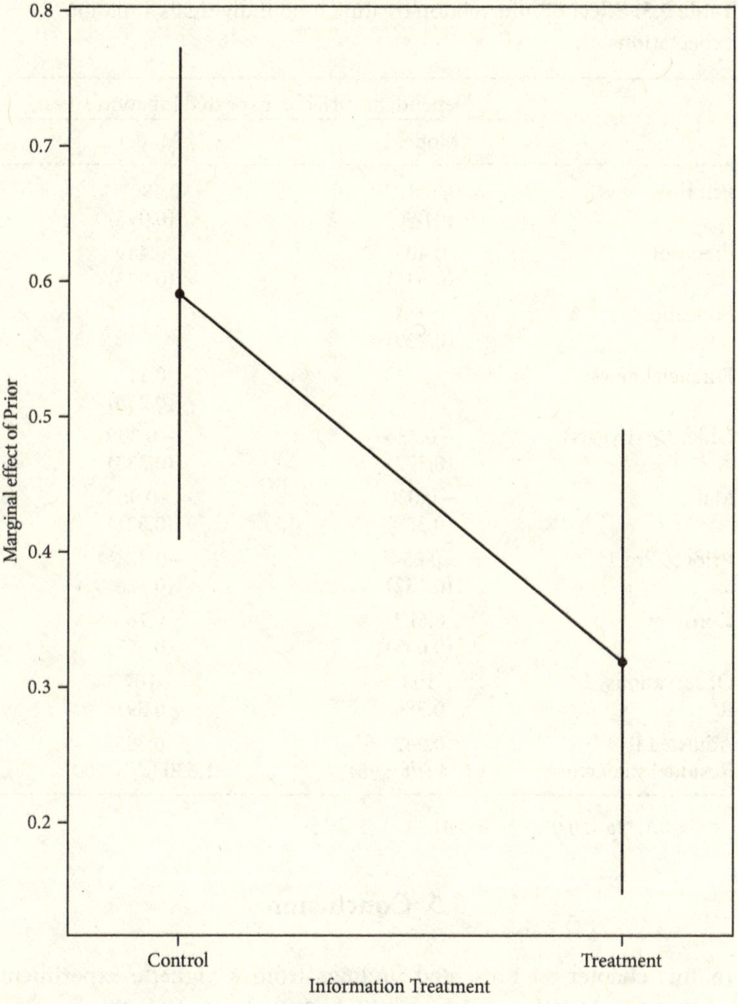

Fig. 5.6 Changes in prior beliefs by information precision. Those who get vague information (control group) have weightier priors than those who get more precise information (treatment group).

and Gender remain statistically insignificant, although they are appropriately signed. Including financial news exposure yields similar results. The interaction term is still statistically significant and stronger than before.

Table 5.3 Effect of information treatment on individuals' inflation expectations

	Dependent variable: Expected inflation 1 year	
	Model 1	Model 2
Prior	0.578***	0.590***
	(0.096)	(0.093)
Precision	0.408	0.449
	(0.546)	(0.523)
Education	0.214	
	(0.229)	
Financial news		0.117
		(0.236)
Older (≥41 years)	−0.384	−0.309
	(0.372)	(0.338)
Male	−0.030	−0.060
	(0.329)	(0.321)
Prior × Precision	−0.254*	−0.271**
	(0.132)	(0.128)
Constant	0.672	0.766
	(0.605)	(0.657)
Observations	103	107
R^2	0.386	0.391
Adjusted R^2	0.347	0.355
Residual std. error	1.654 ($df = 96$)	1.630 ($df = 100$)

*$p < 0.1$. **$p < 0.05$. ***$p < 0.01$.

5.5 Conclusion

In this chapter, I presented findings from a vignette experiment administered to German households in 2014. I tested whether respondents' inflation expectations are influenced by the textual content of monetary policy news released by central bank press releases. I show that households that receive more precise central bank information react more to central bank news than those who receive more vague information. Estimating the average treatment effect across the two experimental groups, I find that more precise information attenuates both short-term (one-year-ahead) and medium-term (five-years-ahead) inflation forecasts but find little evidence of an effect for longer-term expectations (ten years ahead). Also interesting is that while younger people, women, and those less educated and financially literate have higher prior inflation expectations than their older, male, and financially literate counterparts, using a statistical model, I find that information rather than socioeconomic or demographic features matters most of all.

While using a survey experiment has significant benefits, it also has some important limitations. One important concern with this specific design is the omission of an actual control group, or respondents who received no central bank information at all. On the one hand, theoretically, having no control group is the correct specification. Substantively, I am interested in determining whether two different information frames shape households' expectations of the future economy. On the other hand, having no baseline group means that I am comparing the effect of different types of information across respondents rather than the effects of receiving information in the first place. While this is exactly the mechanism my argument highlights, it is important to stress that the findings in this chapter refer to variation in the *presentation of information* rather than variation in *whether respondents receive information*. It is quite possible that group-level effects in the consumption of different central bank content are statistically significant, and yet, there are no statistically significant differences across groups based on whether they receive information, or not, to begin with (Gaines, Kuklinski, and Quirk, 2007).

Another common concern with survey experiments is that the experiment itself may elicit respondents' behavior rather than respondents' changing beliefs as a consequence of receiving differences in information (Goffman, 1963; Tversky and Kahneman, 1974). For example, if those in the treatment group respond more to the ECB target for reasons other than incorporating new information, such as to please the researcher or because of numerical anchoring, then the results may be a consequence of social desirability bias or heuristics. Additionally, research by Cavallo (2012) shows that individuals in low-inflation environments, such as Germany, are also those most likely to be moved by information. This is because inflation is less costly to respondents, and therefore respondents are also less likely to have strong priors to start with. This might mean that the estimates presented here reflect an upper rather than a lower bound of the effects of precision in central bank communication.

Despite these concerns, the findings suggest that ordinary people respond to variations in the textual content of central bank news. While it is true that more precise communication is more effective, the results here are agnostic about whether more precise information is better for the economy. As outlined previously, the fact that precision matters means that central banks have an incentive to be precise about the "good" things and vague about the "bad" things. Fortunately, as we have seen, diverse policy committees and the possibility for public dissent can go some way toward enabling precise communications, even when incentives pull policy makers in the opposite direction.

6
Testing the Theory in Latin America

6.1 Introduction

At the start of the 1990s, inflation rates in many developed countries, including the United States, Canada, and Germany, were very low. Around the same time, however, in many regions of the world, including Latin America, central and eastern Europe, Africa, and the Middle East, inflation was soaring. Several countries, such as Brazil, Argentina, and Israel, had inflation rates that vacillated between low and stable and high and explosive, and reforms to quell such peaks in inflation were often implemented in haste and then abandoned by future governments. Figure 6.1 shows variation in annual consumer price changes in 1998 around the world.

Moving to today, we see similar variation across the developed and developing worlds. Inflation, and even hyperinflation, continues to plague many countries, particularly those in sub-Saharan Africa, the former Soviet Union, and Latin America. According to the International Monetary Fund (IMF), Venezuela's inflation rate is likely to top 1,000,000 percent in 2018, putting it on track to become one of the worst hyperinflation crises in modern times.

To combat high inflation, countries tried a slew of policy reforms.[1] For example, in 1991, Argentina enacted the Convertibility Program, establishing a currency board with an explicitly legislated exchange rate fixed to the US dollar. This program attempted to improve Argentina's macroeconomic policy credibility and ensure inflation stability. The initial success of Argentina's fixed exchange rate regime brought Argentinian inflation down to annual rates as low as −1 percent in 1999. As early as 2002, however, Argentinian

[1] For an excellent review of inflation stabilization, see Bruno (1993).

Crafting Consensus: Why Central Bankers Change Their Speech and How Speech Changes the Economy. Nicole Rae Baerg, Oxford University Press (2020). © Oxford University Press.
DOI: 10.1093/oso/9780190499488.001.0001

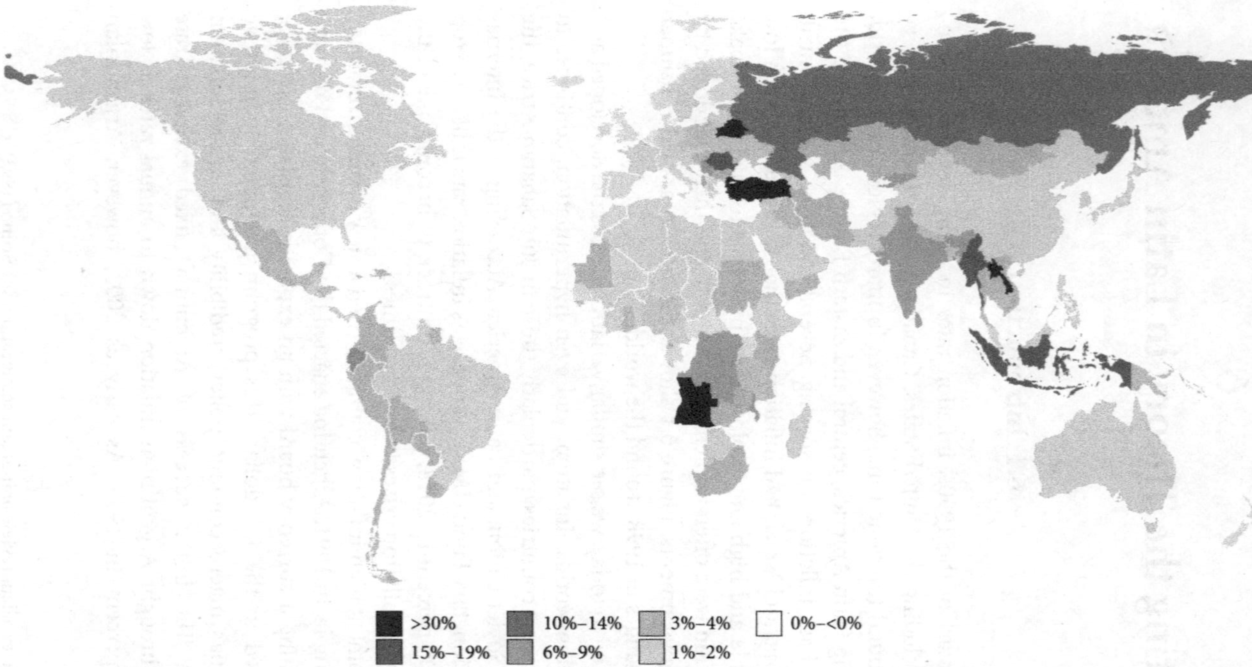

Fig. 6.1 Global inflation rates (annual percentage CPI) in 1998. From the World Bank World Development Indicators (missing data in white).

inflation escalated again, rising to over 25 percent. Around the same time, Mexico and Brazil faced economic crises of their own. Mexico experienced double-digit inflation, averaging approximately 20 percent over the 1990s, whereas Brazil, despite starting the 1990s with a major bout of hyperinflation, managed to keep inflation under 10 percent throughout much of the 2000s. Brazil reported the maximum regional inflation level during the 1990s, with annual inflation reported at over 2,000 percent. Like the earlier attempts to tame hyperinflation in Argentina, Brazil attempted to reform the macroeconomy by adopting the Real Plan. The Real Plan included the introduction of a new currency, unleashed inflation indexation of the economy, implemented an initial freeze of public-sector prices, and finally, tightened monetary policy. These policies sent inflation rates down from 45 percent during the second quarter of 1994 to less than 1 percent in 1996. Venezuela's economy during this period was less volatile despite being similarly plagued with inflationary problems. Inflation in Venezuela rose to a high of 100 percent in 1996 and never fell below this level; however, after 2010, inflation rose faster – so much so that at the start of 2019, experts expect annual inflation to reach an astronomical 1,000,000 percent.

With the exception of a small literature, missing from this earlier research on inflation stabilization policies is an understanding of how central bank information helped (or hindered) inflation stabilization.[2] The reason for this gap is twofold, one substantive and one technical. Most countries experiencing high inflation during this time had such a dire economic policy history that researchers focused on inflation were interested in explaining credibility (or the lack thereof). Unsurprisingly, attention was thus paid not to monetary policy committees and communication by the central bank but rather to questions about how to keep the central bank away from a government that had electoral reasons to inflate the economy and delay costly reforms. Furthermore, the literature on inflation learning was in deep conflict over whether individuals were backward looking or forward looking (Cagan, 1956; Sargent, 1982) when it came to expected inflation; while this debate is not solved, the "Rational Expectations Revolution"

[2] For an exception, see Sargent, Williams and Zha (2009).

had deep effects on policy, especially, but not only, in orienting the debates on monetary policy toward credibility and time inconsistency (Mishkin, 1995). A second reason why the role of communication has not been well studied in historical periods has to do with access to the tools to conduct such research in the first place. Many of the techniques to do quantitative textual analysis, deployed to understand central bank communication, were imported into the social sciences from computer sciences over the last ten years; they have therefore entered into the scholar's toolbox at a time when global inflation is relatively low. For theoretical and practical reasons, therefore, we have very little research that tests whether communication as a policy tool is effective in periods of high and volatile inflation, such as it was throughout the 1990s and 2000s in many countries. By expanding the analysis to include these types of economic conditions, this final empirical chapter tests whether an increase in information precision is associated with lower levels of aggregate inflation even when the economy is doing poorly. To preview the results, I find evidence that an increase in more precise information attenuates forecasters' average expected inflation. A reduction in expected inflation is then associated with a reduction in actual inflation outcomes, suggesting that information is indeed a powerful driver of the economy, even during more volatile periods.

The rest of this chapter is organized as follows. The next section presents the sample of countries considered—Argentina, Brazil, Colombia, Mexico, Peru, and Venezuela—and presents the measurement strategy and the statistical model. I conduct a number of statistical tests. The first tests estimate the relationship between information and inflation using a linear ordinary least squares (OLS) regression model with country and month effects and average forecaster inflation expectations. The subsequent section gives the empirical findings. I find some evidence that an increase in the level of information precision about inflation, as reported by Reuters newswire, lowers the effect of inflation expectations and lowers predicted inflation. Furthermore, I find that the findings hold even when I control for important confounding effects, including credibility, a country's average level of inflation, and monetary policy reforms. Section 6.4 describes further sensitivity analyses. Section 6.5 concludes.

6.2 Data and Analysis

As mentioned, countries in the developing world demonstrated significant variation in their inflation outcomes over the 1990s and early 2000s. The sample that I use for the analysis in this chapter includes six countries located in Latin America: Argentina, Brazil, Colombia, Mexico, Peru, and Venezuela. The time period that I examine comprises the years between 1993 and 2010, which includes three years of the financial crisis; however, the financial crisis does not dominate the series. Inflation, measured by month-over-month changes in annual rates, ranges in this sample from −4 percent to over 4,000 percent.

The data are structured as cross-sectional time series, and the unit of analysis is the country-month.

6.2.1 Dependent Variable: Inflation

The main outcome variable is inflation outcomes, or changes in consumer prices. Changes in prices refers to the rate at which the level of prices for goods and/or services is accelerating or decelerating in the economy. Deceleration in prices, such that the rate of change in prices is positive but slowing, is called *disinflation*. For example, an inflation rate of 20 percent per year means that the price level of goods and services is rising at a rate of 20 percent over the year. If, in the next year, this rate of price changes is 10 percent, there is inflation of 10 percent and year-over-year disinflation of 10 percent. If, instead of being positive, price changes are negative such that the rate at which the level of prices for goods and services is declining, this is called *deflation*. Inflation rates can be likened to driving a car: the driver can either accelerate, decelerate while still moving forward, or move in reverse. Moving forward at an accelerating speed is inflation; moving forward while decelerating to a stop is disinflation; finally, driving in reverse is deflation.

A change in the rate of the "price level" is an abstract concept, where Price Level is an unobserved latent variable. Practically, to construct a measure of price level, national statistical offices measure inflation by considering the rate of change of a representative basket of goods and services in the economy over time. The measure that I use for inflation in this chapter is a weighted basket of goods and services purchased by ordinary households, or the consumer price index (CPI).[3]

As the unit of analysis is monthly, but we tend to think of inflation in annual aggregates rather than monthly aggregates, I used a country's monthly report of annual consumer price measure. This means that inflation in January 1993 is the annual percentage change in inflation from January 1992 to January 1993. These data were collected from the Cleveland Federal Reserve Bank, and the indicator follows the International Labour Organization's methodology for estimating inflation.

6.2.2 Independent Variables: Inflation Expectations

The main independent variable in this study is households' inflation expectations. Unfortunately, to my knowledge, there is no over-time panel of Latin American households asking about their inflation expectations. Instead, to proxy this, I used a panel of professional forecasters' reported expectations about inflation. The professional forecast data are from Consensus Economics, a for-profit organization

[3] According to the OECD, for most countries, the compilation of CPI measures is constructed in accordance with international statistical guidelines and recommendations. Despite international standards, individual countries' statistics can and do depart from international guidelines, leading to a loss of comparability across countries and over time. Some of the across-county or over-time variation is suspected to be due to discrepancies in the choice of weights in the basket used to capture the differences in quality across items; the inclusion of new items (especially technology); and major expenditures, such as rents and housing, which may differ across countries due to government regulation of housing markets and rent controls (OECD, 2011). Furthermore, before consumer price data are released, a country's data are often amended by the country's national statistical office. This means, in theory, removing seasonal variations in prices. In practice, however, seasonal variation is not always taken out, and the methodology used for extracting seasonal variations may vary by country.

In addition to differences in data construction, some national statistical offices have low statistical capacity and/or poor data collection. In other words, some countries have difficulty producing CPI measures at all. Furthermore, countries may misreport their inflation statistics. For example, beginning in 2006, it was thought that Argentina systematically misreported its official CPI measures, reporting official inflation two to three times below actual changes in the price level of consumer products in the country. Unofficial inflation rates in Argentina estimated inflation rates closer to 20 or 30 percent, more than double the official rate (Cavallo, 2012).

that polls individuals and firms each month and surveys their expected changes to key macroeconomic indicators. Consensus Economics reports, on average, 120 prominent Latin American forecasters. While projections are made for a number of indicators, including future growth, inflation, foreign trade, interest rates, and exchange rates, I measure households' expectations using forecasters' current-year expectations of changes in consumer prices.

Measures of consumer price forecasts are December-on-December percentage changes. Coverage starts as early as 1993 and ends in 2010. The number of forecasters polled in a given month varies across the sample, ranging from seven to twenty-three, for a total of 13,829 forecasts. While the frequency of the forecast data is monthly, each month, the forecaster forecasts the current year's annual inflation rate.

I took two summary measures from this panel and used them as independent variables. First, to measure *Expected Average Inflation*, I calculated the average of the forecasters' expectations in a given country-month. For example, if forecasters 1, 2, and 3 had inflation expectations of 10, 12, and 14, then the value of my independent variable was 12. As a second independent variable, I also calculated the *Expected Standard Deviation in Inflation*, which also accounts for the variance. To do this, I calculated the standard deviation in forecasters' expectations for every given country-month. To use the same example, if forecasters 1, 2, and 3 had inflation expectations of 10, 12, and 14, respectively, then the value of my independent variable was 2.

Unsurprisingly, inflation expectations and actual inflation rates are positively related. Figure 6.2 shows a plot of logged expected mean inflation and logged annual consumer price inflation for the six countries in the sample. We can see that inflation is positively associated with inflation expectations, almost at a one-to-one rate. As the variables are both logged, we can interpret that a one-unit change in inflation expectation is associated with an approximate one-unit change in inflation. Also shown in this figure is that the greater the variability of inflation is, the less likely we are to observe a one-to-one ratio.

One possible problem with using forecasters' inflation expectations as a measure for households' inflation expectations is that if forecasters and households are influenced by economic information in different ways, this might invalidate the mechanism. For example, if forecasters

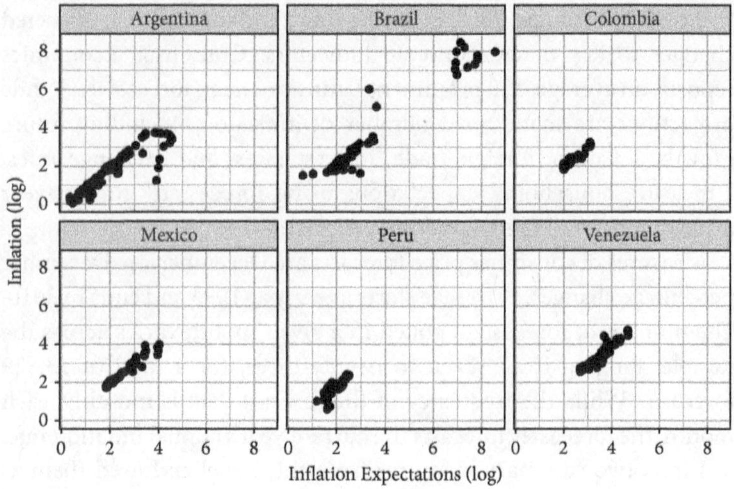

Fig. 6.2 Mean inflation expectations and annual inflation.

derive their economic expectations using economic news but households do not, this might compromise validity. Recent evidence by Menz and Poppitz (2013) finds that households' inflation expectations are positively correlated with professional forecast surveys. Similarly, experimental evidence in chapter 5 shows that those individuals with more financial knowledge are also less rather than more susceptible to central bank communications. Assuming that this is true also for Latin America, this suggests that by using professional rather than household expectations, I have a hard test of my theory and that, consequently, the results in this chapter likely represent the lower rather than upper bounds of the effects.

6.2.3 Information Precision

Clustering

To measure the precision of information in inflation pronouncements, I constructed a new data set of public statements about inflation using Factiva, a news source database. Factiva contains newspaper articles and newswire reports from fourteen thousand news sources.

Using this data set, and following Ehrmann and Fratzscher (2007), I extracted all database entries containing the words "minister and central bank and inflation and 'country name'" from the popular newswire Reuters. The number of newspaper articles returned by Factiva for a given country and a given year is very large. For instance, running the search of "minister and inflation and Argentina and central bank" generates more than one thousand newspaper articles between January 1, 1993, and December 31, 1993, alone. Doing such a search on the entire sample yields more than nine thousand newspaper articles for the six Latin American countries under study here.

With more than nine thousand returns, human coding of each newspaper article is both infeasible and likely to produce error. The use of humans to hand-code each newspaper article introduces the potential for measurement error, which may then cause problems of reliability and validity. In fact, recent scholarship finds that human coding of the Comparative Manifestos Project, the world's largest database on political party manifestos, yields misclassification in serious and systemic ways (Mikhaylov, Laver, and Benoit, 2012). Instead of using human coding, therefore, I depended on machine learning techniques to retrieve, parse, filter, and classify the newspaper articles into difference levels of information precision. I then depended on human coding for validation once the classification is assigned.

A number of different classification algorithms can be used, and I chose an unsupervised learning approach and applied a *K*-means classifier. *K*-means is an iterative clustering algorithm that takes input data, in this case, words contained in the newswire articles and their associated word frequencies, and assigns *K* number of groups based on how well the data fit to that specific grouping. For example, if there are $K = 2$ groups, then the *K*-means algorithm will first randomly choose two means; second, it will assign all the input data closest to that particular mean that mean's label; third, it will determine whether the algorithm can do a better job fitting the data and, if so, it will choose another mean. The algorithm iterates through this process until the best fit is found. It then assigns all data points belonging to that mean a label (Friedman, Hastie and Tibshirani, 2001).

Like many unsupervised techniques, the challenge is assigning a *K* that is both large enough to exploit variation across the clusters and small enough to allow the analyst to interpret the outputs. I ran a series of clustering models[4] and found that the clustering is both most stable and most interpretable when $K = 3$. By most stable, I mean that the algorithm consistently applies the same label when running the clustering algorithm multiple times with the same K, and by most interpretable, I mean that I can observe differences in the texts myself. Because the method is unsupervised, I only assumed the number of groupings; the machine learning algorithm worked to find groupings that were distinguishable due to differences in word correlations across the texts. The classifier then assigned the newspaper articles into groups based on the best fit of the means and the number of clusters to uncover (which is given).

Validation

To validate that the clusters were indeed separating inflation news articles based on the underlying dimension of interest, Information Precision, I used human validation to examine their fit. Two things must be present to ensure that the resulting classifications are meaningful. First, the algorithm must assign inflation articles to clusters in such a way that the resulting clusters rank differences in articles according to variation in information precision; that is, the clusters must identify variation across articles. Second, the cluster outputs must perform well in terms of misclassification error such that the labels are technically valid. One final concern is that in applying a K-means clustering approach, the algorithm treats the clusters as representing discrete outcomes, but the underlying concept, information precision, is latent and continuous. I return to this particular concern in the next section.

Table 6.1 illustrates two typical news items about inflation used for constructing the measure. Each news article is assumed to be a complete text. I do not parse out the articles by topic or by paragraph. As the articles are relatively short and similar in structure, the nature of the texts make them easily comparable across countries and over time.

[4] I ran the clustering model with $K = 2, 3, 4, 5$.

Table 6.1 Example inflation article from Reuters news

City	Date and source	Article text
BUENOS AIRES	Sept. 2 (Reuters)	After decades as a case study in inflation, Argentina has returned to single digit yearly price rises with a bang – nil inflation during August. "Inflation was zero in August," President Carlos Menem proudly told a gala dinner of the Argentine Industrial Union, which groups the country's leading companies. The lowest monthly inflation figure in 20 years also means that in the year ending on August 31, Argentine consumer prices rose less than 10 percent. "For the first time in a quarter of a century, we've broken into single digits," Menem exulted. The August inflation rate of zero percent was even better than Menem's own forecast last week of 0.2 percent or less.
SAO PAULO	April 25 (Reuters)	Brazil's decision to raise bank reserve requirements will have a limited impact on reining in galloping demand, and tougher measures are required to cool the overheated economy, analysts said. The measure, which raises reserve requirements on time deposits from 27 percent to 30 percent, fails to target one of the most important factors fuelling demand, analysts say. "The major factor in the growth of demand is disposable income, and it is pretty hard to control," Ernesto Guedes, partner of MCM Consultores Asociados, said. Analysts said they predict salaries will rise in coming months as annual wage negotiations conclude, and on May 1 the monthly minimum wage will be increased by 42 percent to 100 reais. "The possibility of additional anti-consumption measures is very reduced," Guedes said. Raising taxes is politically difficult and credit restrictions have a "debatable effect." Finance Minister Pedro Malan said additional cooling measures will be adopted this week to curb demand "which generates expectations of future inflation . . . and causes a balance of payments imbalance."

To validate the clusters, I first built a "gold standard" classification or coding rubric. From this master coding, I then employed a graduate student to recode the statements and compare them against my own. The student was given a random sample of 102 newspaper articles from all six countries across all years. The student was asked to classify the documents into three labels, the same number of labels as the *K* clusters assigned by the computer. The student was responsible for hand-coding the data into three latent label types, and, different from the computer, I instructed the student to have an expressed ranking from "Low," "Medium," and "High" information precision. From this identified set of 102 hand-coded statements, I could then calculate which clusters corresponded to the ranked types of information precision and also generate sensitivity and specificity measures to evaluate misclassification error.

Combining each possible value of the machine-coded label and the human-coded label for the 102 subsample, the diagnosis generates statistics presented in the cross-table Table 6.2, and its associated sensitivity and specificity metrics (Enøe, Georgiadis, and Johnson, 2000). The test sensitivity equals the probability that the machine correctly identified the "true cluster" (as determined by humans). In our validation exercise, the computed sensitivity metric for the "High" type is 88 percent. This means that the clustering algorithm selects the "true" (as based on our hand-coded gold standard) "High" cluster 88 percent of the time. Alternatively, however, the specificity, or the

Table 6.2 Machine versus human coding status by diagnostic test

Assigned cluster label	Machine vs. human	Matched status
"Low" precision	0.22	Prevalence in the sample of "1"
	0.65	Percentage of machine-matched cases "1"
"Medium" precision	0.37	Prevalence in the sample of "2"
	0.11	Percentage of machine-matched cases "2'
"High" precision	0.40	Prevalence in the sample of "3"
	0.88	Percentage of machine-matched cases "3"

probability that a cluster will be incorrectly labeled "1" when it is in fact "2" or "3," is 44 percent. As shown in Table 6.2, the machine does a reasonable job matching "High" and "Low" information precision (88 and 65 percent correct, respectively) but not a very good job matching "Medium" levels of information precision (only 11 percent correct). Interestingly, the human coder also "incorrectly" identified the "Medium" label most often.

Measurement

To construct the measure of Inflation Precision, *p*, for a given country-month, I created a dummy variable for each classified newspaper article and aggregated the total number of counts for each information type by country-month. I did this by calculating the total proportion of "precise" articles, or "High," divided by the total number of articles for that quarter. For example, if in country j in M1 1999, there are six articles of "High" type 3; three of "Medium" type 2; and one of "Low" type 1; in that month in country A, the estimated proportion of information precision is equal to 6/10, or 60 percent. Such an aggregation is shown in equation (6.1), where *j* is the country and *m* is the month:

$$p_{j,m} = \frac{\sum_{i=1}^{n} \text{High}_{j,m}}{\sum_{i=1}^{n} \text{High}_{j,m} + \sum_{i=1}^{n} \text{Medium}_{j,m} + \sum_{i=1}^{n} \text{Low}_{j,m}}. \quad (6.1)$$

As we can see, the category counts are converted into a proportion by dividing the total number of certainty articles, or "High," over all articles. These category shares are then interpreted directly as conveying information about the level of precision in the policy environment. If the theory is correct, then what matters is not the exact preciseness of any one news article but the overall precision of information about inflation in any given month. In constructing the variable this way, I can control for the fact that while a given individual may not read a particular inflation news article, people are exposed to economic information in the news, and that the level of precision in inflation-related news varies substantially across countries and over time. Furthermore, by appealing to newswire articles rather than official statements by either the central bank or the finance ministry, I can ensure that the underlying documents have a similar structure both across countries and over time because they are produced according to a standard format. Finally, by looking at newswire articles, I can also expect that newsworthy items that make it into the newswire are more likely to be incorporated into local reports and thus are more likely to be read by households. Depending on another sample of documents, such as official announcements by government agencies, might have more heterogeneous patterns of readership and may therefore represent less well the public's exposure to inflation news.

Figure 6.3 illustrates the distribution of the frequency of newspaper articles by the level of information precision measured according to the share of precise articles across the sample, and Figure 6.4 shows variation in the information precision measure for each country over time.

Because the data set is based on news reports picked up by Reuters newswire, coverage varies across the countries. Relatively large countries, such as Brazil and Argentina, have the most country-month coverage, whereas Peru has the smallest number of inflation-related

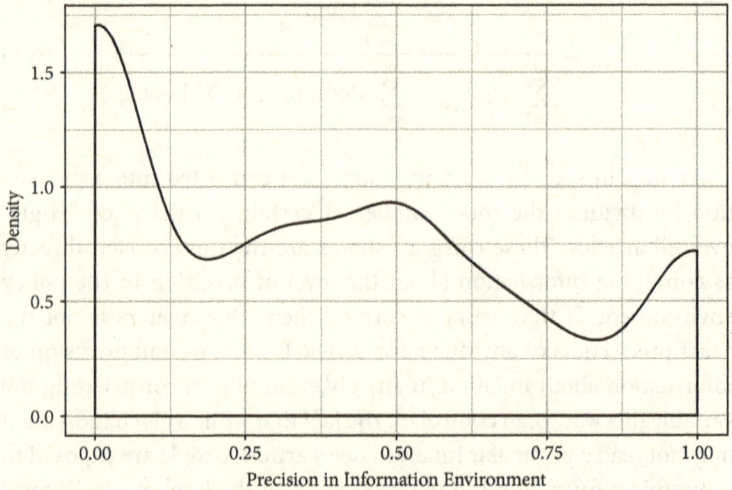

Fig. 6.3 Density of newspaper articles by information precision.

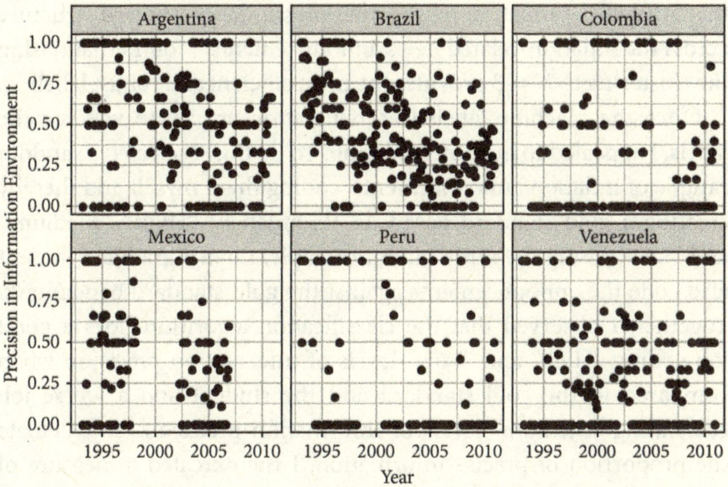

Fig. 6.4 Variation in information precision by country and over time.

news pieces in the corpus. Importantly, from the data presented in Figure 6.4, we observe few obvious time trends in the data. This provides some support for the idea that changes in the precision about inflation reflect underlying domestic incentives and constraints irrespective of changes in the overall level of central bank transparency in the country. This is important, as it is possible that with consolidation of democracy in Latin America, general levels of transparency increased writ large. In other words, the lack of a time trend in the data suggests that the measure is tracking variation in the precision of inflation news across time and by country, which we expect varies as a consequence of monetary committee configurations, rather than broad trends in central bank transparency.

In summary, using Reuters news, I retrieved more than nine thousand inflation-related news articles for six countries in Latin America between 1993 and 2010.[5] I then created a term document matrix of the words used in each article and their word frequency counts. Based on these data, I ran an unsupervised *K*-means clustering technique

[5] I filtered out those newspaper articles that were inflation-related statements, discarding those articles incorrectly identified in the data retrieval.

that labeled the inflation news based on similarity of word structure across the inflation-related news announcements. I found that setting the clustering to $K = 3$ provides the most efficient and robust labeling.

Once the machine labeled each inflation article, to validate the labels, I appealed to human validation. To do this, I selected a random sample of inflation announcements, coding them myself and thereby creating a gold standard based on three labels: "High," "Medium," and "Low." Using the same random sample, I had a graduate student also code the announcements against the gold standard benchmark. Together, I observed that the classification algorithm does a good job coding "High" and "Low" levels of information precision when compared to the gold standard and the student and a worse job calculating "Medium" levels of information precision. To calculate the proportion of precise information, I then created a measure of information precision based on the share of inflation news statements labeled as "High" as a proportion of the total amount of inflation news by county-month. The proportional is therefore a measure of the proportion of precise inflation-related news articles over not precise. I then used this measure in the statistical analysis reported in the next section as a measure for $p_{j,m}$. This effectively created a proportion of the level of information precision in the economy for each country-month.

6.2.4 Control Variables

Inflation Three-Month Moving Average

The analysis also needs to control for a number of important alternative explanations and for the persistence in the average level of inflation. To account for the relative persistence in inflation, I include the moving average of inflation on the right-hand side of the equation. Similar to a lagged dependent variable measure, this implies that the estimated model evaluates changes in inflation from the moving average level of inflation rather than evaluating the level of inflation. The rolling average monthly inflation rate is constructed using the inflation data from earlier.

Credibility

One possible alternative explanation is that a country's level of inflation is determined by the government's policy credibility and is not related to changes in the information environment at all. To account for this, I included two measures. As a first measure, I collected new data that count the number or frequency of monetary policy changes, including changes to the exchange rate and exchange rate regime, which therefore accounts for both changes in the central bank's relationship with the government and changes to the exchange rate regime. These data came from the IMF. The IMF in its publication *Exchange Rate Agreements and Exchange Rate Restrictions* reports institutional policy changes according to seven topics: the exchange rate regime, imports, exports, invisibles, capital, gold, nonresident accounts, and changes to the payments system. I count a policy change by topic as equal to 1 if there was a policy announcement reported by the IMF in a specific quarter. If there was no announcement in a quarter, I code it as 0. For example, if Mexico announced a change to its import restrictions with Argentina in Q1 1999, I code this as 1 import announcement for Mexico. I do not include the Mexican announcement in Argentina's tally, as I am interested in the relative frequency for which there is an announced policy change for a given country, not in bilateral changes. Because the IMF data are reported quarterly, whereas the rest of the data that I am using are monthly, I interpolate the monthly number of policy changes from the quarterly data using a cubic spline. I then use this cubic spline measure to proxy for a country's level of monetary credibility. The interpretation is that a higher number of institutional reforms is associated with higher levels of policy credibility. There are certainly other measures that I could use. Unfortunately, however, most of the institutional variables, such as the level of central bank independence (CBI) and a country's official exchange rate regime, change at much lower frequencies than my monthly panel. These institutional constraints will however, be likely picked up in the average inflation rate across the sample as well as in the country effects in the statistical analysis.

To ensure that the results do not hinge on the measure of credibility that I use, as a second measure of credibility, I include a measure of contract intensive money (CIM). This measure has been used elsewhere in the literature, especially to proxy contract enforcement and the secureness of property rights, including an inflation tax, which erodes the value of assets (Clague et al., 1999). At any given time, firms and individuals decide in what form they want to hold money. If firms and individuals trust that their assets are safe from appropriation, then they are more likely to allow banks to hold their money. When trust in the system occurs, therefore, the level of CIM is higher. Alternatively, when individuals are more likely to hold their assets as cash or in foreign currency that cannot be taxed by the domestic government, CIM is expected to be lower. In this way, CIM is a high-frequency behavioral measure for credibility. CIM is operationalized as the ratio of noncurrency money to the total money supply, or $(M2 - C)/M2$, where $M2$ is a broad definition of the money supply and C is currency held outside of domestic banks, such as in cash. The data are constructed using monthly data available from the IMF's International Financial Statistics (IFS) for both series and for all countries.[6]

Output

As another possible confounding variable, I also included output. One reason why a country may have relatively high levels of inflation is that the country is also experiencing rapid economic expansion. This is especially true for emerging markets. To account for this, I gathered data from the IMF on monthly per capita output as measured by GDP, normalized to 2005 prices.

6.3 Main Results

The main results from the OLS model are shown in Table 6.3. Models 1 and 3 estimate monthly, year-over-year inflation as a function of expected mean inflation conditional on the level of precision in the information environment. Models 2 and 4 estimate a similar model,

[6] This is constructed using the following lines from the IMF's IFS: CIM = lines ((34 + 35) − 14)/(34 + 35).

Table 6.3 Linear OLS regression model

	Dependent variable: Monthly inflation			
	Model 1	Model 2	Model 3	Model 4
Average inflation	0.928***	0.942***	0.929***	0.944***
	(0.013)	(0.009)	(0.013)	(0.009)
Mean expected inflation	0.170***		0.170***	
	(0.065)		(0.065)	
SD expected inflation		0.942***		0.943***
		(0.129)		(0.128)
Information precision	−3.671	0.416	−3.305	0.864
	(8.774)	(8.396)	(8.696)	(8.320)
Output	0.004	−0.000	−0.005	−0.009
	(0.008)	(0.008)	(0.008)	(0.008)
CIM	79.709	86.777		
	(94.063)	(91.419)		
No. policy changes			−2.465**	−2.493**
			(1.132)	(1.101)
Mean Expected Inflation × Precision	−0.099		−0.098	
	(0.094)		(0.093)	
SD Expected Inflation × Precision		−1.272***		−1.272***
		(0.184)		(0.183)
Country and month effects	✓	✓	✓	✓
Observations	519	519	519	519
R^2	0.976	0.977	0.976	0.977
Adjusted R^2	0.974	0.976	0.975	0.976
Residual std. error ($df = 496$)	61.885	60.172	61.636	59.918

$^{*}p < 0.1$. $^{**}p < 0.05$. $^{***}p < 0.01$.

but instead of using mean inflation expectations, I use the standard deviation in expected inflation. The variable information precision is the key conditioning variable in all models. Models 1 and 2 include the possible confounding variable output and the CIM measure as a measure of policy credibility. Alternatively, models 3 and 4 include the possible confounding variable output and, alternatively, the number of policy changes as reported by the IMF as a measure of credibility. All models control for the moving average of monthly inflation on the right-hand side, and all models also include country and month effects.

In interpreting the results, we see that average levels of monthly rolling inflation are positively and significantly related to inflation. This is to be expected. We also see that both average mean expected inflation and the standard deviation of expected inflation are positively and significantly related to inflation as well. In terms of our controls, we see no evidence that either CIM or output is systemically related to inflation. Interestingly, output is both substantively and statistically insignificant. Note, however, that the CIM estimate is very large with very large associated error. Alternatively, the measure of the count of policy changes is negative and significantly related with the inflation variable in both models, and has the expected sign. A higher level of policy credibility, as measured by more policy reforms, is negatively associated with lower values of inflation even when controlling for the average level of inflation.

Our main variable of interest is the interaction between the mean and standard deviation in inflation expectations and information precision. While the results in the table suggest that the effect is negative, to understand the relationship, we must examine the estimated effects of information across the range of values that information precision can take. Figure 6.5 and Figure 6.6 plot the estimated relationship for both measures of expectations. Here we find evidence that, indeed, an increase in information precision attenuates the effects of expectations. For those cases when the information environment is vague (defined as equal to 0), the marginal effect of inflation expectations is 1.7. When information is precise, however (defined as equal to 1), the marginal effect of mean inflation expectations is much lower, closer to 0.7. This suggests that conditional on the information environment being precise, by reducing the weight on inflation expectations, actual inflation outcomes attenuate compared to when the information environment is more vague.

Furthermore, we see that this attenuating relationship is even more pronounced when we examine the standard deviation in expectations rather than the mean. Here we find that when the information environment is vague (defined again as equal to 0), the marginal effect of the standard deviation in expectation is close to 1. Alternatively, when the information environment is precise (defined again as equal to 1), we see that the magical effect is not only lower but negative.

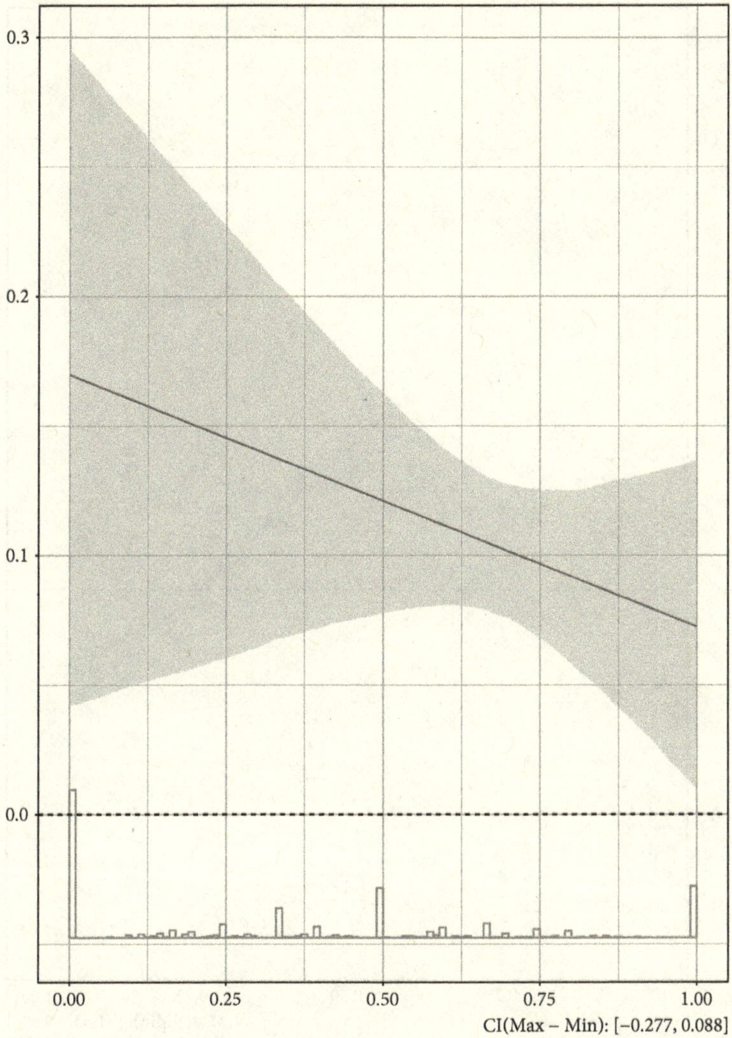

Fig. 6.5 Attenuation in Marginal Effect of Mean Expected Inflation.

Such a finding suggests that conditional on the information environment being precise, by reducing the weight on inflation expectations, actual inflation outcomes are predicted to be lower than when the information environment is more vague. In other words, more precise

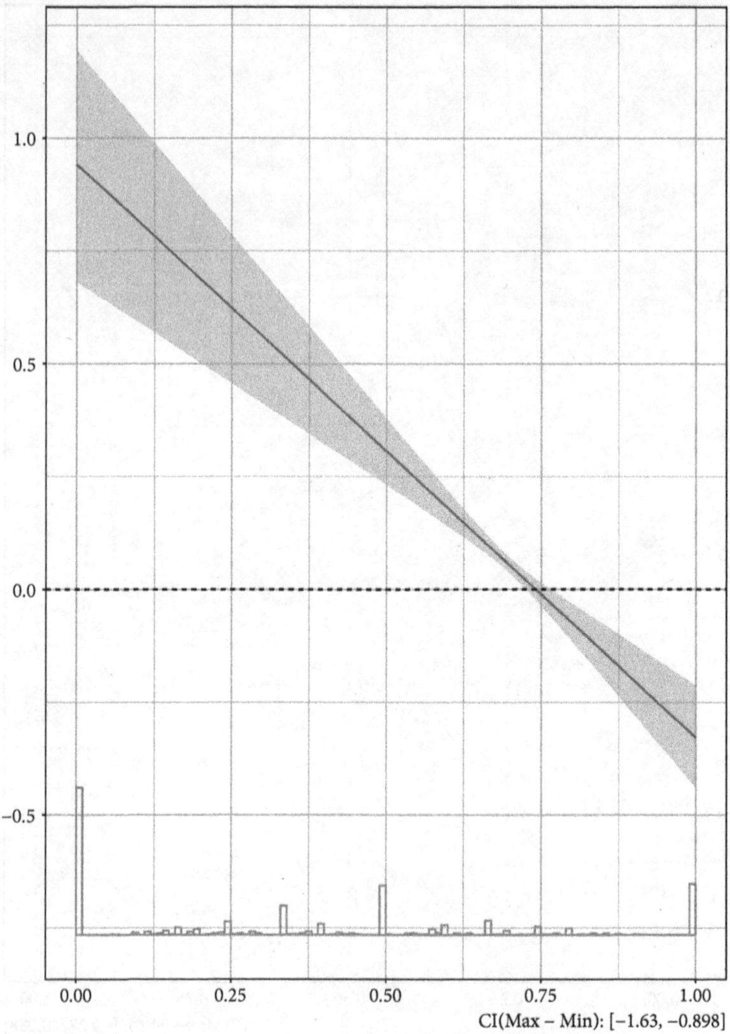

Fig. 6.6 Attenuation in Marginal Effect of Standard Deviation in Expected Inflation.

information is associated with lower inflation, and the channel or mechanism that this works through is by lowering the variance in expected inflation.

6.4 Sensitivity Analysis

In this section, I rerun the analysis using an instrumental variable (IV) approach. IVs are used to control for confounding and measurement error in observational studies. The purpose is to allow for the possibility of making causal inferences with observational data. IVs can adjust for both observed and unobserved confounding effects. In this section, I run the results again using a two-staged least squares (2SLS) model.

I use the level of ethnic and religious fractionalization and the level of internal conflict as instruments. The choice of these instruments is driven by early political economy explanations of the timing of inflation reforms. Researchers argue that sociodemographic features of a country, or factions, may explain why countries delay costly inflation stabilization policies (Alesina and Drazen, 1991). Using a "War of Attrition" model, these authors show that countries with relatively balanced societal factions are more likely to agree to costly economic reforms and stabilize inflation sooner than countries without balanced factions. As ethnic and religious conflict likely predates contemporaneous inflation levels, these variables are likely exogenous to a country's level of current inflation. The expectation is that countries with higher levels of ethnic, religious, and internal fractionalization are more likely to have longer delays in stabilizing inflation and, consequently, that greater societal cleavages will be positively related to expectations of future inflation. Importantly, these factors feed through expectations rather than affecting inflation directly, thus making them good instruments.

The data for these measures are from the international country risk data set and, like the other data, are monthly. The components that I use are *Ethnic Tensions*, *Religious Tensions*, and *Internal Conflict* (Howell, 2011). The first variable, Ethnic Conflict, is scored based on the level of tension in the economy resulting from racial, national, or linguistic divisions. Importantly, lower ratings are given to countries where racial and national tensions are high and directly relate to a perception of unwillingness to compromise. Consequently, we should see a negative relationship between ethnic conflict and inflation. The second measure, Religious Conflict, is similar and includes to what extent a religious majority dominates society as well as the willingness for societal groups to replace secular institutions with religious ones (Howell, 2011). Finally, the Internal Conflict variable has lower levels the more risk there is of civil war. A high score (4) indicates that there is little risk of civil conflict, whereas a low score (0) suggests a greater risk of conflict (Howell, 2011).

Using a 2SLS model,[7] Table 6.4 shows the results from the OLS model 3 alongside the IV results using the instruments discussed. I report only the models that use the mean (and not the standard deviation) of expected inflation, as when I analyze the models using

Table 6.4 Effect of information precision on inflation using both OLS and IV regression

	Dependent variable: Monthly inflation			
		Instrumental variable		
	OLS Model 1	Model 2	Model 3	Model 4
Average inflation	0.929***	0.891***	1.162	0.992**
	(0.013)	(0.295)	(2.740)	(0.458)
Mean expected inflation	0.170***	0.244	0.230	−0.017
	(0.065)	(0.778)	(1.161)	(1.093)
Precision	−3.305	0.215	4.848	−2.456
	(8.696)	(23.246)	(66.424)	(21.017)
Output	−0.005	−0.007	−0.003	−0.010
	(0.008)	(0.012)	(0.059)	(0.016)
No. policy changes	−2.465**	−1.936	−3.412	−1.963
	(1.132)	(1.214)	(15.673)	(1.289)
Mean Expected Inflation × Precision	−0.098	−0.210	−0.578	−0.003
	(0.093)	(1.136)	(4.745)	(1.112)
Observations	519	519	519	519
R^2	0.976	0.975	0.946	0.971
Adjusted R^2	0.975	0.974	0.944	0.970
Residual std. error ($df = 496$)	61.636	62.916	91.541	67.176
F-statistic ($df = 23; 496$)	866.811***			

*$p < 0.1$. **$p < 0.05$. ***$p < 0.01$.

[7] I ran the 2SLS model using the AER package in R.

the standard deviation, I cannot reject the *F*-test on the instruments in the first stage, suggesting that the instruments are weak in explaining the variance in expected inflation. Weak instruments are known to generate even worse problems than estimates with OLS, and so I proceed with the mean expectations (Angrist and Pischke, 2008) where I cannot reject the null of weak instruments.

I also ran other tests suggesting that the Ethnic Tensions variable is a stronger instrument than either the Religious Tensions or Internal Conflict variable. Consequently, in all the IVs, I paired this variable with one of the other instruments. In terms of the relationship between the instruments, the ethnicity instrument is weakly and positively correlated with internal conflict (0.11), showing that lower levels are associated with more conflict, yet it is only weakly and negatively correlated with religious conflict (−0.13). This implies that there is an inverse relationship between ethnic and religious conflict in my data. Interestingly, religious and internal conflict are more strongly positively correlated (0.46) than across the other variables.

Model 1 reports the main results from Table 6.3 in column 3. Model 2 shows the results of the IV when ethnic conflict and internal conflict are included as instruments. All of the variables retain their expected signs, with the exception of the information precision variable, which is insignificant across all models. None of the variables, with the exception of average inflation, are statistically significant, however, and the estimated uncertainty around the estimates is larger rather than smaller, implying that the IV model may not be as well fit as the OLS model (IV models are supposed to increase the estimate size and decrease the uncertainty, which we do not see here). Model 3 includes as instruments religion and internal conflict and, according to the residual standard error, is the model least well fit to the data. Model 4 recovers more similar estimates to the OLS model, but again, none of the variables are statistically significant due to the larger estimated uncertainty of the coefficients. Given these concerns, I conducted a Wu–Hausman test on the IV regressions and found that I could not reject the null that the OLS estimates are more efficient than the IVs. I also removed the rolling average inflation variable across all the IV estimates and then reran the sensitivity analysis. Once the rolling moving average variable was excluded, using the Wu–Hausman test again, I found that I could then reject the null that the OLS model performs better and that there is possible endogeneity that needs to be accounted for. These sensitivity tests suggest that by including the average rolling inflation variable on the right-hand side in the OLS model, I am already accounting for significant persistence in inflation and therefore for the possibility of endogeneity, leading me to favor the results from the simple OLS regression, which are more efficient.

In summary, I find evidence that an increase in the information environment, in terms of its level of precision, exerts an attenuating and significant effect on mean inflation expectations and the standard deviation in expected inflation as well. I find that this holds even when I account for alternative explanations of inflation, such as the level of a country's policy credibility, persistence in inflation, economic output, and month and country effects. In running an instrumental variable analysis, I find similarly signed results; however, the results are no longer statistically significant. I also find reason to reject the IV estimates in favor of the more efficient OLS results especially when the model accounts for average levels of inflation. The main results in this chapter imply that an increase in information precision can indeed help to lower aggregate levels of inflation and that the channel that this works through is by lowering the weight of prior expectations, as predicted by my theoretical argument. Importantly, the results hold even when we consider a sample of countries with relatively variable inflation outcomes and less established (and therefore less credible) economic institutions.

6.5 Conclusion

This chapter statistically evaluates the relationship between information precision and inflation outcomes in a panel of six Latin American countries from 1993 to 2010. To measure information precision in a way that is comparable across countries and over time, I develop and validate a new measure of inflation-related information about the economy from Reuters newswire reports. I cluster these newswire reports into three levels of information precision using a *K*-means clustering algorithm and computational textual analysis techniques. I then use human coding to validate the classification and then generate an information precision variable that measures the proportion of precise news articles about inflation in a given country-month. I then use this variable as an important conditioning variable, interacting it with average inflation expectations and the standard deviation in inflation expectations from a panel of expert forecasters, whom I use to proxy households' inflation expectations. I find significant (both substantively and statistically) evidence that an increase in the level of information precision in the information environment about inflation attenuates inflation expectations and negatively contributes to inflation.

The analyses in this chapter make a number of contributions to the literature. The first contribution is that, by conducting the analysis on a set of countries with wider variability in inflation experiences, we learn that more precise information works to influence the economy even for those countries where aggregate inflation outcomes are relatively high. This is especially important as emerging markets and developing countries often have significantly less stable economies than economies in developed countries and also have governments with lower levels of credibility about their economic policies. Alternative explanations of inflation have generally focused on the role of credibility and the time-inconsistent nature of economic policy as being one reason why we observe variation in inflation. Consequently, we might find that credibility is a more important predictor of inflation than a mechanism based on information. Interestingly, I find evidence in support of both arguments. Using a new measure of policy credibility based on the number of policy changes, I do find evidence that an increase in credibility is inversely related to inflation outcomes, suggesting that policy and the institutions that make them are important bellwethers for the economy. Additionally, I also find that even accounting for this, information exerts its own effect on inflation through the expectations channel.

A second contribution to the literature relates to the historical role that information has played in stabilizing expectations. Much of the literature on central bank communication focuses on the effectiveness of communication starting with the 2008 financial crisis. While global average inflation in developed and developing countries is historically very low, in many developing countries, especially Venezuela, inflation continues to be a problem. Thus, while recent research shows that central bank information helps drive the economy in low-inflation conditions, previously untested is whether this mechanism can work in countries facing higher rather than lower levels of inflation. By analyzing a sample of countries in a historical setting where communication was less likely to be an explicit policy tool of either central banks or government, I offer a more general test of the effectiveness of information on inflation, and one that has important implications for a wider range of countries and economic conditions.

7
Putting It All Together

More than a decade has passed since the beginning of the US financial crisis, and yet, we still live with its consequences. Also called the Great Recession, the US financial crisis was both an American and a global economic downturn that devastated world markets. Not only did the crisis shatter financial markets but it also reverberated across other markets as well, including banking, stocks, and real estate. The crisis led to increases in home mortgage foreclosures; caused people to lose their jobs and their savings; and eroded trust in many institutions, including central banks.

Throughout the crisis, central banks and governments imagined new (and not so new) tools to deal with it. One of the most heralded tools of crisis-driven central banking was the strategic deployment of central bank communication—where central bank officials publicly communicated their future policy moves and their rationale to private actors, with an aim to quell uncertainty. While even as early as 1602, monarchs were known to use communications to cry up and cry down the value of coinage (Sargent and Velde, 2003), communication as an intentional arm of monetary policy took center stage throughout the Great Recession.

Alongside, there was an explosion of academic and market research about the effects of central bank communications. Generally, research shows that central bank communication can move markets, and in ways that policy makers intend (Ehrmann and Fratzscher, 2007). Less understood, however, is why the content of central bank communications varies across time and across countries, and in this book, I focus on how the composition of MPCs can affect the content of central bank communications. Finally, while most previous studies focus on how central bank communication policy exerts influence on financial markets, much less is known about how or whether official communications shape the expectations of the mass public (for

Crafting Consensus: Why Central Bankers Change Their Speech and How Speech Changes the Economy. Nicole Rae Baerg, Oxford University Press (2020). © Oxford University Press.
DOI: 10.1093/oso/9780190499488.001.0001

exceptions, see Cavallo, 2012; Ehrmann, Eijffinger, and Fratzscher, 2012). What influence, if any, do changes in central bank proclamations have on everyday households? How do households' expectations, and by extension, central bank communications, change the economy? The answers in this book aim to fill these gaps, and I summarize my findings in the next section.

7.1 Summary of the Findings

Does variation in the preferences of MPC members affect the content of central bank communications?

My argument takes us into the policy cycle of monetary policy meetings. In particular, I take seriously the structures and institutions where central bankers deliberate and the committee rules that govern policy decision-making. In chapter 3, using a simple bargaining model, I show how the preferences of central bank committee members, in particular, the preference alignment of the committee chair and the median committee member, impact the level of *strategic vagueness* in official communications. The theoretical chapter provides a new explanation for why central bank communication varies in its content and argues that policy makers' internal bargaining process matters. In particular, I show that when these two pivotal actors have opposing preferences, such as when one is an inflation "hawk" and the other an inflation "dove," the level of strategic vagueness is lower than when they have like preferences. Additionally, I show that as these pivotal actors increase in their dissimilarity, there is an associated rise in the number of edits to the policy statement. My argument is different from other accounts that suggest that central bank communications arise due to demand-side reasons for greater central bank transparency (Crowe and Meade, 2007); policy diffusion and learning accounts, which focus on the globalization of ideas (Helleiner, 2014; Johnson, 2016; Meseguer, 2010); and supply-side accounts that focus on new technologies that facilitate more direct communications, such as the advent of social media.

To empirically evaluate my argument, in chapter 4, I examine the FOMC in the United States. Using quantitative text analysis to measure lexical uncertainty in a sample of FOMC-issued official policy announcements and a measure of committee members' inflation preferences, I find some evidence in support of my argument. When the committee chair and the median member have opposing inflation preferences, the official policy statement contains less uncertainty language than when these members have similar preferences. Interestingly, however, I find that this only holds when I consider the median member with voting rights. This finding is consistent with the idea that the median committee member must have a credible outside offer to constrain the committee chair. Unlike her counterparts not on schedule to vote, the median voting member can publicly dissent, thus giving her a credible threat when bargaining in committee deliberations.

As a second prediction, my theory suggests that the sheer number of changes to the official policy announcement also depends on the preference configuration of the MPC. Again using quantitative text analysis and a new measure of textual changes to the official policy statement, I examine whether there is an associated increase in the number of textual changes made to the policy statement as the distance between the chair and the median member grows larger. Here I find evidence that a one-unit increase in the distance between the chair and the median member is associated with eleven additional edits to the monetary policy statement. This is a substantively large finding, as official monetary policy statements are often very short and slow changing, with significant status quo bias in their content.

The theoretical and empirical findings demonstrated in chapters 3 and 4, therefore, are important in that they suggest that central bank communications depend on policy makers' interests and the decision-making rules that aggregate members' interests. The fact that interests and institutions together matter implies that crafting consensus on an MPC is an inherently political exercise and not just a technical one. Applying the language of March (1962), MPCs function in a *conflict system*, where members have identifiable preferences and yet only some members' preferred outcomes are realizable at any given time. Furthermore, as MPCs are part of a conflict system, managing internal conflict, that is, conflicts of interest between colleagues, matters for central bank communications. Importantly, I find that the median member's power is strongest when she holds opposing views to the committee chair and is simultaneously able to cast a public dissenting vote even if dissenting is only used as a threat. The statistical evidence in chapter 4 implies that policy makers' preferences and the voting rotation system work together to produce the level of uncertainty in central bank communications.

The fact that internal, committee-level conflict matters for central bank communication makes a new contribution to the study of monetary policy. Often scholars depict central bankers as managing external rather than internal conflicts. Previous research, for example, focuses on conflicts that central bankers have with other political actions, such as internal governing factions, different political parties and branches of government, and domestic political actors (Chang, 2003; Johnson, 2016; Shih, 2008). The fact that internal conflict matters is not to say that managing external conflict does not matter as well. Conflicts between the central bank and outside actors can and do occur. Yet, in addition to public conflicts, private, internal, committee-level conflicts play a defining role in the conduct of monetary policy. And while some previous literature has looked at internal conflict, it has mainly focused on how committee members' preferences matter for deciding on interest rates (Adolph, 2013; Ainsley, 2016; Chappell, McGregor and Vermilyea, 2005; Schonhardt-Bailey, 2013). Thus a main contribution of this book is that I show how committee-level conflict and institutional rules matter when crafting central bank communications.

Do changes in the content of central bank announcements impact households' inflation expectations?

A significant body of research examines the influence of central bank communications on financial markets, yet much less is known about whether official communications can influence everyday people as well. In chapter 5, using a survey experiment, I show that subtle changes to the lexical content of official communications influence households' expectations of the future economy. In particular, I find that by using more precise language, central banks can both engender lower average expected inflation and lower the variance in citizens' inflation expectations. I also find that this is true in a country where disinflationary risks are evident. The testing of this hypothesis under crisis conditions is important for understanding when communications might matter, as during disinflationary risks, the public might be more rationally inattentive, willing to ignore central bank information, or more attentive, owing to higher levels of uncertainty in the economy. At the same time, however, previous studies point to possible limits of more precise central bank information. While greater lexical precision seems to generate particularly strong effects on households, we know very little about the bounds of such an effect. Furthermore, we do not know whether such effects vary across different audiences. For instance, in using forecast data, researchers found that the dispersion in expectations among the general public is more affected by central bank transparency than is the dispersion in expectations of professional forecasters (Ehrmann, Eijffinger, and Fratzscher, 2012). Future research might well consider additional experiments that try to identify possible ceiling and floor effects of central bank communications. Another avenue worth exploring is testing for heterogeneity across different audiences, which might matter for communication effectiveness.

Also important is that I find that changes in information are a stronger predictor of expected future inflation than sociodemographic characteristics like age and gender. A large share of the population has low levels of financial literacy, even in OECD countries. If information can help inform the mass public, then financial literacy might improve alongside increases in central bank precision. By using more precise language, central bank communication may better inform, helping to shape consumers' expectations about the economy and making policy success more likely.

Relatedly, another finding is that despite their low levels of financial literary, households act in a relatively sophisticated manner when receiving and incorporating even technical central bank announcements. According to the survey results, more precise information influences short-term and medium-term expectations, defined as one to five years ahead. Households do not, however, incorporate central bank announcements into their longer-term expectations, defined as ten years ahead. Thus, while information has the ability to influence individuals' immediate to medium-term price expectations, information alone does not explain why citizens vary in their fundamental beliefs about the economy in the first place. Because individuals' prior beliefs are likely driven by both economic and political factors, such as personal economic experiences, trust in institutions, and expectations of future policy success, further research into the possible mediating role of economic and political factors on citizens' inflation beliefs is warranted.

Finally, other dimensions of information aside from information precision can vary across central bank pronouncements, but these remain untested in this book. While the survey experiment in chapter 5 focuses on lexical uncertainty, other dimensions, such as textual complexity and readability (Jansen, 2011), the length of the text, and the use of audio and visual information, may also matter. For example, with the advent of social media, central banks increasingly communicate using tools like Twitter and Facebook. These platforms constrain communications into shorter and less formal messages; understanding whether and how communications may differ across informal and formal channels is also an avenue worth exploring. Another exciting direction is the influence of nonverbal communication. One pathbreaking study by Schonhardt-Bailey (2017) finds that central bankers reporting to the government in oversight hearings use appeasing body language when questioned. As internal committee meetings do not offer visual records of what transpires, it is more difficult to evaluate nonverbal cues in MPC deliberations. Yet, mining textual information for humor, appeasement, and rousing can offer researchers an additional way to analyze textual records for meaning, taking us beyond the analysis of words and word phrases.

While central bank communication policy was deployed as a strategic tool during the Great Recession, inflationary rather than deflationary crises are more common. Testing the theory in other economic environments is therefore paramount. As I am also interested in explaining economic performance, specifically, inflation performance, chapter 6 extends the empirical analysis to a sample of six Latin American countries between 1993 and 2010. Importantly, this period covers a wide range of inflation experiences: deflation, inflation, and exploding hyperinflation.

To test whether more precise information acts as a mediator for expectations even in such diverse conditions, I develop a new measure of the preciseness of the information environment at the country-month level. I build this measure using a *K*-means, unsupervised machine learning classification applied to a corpus of Reuters newswire reports. To validate the measure, I compare the classification with a human-coded "gold standard." To proxy households' inflation expectations, I use the mean and standard deviation of expected inflation from a panel of professional forecasters located in Latin America. I then test whether a more precise information environment helps attenuate inflation expectations and lowers inflation. I find that information is crucial in lowering short-term expectations. Because inflation expectations may not only be about information but may also capture beliefs about the central bank's long-run inflation target and its credibility to achieve inflation stabilization, I also include a new measure of monetary policy changes to account for credibility. Yet, even when I include a measure of credibility, I find that an increase in the preciseness of the information environment continues to exert a significant attenuating effect on short-term inflation expectations.

7.2 Accountability and Transparency

Former policy makers, academics, and the media have started to question the significant powers handed over to today's central bankers. One of the most concerning features is their *unelected power* (Tucker, 2018). Central banks are nonmajoritarian institutions, or "governmental entities that... possess and exercise some grant of specialized public authority, separate from that of other institutions, but... are neither directly elected by the people, nor directly managed by elected officials" (Thatcher and Sweet, 2002). Because central bankers are unelected and are also not directly managed, how does one ensure that they are held accountable?

Previous literature often focuses on *vertical* accountability. Vertical accountability describes a hierarchical chain where each link provides a step in an accountability relationship. Applied to central banking, this chain is thought to run first from the electorate to the government and then second from the government to the central bank. In the first step, vertical accountability occurs through the formal process of elections between voters and the government in democracies and between elite factions in new and nondemocracies (Johnson, 2016; Shih, 2008). In the second step, the central bank accounts to the government, and this usually occurs through formal reporting. For example, the chair of the FOMC offers semiannual oral testimony about the activities of the US central bank to the Committee on Banking, Housing, and Urban Affairs of the Senate and the Committee on Financial Services of the House of Representatives.[1] In the United Kingdom, the governors, executive directors, and external Monetary Policy Committee and Financial Policy Committee members regularly appear before the government, and new members of the Monetary Policy Committee and Financial Policy Committee also have hearings at the Treasury Committee before they are appointed.[2]

In vertical accountability relationships, transparency and accountability are embedded in the principal's monitoring problem. In vertical accountability, an increase in transparency helps those actors up the hierarchy better monitor those actors down the hierarchical chain. And sometimes the relationship between those up and down the chain is adversarial as well as appeasing. In this vein, at times, members sitting on MPCs want more numerous and like-minded allies to prevent pressure from the government. For example, in 2007, Lorenzo Bini Smaghi, a member of the Executive Board of the ECB, stated that "a collegial decision-making body, composed of several members is more likely to resist external pressures and partisan behaviour." According to this view, a more homogeneous MPC makes it easier for the MPC to hold its own against the government and limits any friction on the MPC itself.[3]

Missing from this, however, is consideration of the role that *horizontal* accountability can play in central bank decision-making. Horizontal accountability is when actors are held to account for their behaviors and decisions to peers rather than superiors (Mainwaring and Welna, 2003; O'Donnell, 1998; Schillemans, 2008). In this book,

[1] Testimony of Federal Reserve Officials.
[2] Bank of England Appearances before Parliament.
[3] https://www.ecb.europa.eu/press/key/date/2007/html/sp070419.en.html

I show how diverse, rather than like-minded, peers induce horizontal accountability. In other words, a truly collegial decision-making body with horizontal accountability is one where competition of interest is encouraged and dissent is possible.

Why does horizontal accountability matter? What does it mean for the politics of central bank appointments? One implication of the book is that appointing a diverse MPC improves horizontal accountability as well as central bank transparency. While I am not the first to suggest that MPCs ought to be staffed with members with diverse interests, previous literature has focused on alternative explanations for why. Scholars have pointed out that diversity on committees protects against groupthink, helps to overcome cognitive limitations, and enhances deliberations (Blinder, 2007; Dhir, 2015; Hong and Page, 2004). Rather than focus on these cognitive benefits, my argument instead suggests that committee diversity ensures greater horizontal accountability by encouraging political competition and constrains its members. While it may be true that a collegial decision-making body is more able to resist external pressures, on the other hand, a contentious decision-making body with diverse membership may be more able to resist internal pressures toward collusion.

Horizontal accountability is also especially important in the context of unelected power (Tucker, 2018) because vertical accountability, through formal reporting, occurs relatively infrequently. Another concern is that expertise may not be shared by those up the chain, limiting the level of technical oversight that can be performed by superiors in the first place. Alternatively, horizontal accountability happens more frequently among those who share information and expertise. For example, in the United States, FOMC members meet to decide on policy every six weeks, or eight times a year, which allows for much greater frequency in horizontal accountability than the semiannual reporting that the committee chair performs for the government.

7.3 Horizontal Accountability and Central Bank Appointments

In his canonical model of central bank delegation, Rogoff (1985) argues that the government is better off delegating responsibility to a single, conservative (hawkish) central banker. In delegating authority to the central bank, the government enters into a costly relationship of vertical accountability. In exchange, by appointing a conservative central banker, citizens' inflation expectations are stabilized, and inflation is lower than otherwise.[4] What this means is that the government trades off greater independence in governance for economic stability. The central problem for the government is that in delegating responsibility to stabilize households' inflation expectations, it is left with what Tucker (2018) terms "unelected power": the conservative central banker wields authority that the government is required to check somehow. Consistent with notions of vertical accountability, checking the central bank is usually, although not exclusively, performed by formal reports to the government.

Instead of appointing Rogoff's (1985) conservative central banker, my argument suggests that the government would do better to appoint one hawkish central banker and one dovish central banker to an MPC, or equivalently, one hawkish and one dovish faction. If the government appoints not one but two committee members, and these members have conflicting rather than consensual interests, then, according to my theory, the committee members themselves will generate horizontal accountability on the MPC. Furthermore, as this is an equilibrium condition, such benefits are self-reinforcing. As I have demonstrated in previous chapters, one important byproduct of MPC horizontal accountability is the production of more precise policy communications. Assuming that more precise communications stabilize expectations as equally well as Rogoff's conservative central banker (this is untested in the manuscript but is an interesting empirical question), then the government receives an additional benefit of better oversight. This is first because the MPC itself better communicates what it will do (more precision), and second, the MPC communicates at more frequent intervals (eight rather than two times a year). In other words, as in Rogoff, the government benefits from economic stability as a consequence of information-stabilizing expectations, and

[4] For an argument that suggests that such economic benefits do not ensue, see Ainsley (2016).

additionally, it benefits in more frequent monitoring of the central bank. Compared against Rogoff's single conservative central banker, the government's hand is strengthened.

So why don't governments always appoint two central bankers who have competing interests? The fact that governments can appoint central bankers with competing interests and yet, sometimes choose not to, implies either that the government does not want to or that it cannot. For example, assuming that the government has an incentive to stack the MPC with members that it favors, the government might now appoint two rather than one member it prefers. Doing so, however, will make its monitoring problem harder and may also not stabilize expectations. The government, and by extension, the citizenry, thus faces a conundrum: if the government appoints two central bankers both with similar preferences, it not only loses central bank transparency but also fails to solve its credibility problem. If, alternatively, the government appoints one dovish and one hawkish central banker, the government gains in horizontal accountability and also benefits from more informed citizens with lower inflation expectations. While addressing the empirical question of who appoints diverse MPCs and who does not is outside the scope of this book, the next section considers some possible extensions and applications for future research to tackle this question.

7.4 Future Research

7.4.1 Rotational Voting

As I have shown, a combination of interests and institutions matters for communication policy. It is not just who sits on the MPC but also who has the right to vote on policy outputs that matters for the level of precision in central bank communications. Some central banks around the world have one-member, one-vote systems, whereas other countries, such as the United States and the Eurozone, have rotational voting. Rotational voting means that only a subset of the MPC has formal voting power at any given time. Being on schedule to vote is usually exogenously determined, with members unable to select into or out of voting rotation, which makes comparing on-schedule and off-schedule voting patterns particularly useful.

In 2015, with the inclusion of Lithuania into the Eurozone, the ECB changed from a one-member, one-vote system to rotational voting. Importantly, this change was envisaged early on by the Governing Council, in 2002, as a way to deal with growing European membership and therefore not as a consequence of internal politics on the MPCs or debates between member states. Examining the ECB's rationale for changing the voting system, we see that the ECB itself expected little change to decision-making as a consequence of new voting rules. Such a rationale is likely due to considering vertical rather than horizontal accountability. According to information provided on its website,

> *With the rotation system there are three different classes of Governing Council members. Does that affect the discussion among the members and the decision-making process?* Because all members of the Governing Council attend the meetings and have the right to speak, so in terms of the discussion nothing has changed. Since the Governing Council takes most decisions on a consensual basis, in a spirit of cooperation, the decision-making process has not changed either.[5]

Whether or not this is true, however, is an empirical question. If my theory is correct and horizontal accountability on MPCs matters for communication policy, we would expect changes to the voting system to lead to changes in the level of uncertainty expressed in the policy statement. In particular, we would expect changes in the voting system to alter the content of ECB official communications once the new rotational voting system had been put into place.

The voting reform in 2015, therefore, generates a discontinuity in MPC membership before and after the reform. Indeed, because the previous one-member, one-vote system included a relatively large number of actors, we might expect that the preferences of the chair and

[5] Rotation of voting rights in the Governing Council, December 1, 2014.

the median member before the reform were relatively more similar.[6] However, with the adoption of rotational voting in 2015, now only a smaller subset of committee members can vote. Given the smaller number, this increases the likelihood that at some point, the chair and the median committee member will have dissimilar preferences. If my theory is correct, we should expect to see higher variability in the level of expressed uncertainty in the ECB policy statement after the ECB changed to rotational voting in 2015. Employing a research design to test whether this has occurred is one possible avenue for future research.

7.4.2 Qualifications

Who gets to sit on the MPC in the first place? What sorts of professional qualifications must individuals have to be appointed, and how do we ensure a diverse MPC? Central banks often argue that appointees must necessarily be central bankers, economists, or individuals with expertise in banking and finance. This is not only a norm but also a legal requirement for some central banks. The Statute of the European System of Central Banks, for example, states, "In accordance with Article 109a(2)(b) of this Treaty, the President, the Vice-President and the other Members of the Executive Board shall be appointed from among persons of recognized standing and professional experience in monetary or banking matters" (ESCB, 1992). Empirically, however, we observe much larger variation in the vocational backgrounds of who is appointed to central bank committees. As shown in chapter 2, while the bulk of MPC members are economists and central bankers, others have backgrounds in industry

[6] Unfortunately, to my knowledge, there is no measure of ECB members' preferences before and after, and the ECB does not yet publish meeting transcripts. The ECB publishes an account of the Governing Council's monetary policy discussions four weeks after each monetary policy meeting to make the rationale behind the decisions more transparent. Unfortunately, the texts of these discussions often refer to MPC members as "Members" and not individually by name, making preferences hard to measure.

and even in government. How the appointment process works is essential to committee composition.

Previous literature finds that both the partisan nature of the appointer and the economic conditions of the country matter for central bank appointments. According to one recent study, Hallerberg and Wehner (2018) find that left-partisan leaders appoint economic policy makers who are more highly trained in economics and that an appointer's exposure to economics training is also related to the background of those appointed. In Kaplan (2017), left-leaning parties use information about the educational background of central bankers to infer whether appointees hold heterodox or mainstream policy preferences; left governments then appoint mainstream economists when the economy is doing poorly. Even in nondemocracies, the economy matters for appointments. Shih (2008) shows that Chinese party cadres hand over monetary policy to an elite faction that does not want to expand the monetary base and trigger short-term growth, but they do so only when the economy is doing poorly. While partisanship and bad economic times might mean that central bank committees are staffed by economists, these factors do little to ensure that staffing is diverse.

In addition to concerns about the economy, political calculations may matter to the appointer. Baerg, Gray and Willisch (2019) argue that who gets appointed depends on the reelection strategy of the appointer and especially on the level of electoral competition for the appointer's post. Meanwhile, Chang (2003) shows that the appointer's choice is conditioned by the likelihood that the candidate will be confirmed by other levels of government. When the president and the senate are divided, the president must either appoint a candidate the senate will confirm or delay appointments. If the president always needs to consider the preferences of the confirming body, it might be that we end up with greater homogeneity in candidates than what we would observe if the president and the senate had always the same party. Consequently, if divided governments make the MPC more homogeneous by appointing more moderate (and therefore more similar) members, it may also be the case that divided governments indirectly create MPCs with lower levels of diversity and lower levels of horizontal accountability. As we know that diversity and horizontal accountability are related to more precise information, divided governments may unknowingly create MPCs that are less accountable and communicate less precisely.

Ensuring diversity through the appointment process is therefore likely to be tricky. A number of institutional practices, such as staggering the length of tenure, implementing quotas, or widening the definition of professional qualifications to include others outside of economics and finance, may be warranted. Yet we know very little about how such mechanisms might work and little empirical evidence of their consequences. Further research into identifying appointment mechanisms that may better construct competing interests on MPCs is an exciting avenue worth exploring.

7.5 Applications beyond Central Banking

While the focus of this volume is on central banking, the argument and empirical findings are also relevant for other institutions. In this section, I consider relevant literature and the implications for my findings for studies of judicial politics and governance on corporate boards. My goal in mentioning these other applications is to offer some additional ideas for future research and to broaden my argument.

7.5.1 Judicial Politics

In their seminal paper on judicial lawmaking, Staton and Vanberg (2008) ask why judges sometimes choose to be clear in their rulings, whereas at other times, judges decide to be vague. While these authors answer this puzzle by focusing on the court's external relationships rather than focusing on internal deliberations among justices, other scholars examine internal reasons for vagueness. Just as central bankers deliberate over policy communications, court justices bargain and negotiate with one another to create binding legal precedent. Indeed, Maltzman, Spriggs, and Wahlbeck (2000) argue that court justices act strategically with their colleagues on the court to get their preferred rulings. Unfortunately, however, these authors are more interested in evaluating whether judges act strategically than in evaluating the impact strategic behavior has on the court's decisions. Consequently, the empirical treatment of the court does not answer the question why some judicial rulings are more vague than others; however, it does provide significant evidence that intercommittee deliberation matters for judicial rulings.

More recently, Owens and Wedeking (2011) provide an empirical investigation into those internal factors that might matter for the level of clarity in judicial rulings. These authors test whether the size of the court and the ideology of the members on the court matter for clarity. Importantly, their argument on the role of ideology makes the opposite prediction as my model. According to their argument, judicial members are engaged in coalition building. Justices are motivated to build coalitions with other, like-minded justices. An increase in connectivity among those in the coalition (i.e., less ideological dispersion) reduces the need for members to appease conflicting views, which, they argue, manifests through opinion complexity. As a result, an increase in ideological dispersion among justices will lead to a decline in clarity (increase in vagueness) as justices have to be more accommodating through the strategic deployment of complexity, whereas a decrease in ideological dispersion will lead to an increase in clarity (i.e., a decrease in vagueness) as the justices can better write what they want without appeasing conflicting views.

To assess their argument empirically, the authors use readability measures and a dictionary approach with ten Linguistic Inquiry and Word Count (LIWC) indicators. These ten dimensions of complexity are associated with cognitive complexity: *causation, insight, discrepancy, inhibition, tentativeness, certainty, inclusiveness, exclusiveness, negations*, and *percentage of words containing six or more letters*. While the dimension *certainty* is included in their measure, other types of complexity contribute to vagueness as well. These authors find that judicial opinions written by minimum-winning coalitions are clearer (less vague) than opinions written by unanimous coalitions.

Different from my model, these authors do not account for key roles played by certain members of the committee. For example, the chief justice and the median justice have the same power as all other members, and all justices' preferences contribute equally. It is perhaps fair to say that despite looking at internal deliberations, in their model, the internal committee is institutionless in terms of rules. Judges face no problem in aggregating interests other than the accommodation of preferences, and the rules of the game do not benefit some members at the expense of others. While this is certainly not true for MPCs, whether or not this is true for judicial committees is untested in the paper. Furthermore, it could be the case that the chief justice and the median justice have more similar orientation in relatively large coalitions. If this is true, then an increase in opinion vagueness, which is associated with large coalitions, might merely be measuring the median justice reverting to the chief justice's opinion, rather than ideological cohesion. To better understand which mechanism is at work, future research could compare competing expectations across the theories. Analyses that not only account for the preferences of all actors but also include the preference similarity or dissimilarity of the chief justice and median justice in addition to the size of the coalition would go a long way toward determining whether cohesion or conflict is a better predictor of vagueness in judicial opinions.

7.5.2 Corporate Governance

Diversity on corporate boards, especially gender diversity, is of growing importance to industry groups and governments. In the United Kingdom, public companies will need to appoint women to 40 percent of their board positions before 2020 if they are to meet government-backed targets to improve gender diversity.[7] For example, some research indicates that having more women and minorities on corporate boards is good for firm productivity and also generates more conservative financial reporting (for a review, see Francis et al., 2015).

Little research, however, questions whether board diversity between the board director and the median board member matters for firm reporting transparency. Loughran and McDonald (2011) use

[7] Sarah Gordon. UK plc behind target for number of women on boards, Financial Times, June 27, 2018.

a measure of uncertainty words to examine 10-K filings, which are annual reports required for filing with the Securities and Exchange Commission (SEC). Importantly, 10-K filings report on companies' performance and finances. In addition to varying in their level of transparency, they often include information about board members and, combined with personnel information, could be used to test the argument in another application. The most supporting research is a study by Gul, Srinidhi, and Ng (2011). These authors find that stock prices of firms with gender-diverse boards reflect more firm-specific information after controlling for alternative explanations. Like the judicial politics literature highlighted earlier, however, the authors do not account for the preferences of key actors, such as the board director and the median board member. Future research that applies my model to see whether board diversity can act as a substitute mechanism for corporate governance that would be otherwise weak is a fruitful avenue for future research.

7.6 Final Thoughts

In an important symposium on monetary policy in political studies published in 2018, Adolph (2018, p. 737) argues that we must stop thinking of central bankers as "neutral technocrats, without interests of their own." In this book, I go one step further and argue that it is the combination of central bankers' *interests* and *institutions* that matters for understanding the politics of monetary policy. While recent literature has examined the political economy of central bankers being beholden to external actors, such as government factions, shadow principals, and epistemic communities, my argument takes us back into the everyday politics of monetary policy in the institutions where central bankers deliberate on policy, instead focusing on the internal politics of decision-making. Anyone who has performed some kind of committee work, whether it be for work, school, or a community organization, knows that internal committee politics often plays a role in decision-making.

One key element of my model is that it is the committee chair and the median committee member who yield enormous power in deliberations, as their preference configuration is the driving force behind the content of central bank announcements. An alternative explanation is one where all members' interests are important to committee decision-making and where members contribute equally. Absent of power, in this view, institutions do very little and instead act as empty vessels, holding the interests of actors rather than shaping outcomes. Conceiving of monetary policy committees this way is akin to traditional pluralistic models of monetary policy making (Frieden, 1991). Just as we now understand that institutions matter for the conduct of monetary policy at the national level (Bearce, 2009; Bernhard, Broz, and Clark, 2002; Bodea and Hicks, 2015; Hallerberg, 2002; Hallerberg and Clark, 2002), it is perhaps intuitive that institutions should matter at the monetary policy committee level as well. The most direct evidence I found of institutions mattering is presented in chapter 4. If I consider only committee members' interests, committees with more dissimilar preferences are more likely to have higher levels of uncertainty language contained in the policy statement. When I consider both interests and institutions, however, I find the opposite: dissimilarity in preferences is associated with lower levels of uncertainty language in the policy statement, or greater central bank transparency.

Irrespective of whether members of central bank committees think that they are technocrats, the very institutions where they work and the rules that govern how they work, in addition to their interests, matter for policy outputs. A key implication of this is that rather than encouraging committee members to be collegial, this volume points to important byproducts in transparency that result from having conflicting interests on monetary policy committees. Monetary policy committees may do well to strengthen diversity of interests. Removed from the shackles of committee homogeneity, a more diverse committee might go some length toward generating greater monetary policy transparency and, through its encouragement of horizontal accountability, toward reducing the "democratic deficit" of central banks as well.

Appendix

Table A.1 gives a summary of the main characteristics of the corpus of official policy statements used to construct one of the dependent variables in chapter 4.

I use the share of uncertainty and certainty words and word phrases as the main dependent variable. This proportion is constructed from a custom made dictionary of certainty and uncertainty words. As discussed in the chapter, the

Table A.1 Descriptive statistics for corpus of official FOMC policy statements adopted

Meeting Number	Types	Tokens	Sentences	Selected Statement	Meeting Date
1	110	174	7	B	February 2005
2	130	213	7	B	March 2005
3	124	201	9	B	May 2005
4	119	193	8	B	June 2005
5	124	193	7	B	August 2005
6	161	272	11	B	September 2005
7	120	197	9	B	November 2005
8	91	137	6	B	December 2005
9	98	135	6	B	January 2006
10	121	194	7	B	March 2006
11	137	254	10	B	May 2006
12	115	185	8	B	June 2006
13	104	155	5	B	August 2006
14	103	162	6	B	September 2006
15	111	175	7	B	October 2006
16	118	184	7	B	December 2006
17	104	160	7	B	January 2007
18	104	164	8	B	March 2007
19	93	136	7	B	May 2007
20	95	137	7	B	June 2007
21	111	162	9	B	August 2007
22	101	151	6	B	September 2007
23	110	190	8	A	October 2007
24	116	187	8	B	December 2007

dictionary "keys" are determined by human annotation of the FOMC official meeting transcripts. A random sample of sentences are coded for whether or not sentences use hedging language. Human annotators highlighted those vocabulary words that triggered their decision-making for classifying the sentences. The list of trigger words and phrases are then applied to the out of sample corpus of FOMC official policy statements shown in Table A.1. For completeness, I include the full list of keys (136 uncertainty words, 154 certainty words), however, in the empirical analysis presented in chapter 4, I present results using words and word phrases that are of length $n = 3$ or less. As longer word phrases are unlikely to show up verbatim in the official statement, there is likely to be little difference between using the full set of keys including longer phrases and phrases with length smaller than three.

Alternative measures of uncertainty are also considered. One dictionary, the LIWC dataset is proprietary, and so I cannot publish the list of keys associated with this dictionary, however, I use both the certainty and uncertainty lists from LIWC.[1] As a second check, I also use a dictionary of uncertainty keys generated from a paper that examines 10-K filings to the Securities and Exchange Commission (SEC) and which are published in the Appendix of Loughran and McDonald (2011).

My dictionary includes the following keys:

Certainty words keys:

grew
we should continue
The negotiations are
is now 4.5 percent
there remains widespread concern
have been on the upside
We have
could lead
remained strong
seems likely to moderate
at a
would expect
could slow
also point to
I say this not because
running a little behind
potential shortages over the winter
could keep
have not changed
continues to
have served to
show
is slower
surged by more than
suggests
remains quite robust
reports a
had
remains
It's clear
widespread use of
has been reported
they will not be able to meet demand
are seeing
came in at
continuing
is reported to be
rose 1.6 percent
Several members
have served to
reinforce
addresses the policy issues
I would say
with more
shift taking place
by more than
they will not be able

[1] Those interested in this data, please see LIWC2015.

the tightest capacity rate
still have not had
increased at an annual rate of
continues to have
paradigm shift taking place
has been
lagged
I think
have served
seems to be able
I take to imply that
think the economy is likely to grow
they are concerned
is possible
reports a 6 percent
then a pickup
have been
rose strongly
has been accompanied
by
led
because
stronger than we thought
would be
didn't come
A second possibility
we're seeing
could
is affecting
I have not changed
I guess
have used
received since
half a month since the beginning of the year
continues to expand
going into
I was
they will need
by more than 13
000 jobs
is now
creating
made
rebounded
continuing at a high rate
perhaps due to
results from
is planning to expand
should continue to increase
reports a 6 percent volume
a number of indications
think
attempt
is at least
remained
will not do so
supply has risen
there may be forces at work that could
suppose
was raised
spoke of
I don't believe
are likely to be
was optimistic
is planning to
seems reasonably strong
We have seen
tightened
employment grew
was referring to earlier
appears
seems
has some
feel that risks
have seen very strong
perhaps as a consequence of
is even less clear
this has been
I continue to
likely feeding
than they have ever seen
have seen
at an annual rate of 3 percent
increased notably
is
a bit stronger
now running
have not had
has softened
causing
held steady
productivity rose
good idea about
seems to me
half of the effect due to seeing
are seeing increased demand
still have not
seem
face the familiar sources
very strong
as well as
Indeed
are
do not see
hint at some moderation
do expect a temporary
slowdown
since December of 1985

Uncertainty words keys:

Should
are divided
This view
I would expect to see
pretty
commented
I suppose
could slow
only small
there may be forces
is likely to
my sense is
especially if
could have a
we think the
there may be forces at work
Some
have been quite encouraging
suggests
remains quite robust
has held up
will need
spoke of a
any time soon
could keep
increases in interest rates
will not do so now
at least to me seems likely
indicated
with more forward momentum
quite close
is reported to be
want to strengthen
Are we
although I think that's
I would say
appears to be
hint at
is expected to depress
somewhat higher
that's more a
Are we at the point
generally
point to
I think
has been
should
I take to imply that
we do expect
anecdotal evidence
is possible
we have a good idea about
taking place
somewhat optimistic
we should
greater business optimism
also point to some
have been
even less clear
seems reasonably
at least beginning
somewhat
running so far this year at about the
have provided
seems to be able to
it seems to me
should continue
would be
likely
could
perhaps
could lead to
I guess
quite
make the case
suggests that
as far as policy is concerned
appropriate course
seems quite reasonable
looking out a year
characterize
overall rebounded
could slow even more
and yet there's
perhaps as
would entail
likely feeding into
suppose
guardedly optimistic
are likely to be
thinking
seems reasonably strong
is planning to
relatively
seem sensitive
seems
continue
seems to
seems to be
illustrates
it could lead
see some pressure
would expect to see
could have
little bit less
something closer
familiar sources
A second possibility is about
about the same
expected
overall
some weakening
quite well

could be	seem	suggests to us
at least to me	really didn't	elevated level of house prices
has some labor concerns	is expected to	relatively lean
reflect	possibility	seems mostly
potential	seems likely to	perhaps due
should continue to	has held up quite well	have a good idea
I think this	a bit	expect
	hint at some	

Dictionary Robustness

This section reports the robustness of the findings presented for the certainty/uncertainty measures in chapter 4, Table 4.1. I apply three different dictionaries to determine the stability of the findings: the list of uncertainty words in the finance dictionary just cited; the LIWC dictionary of uncertainty words (recall there are no certainty words in the FOMC statement using the LIWC keys); and finally a larger dictionary from the FOMC human annotations (184, 234).

When I use the finance dictionary, I find evidence that is inconsistent with the evidence I present in the chapter. Instead, I find that in the model with all FOMC members, when the median committee member has opposing bias (model 2), there is a negative predicted relationship with the number of uncertainty words, however, this measure is neither substantively large nor statistically significant. Some of the models also report a negative relationship (model 4 and model 6), but again, the coefficients are close to zero. When I move to a model that examines only those members on schedule to vote, again, I find the opposite results than what I present in chapter 4. Here I find a positive relationship between the level of expressed uncertainty and the opposing bias of the median member.

When I use the LIWC dictionary to measure uncertainty, however, and unlike the finance dictionary, I find very similar results to the main specification in Table 4.1. As in chapter 4, I find a positive relationship between the median member having opposing bias and the number of uncertainty words expressed in the policy statement. As there are no certainty words, I just use uncertainty words and this model has a count (Poisson) link function rather than the binominal link function used to estimate the proportion. Similarly, when I restrict the sample to only those FOMC members on schedule to vote, as in the main specification, I find that there is a negative predicted relationship between the median having opposing bias and the number of uncertainty words contained in the policy statement. This makes me somewhat more confident that the results are not completely dependent on my dictionary.

One additional concern may be because the custom dictionary is designed from FOMC transcripts and then applied to FOMC policy statements, the dictionary may be over-fit to the texts. In order to check this, I constructed a larger, more unstructured dictionary with an even larger number of certainty and uncertainty keys. In this case, the number of uncertainty words is 184 (rather than 136) and the number of certainty words 234 (rather than 154). The unbalanced nature of the keys also now means that the dictionary is stacked in favor of finding more certainty rather than uncertainty words. This imbalance should therefore make this a more conservative test of the results presented in the main specification.

As with the main findings, I find a positive relationship between opposing biases and the proportion of uncertainty words and word phrases expressed in the policy statement when the sample includes all members. The positive relationship is robust to a variety of specifications, including those models where I control for the number of dissents, which is unrelated to the level of uncertainty in the policy statement. In contrast to the preceding results, when I restrict the results to only those members on schedule to vote, I find some evidence in support of the first hypothesis, although as before, likely due to the low sample size, the results are not statistically significant at conventional levels. When the chair and the median (mean) member have opposing bias, we see a reduction in the level of uncertainty expressed in the policy statement. The negative relationship is also robust to a variety of different model specifications, including controlling for the number of dissents. The dissent variable continues to be unrelated, either substantively or statistically, to the level of uncertainty in the policy statement.

In chapter 5, I present findings from a survey experiment and here I include further details of the experiment, including the full text of the experiment.

Sample

- Number of invitations sent: 120
- Number of completed questionnaires: 108
- Selection of target population: Quota sampling. The participants were recruited from the nonprobability online panel "GESIS Online Panel Pilot."
- Quotas: The selection of the target population was based on age-group (18–40 years; 41 years and older), education (Fachhochschulreife/Abitur; no, Abitur) and gender quotas.

Methods

Field time: 16th of July to 13th of August 2014
Procedure: Usage of an online questionnaire with additional open and closed probing-questions
Incentives: 5 euros

Table A.2 Effects of committee heterogeneity on uncertainty (Finance Dictionary) in FOMC statements: All members

	Model 1	Model 2	Model 3	Model 4	Model 5	Model 6
Opposing Biases (mean)	0.125			0.140		
	(0.188)			(0.201)		
Opposing Biases (median 1)		−0.016			−0.024	
		(0.184)			(0.203)	
Opposing Biases (median 2)			0.071			0.074
			(0.205)			(0.215)
No. of Dissent				−0.008	0.004	−0.002
				(0.041)	(0.043)	(0.041)
Constant	1.526***	1.609***	1.551***	1.538***	1.604***	1.553***
	(0.147)	(0.135)	(0.174)	(0.158)	(0.147)	(0.182)
Chair and year effects	✓	✓	✓	✓	✓	✓
Observations	24	24	24	24	24	24
Log Likelihood	−49.193	−49.413	−49.357	−49.173	−49.408	−49.355
Akaike Inf. Crit.	106.386	106.826	106.713	106.346	106.816	108.710
Bayesian Inf. Crit.	111.098	111.538	111.425	111.058	111.528	114.600

*$p < 0.1$. **$p < 0.05$. ***$p < 0.01$.

Table A.3 Effects of committee heterogeneity on uncertainty (Finance Dictionary) in FOMC statements: Voting members only

	Model 1	Model 2	Model 3	Model 4	Model 5	Model 6
Opposing Biases (mean)	0.161			0.167		
	(0.189)			(0.194)		
Opposing Biases (median 1)		0.288			0.316	
		(0.185)			(0.195)	
Opposing Biases (median 2)			0.224			0.250
			(0.187)			(0.198)
No. of Dissent				−0.005	−0.019	−0.016
				(0.040)	(0.042)	(0.042)
Constant	1.504***	1.447***	1.473***	1.514***	1.478***	1.497***
	(0.149)	(0.140)	(0.144)	(0.165)	(0.155)	(0.157)
Chair and year effects	✓	✓	✓	✓	✓	✓
Observations	24	24	24	24	24	24
Log Likelihood	−49.050	−48.198	−48.686	−49.040	−48.091	−48.615
Akaike Inf. Crit.	106.099	104.396	105.372	108.081	106.181	107.230
Bayesian Inf. Crit.	110.812	109.108	110.085	113.971	112.072	113.120

$^{*}p < 0.1$. $^{**}p < 0.05$. $^{***}p < 0.01$.

Table A.4 Effects of committee heterogeneity on uncertainty (LIWC) in FOMC statements: All members

	Model 1	Model 2	Model 3	Model 4	Model 5	Model 6
Opposing Biases (mean)	0.109			0.109		
	(0.236)			(0.248)		
Opposing Biases (median 1)		0.149			0.178	
		(0.247)			(0.272)	
Opposing Biases (median 2)			0.068			0.177
			(0.252)			(0.274)
No. of Dissent				−0.032	−0.036	−0.056
				(0.053)	(0.053)	(0.057)
Constant	0.885**	0.873**	0.902**	1.055***	1.036***	0.933**
	(0.398)	(0.381)	(0.417)	(0.351)	(0.335)	(0.448)
Chair and year effects	✓	✓	✓	✓	✓	✓
Observations	24	24	24	24	24	24
Log Likelihood	−43.515	−43.439	−43.584	−43.835	−43.718	−43.094
Akaike Inf. Crit.	95.031	94.879	95.168	95.671	95.436	96.188
Bayesian Inf. Crit.	99.743	99.591	99.881	100.383	100.148	102.078

*$p < 0.1$. **$p < 0.05$. ***$p < 0.01$.

Table A.5 Effects of committee heterogeneity on uncertainty (LIWC) in FOMC statements: Voting members only

	Model 1	Model 2	Model 3	Model 4	Model 5	Model 6
Opposing Biases (mean)	−0.290			−0.264		
	(0.231)			(0.234)		
Opposing Biases (median 1)		−0.165			−0.100	
		(0.245)			(0.266)	
Opposing Biases (median 2)			−0.193			−0.138
			(0.237)			(0.258)
No. of Dissent				−0.031	−0.033	−0.029
				(0.054)	(0.058)	(0.058)
Constant	1.107***	1.050***	1.069***	1.156***	1.074***	1.090***
	(0.382)	(0.378)	(0.379)	(0.405)	(0.398)	(0.395)
Chair and year effects	✓	✓	✓	✓	✓	✓
Observations	24	24	24	24	24	24
Log Likelihood	−42.846	−43.393	−43.288	−42.676	−43.233	−43.161
Akaike Inf. Crit.	93.692	94.786	94.576	95.352	96.466	96.322
Bayesian Inf. Crit.	98.404	99.498	99.288	101.243	102.356	102.213

$^{*}p < 0.1$. $^{**}p < 0.05$. $^{***}p < 0.01$.

Table A.6 Effects of committee heterogeneity on certainty and uncertainty (Longer FOMC Dictionary) in FOMC statements: All members

	Model 1	Model 2	Model 3	Model 4	Model 5	Model 6
Opposing Biases (mean)	0.292 (0.219)			0.289 (0.235)		
Opposing Biases (median 1)		0.366* (0.218)			0.388 (0.242)	
Opposing Biases (median 2)			0.219 (0.239)			0.199 (0.250)
No. of Dissent				0.002 (0.054)	−0.012 (0.055)	0.014 (0.052)
Constant	−0.026 (0.162)	−0.047 (0.153)	−0.020 (0.201)	−0.030 (0.180)	−0.031 (0.172)	−0.038 (0.212)
Chair and year effects	✓	✓	✓	✓	✓	✓
Observations	24	24	24	24	24	24
Log Likelihood	-40.476	−39.960	−40.950	−40.475	−39.937	−40.915
Akaike Inf. Crit.	88.952	87.919	89.900	88.950	87.874	91.830
Bayesian Inf. Crit.	93.664	92.632	94.613	93.662	92.586	97.720

$^{*}p < 0.1$. $^{**}p < 0.05$. $^{***}p < 0.01$.

Table A.7 Effects of committee heterogeneity on certainty and uncertainty (Longer FOMC Dictionary) in FOMC statements: Voting members only

	Model 1	Model 2	Model 3	Model 4	Model 5	Model 6
Opposing Biases (mean)	−0.092			−0.121		
	(0.222)			(0.226)		
Opposing Biases (median 1)		−0.013			−0.056	
		(0.217)			(0.230)	
Opposing Biases (median 2)			−0.042			−0.095
			(0.218)			(0.234)
No. of Dissent				0.032	0.031	0.034
				(0.051)	(0.053)	(0.054)
Constant	0.190	0.141	0.158	0.133	0.092	0.108
	(0.172)	(0.154)	(0.163)	(0.194)	(0.176)	(0.180)
Chair and year effects	✓	✓	✓	✓	✓	✓
Observations	24	24	24	24	24	24
Log Likelihood	−41.284	−41.369	−41.353	−41.089	−41.202	−41.148
Akaike Inf. Crit.	90.569	90.739	90.706	92.178	92.404	92.297
Bayesian Inf. Crit.	95.281	95.451	95.418	98.068	98.294	98.187

$^{*}p < 0.1$. $^{**}p < 0.05$. $^{***}p < 0.01$.

Education Codes

Low: Schüler/-in, besuche eine allgemeinbildende Vollzeitschule Von der Schule abgegangen ohne Hauptschulabschluss (Volksschulabschluss) Hauptschulabschluss (Volksschulabschluss) + Polytechnische Oberschule der DDR mit Abschluss der 8. oder 9. Klasse

Medium: Realschulabschluss (Mittlere Reife) + Polytechnische Oberschule der DDR mit Abschluss der 10. Klasse

High: Fachhochschulreife, Abschluss einer Fachoberschule Allgemeine oder fachgebundene Hochschulreife/Abitur (Gymnasium bzw. EOS, auch EOS mit Lehre)

Missing: Einen anderen Schulabschluss, und zwar

Questions

1. Eine Person bezahlt aktuell, also im Juli 2014, 1.500 Euro pro Monat für Lebensmittel und Kleidung. Was schätzen Sie: Wie viel Euro wird diese Person für die gleichen Lebensmittel und die gleiche Kleidung im Juli 2015 bezahlen? Gehen Sie bitte davon aus, dass sich weder die Lebensumstände, noch das Konsumverhalten der Person verändern wird, d.h. sie wird in 12 Monaten ähnliche Produkte und Dienstleistungen im gleichen Umfang wie derzeit nutzen. Bei dieser Frage können Sie nur eine Antwort geben.
2. Die Europäische Zentralbank (EZB) erwartet, dass die wichtigen Zinssätze für eine längere Zeit auf dem gegenwärtigen Level oder darunter liegen werden. Diese Einschätzung beruht auf den insgesamt gedämpften Inflationsaussichten (Bedingung 2: von derzeit 1 Prozent pro Jahr).

Bedingung 1: Die Inflationserwartung für die Eurozone deckt sich mit dem Ziel der Europäischen Zentralbank, die Preissteigerung auf angemessenem Niveau zu halten.

Bedingung 2: Die Inflationserwartung für die Eurozone deckt sich mit dem Ziel der Europäischen Zentralbank, die Preissteigerung nahe 2 Prozent zu halten.

Bei der vorherigen Frage haben Sie angegeben, dass eine Person im Juli 2015 [XXXX] EUR für Lebensmittel und Kleidung ausgeben wird. Dieser Betrag entspricht einer jährlichen Inflationsrate von [X] Prozent. Wenn Sie nun die Erwartungen der EZB berücksichtigen, was schätzen Sie: Wie viel Euro wird diese Person für die gleichen Lebensmittel und die gleiche Kleidung im Juli 2015 bezahlen? Gehen Sie bitte davon aus, dass sich weder die Lebensumstände, noch das Konsumverhalten

Table A.8 Frequency distribution ($N = 108$)

Prior Inflation	Frequency	Percentage
Less than 1500€	7	6.48%
1500€	6	5.56%
1515€	12	11.11%
1530€	26	24.07%
1545€	16	14.81%
1560€	9	8.33%
1575€	11	10.19%
1590€	5	4.63%
1605€	11	10.19%
1620€	2	1.85%
1635€	0	0%
1650€ or more	3	2.78%

der Person verändern wird, d.h. sie wird in 12 Monaten ähnliche Produkte und Dienstleistungen im gleichen Umfang wie derzeit nutzen. Bei dieser Frage können Sie nur eine Antwort geben.

3. Mit welcher jährlichen Inflationsrate rechnen Sie in 5 Jahren? Bei dieser Frage können Sie nur eine Antwort geben.
4. Mit welcher jährlichen Inflationsrate rechnen Sie in 10 Jahren? Bei dieser Frage können Sie nur eine Antwort geben.
5. Weiter oben haben Sie folgende Informationen gelesen:
   Bedingung 1: Die Inflationserwartung für die Eurozone deckt sich mit dem Ziel der Europäischen Zentralbank, die Preissteigerung auf angemessenem Niveau zu halten.
   Bedingung 2: Die Inflationserwartung für die Eurozone deckt sich mit dem Ziel der Europäischen Zentralbank, die Preissteigerung nahe 2 Prozent zu halten.
6. Für wie detailliert halten Sie diese Information?
7. Wie oft schauen oder lesen Sie Nachrichten? Bei dieser Frage können Sie nur eine Antwort geben.
8. Wie oft schauen oder lesen Sie Nachrichten zu wirtschaftlichen Themen? Bei dieser Frage können Sie nur eine Antwort geben.

Table A.9 Frequency distribution by treatment group

Posterior Inflation	Vague Frequency	Vague Percentage	Precise Frequency	Precise Percentage	Total Frequency	Total Percentage
Less than 1500 €/ -1%	1	1.92%	1	1.82%	2	1.87%
1500€/ 0%	5	9.62%	2	3.64%	7	6.54%
1515€/ 1%	9	17.31%	14	25.45%	23	21.50%
1530€/ 2%	15	28.85%	24	43.64%	39	36.45%
1545€/ 3%	5	9.62%	7	12.73%	12	11.21%
1560€/ 4%	7	13.46%	3	5.45%	10	9.35%
1575€/ 5%	2	3.85%	1	1.82%	3	2.80%
1590€/ 6%	2	3.85%	2	3.64%	4	3.74%
1605€/ 7%	4	7.69%	1	1.82%	5	4.67%
1620€/ 8%	0	0.00%	0	0.00%	0	0.00%
1635€/ 9%	0	0.00%	0	0.00%	0	0.00%
1650€ or more / 10% or more	2	3.85%	0	0.00%	2	1.87%
N	52	100%	55	100%	107	100%

References

Acosta, Miguel, and Ellen E. Meade. 2015. *Hanging on Every Word: Semantic Analysis of the FOMC's Postmeeting Statement*. Feds note, Board of Governors of the Federal Reserve System, Washington, DC.

Adolph, Christopher. 2013. *Bankers, Bureaucrats and Central Bank Politics: The Myth of Neutrality*. Cambridge University Press.

Adolph, Christopher. 2018. "The Missing Politics of Central Banks." *PS: Political Science and Politics* 51(4):737–742.

Ainsley, Caitlin. 2016. "The Politics of Central Bank Appointments." *Journal of Politics* 49(4):1205–1219.

Aksoy, Yunus, Paul De Grauwe, and Hans Dewachter. 2002. "Do Asymmetries Matter for European Monetary Policy?" *European Economic Review* 46(3):443–469.

Alesina, Alberto, and Alex Cukierman. 1990. "The Politics of Ambiguity." *Quarterly Journal of Economics*' 105(4):829–850.

Alesina, Alberto, and Allan Drazen. 1991. "Why Are Stabilizations Delayed?" *American Economic Review* 81(5):1170–1188.

Alesina, Alberto, Nouriel Roubini, and Gerald D. Cohen. 1997. *Political Cycles and the Macroeconomy*. MIT Press.

Angrist, Joshua D., and Jörn-Steffen Pischke. 2008. *Mostly Harmless Econometrics: An Empiricist's Companion*. Princeton University Press.

Armantier, Olivier, Wändi Bruine de Bruin, Giorgio Topa, Wilbert Klaauw, and Basit Zafar. 2015. "Inflation Expectations and Behavior: Do Survey Respondents Act on Their Beliefs?" *International Economic Review* 56(2):505–536.

Armantier, Olivier, Scott Nelson, Giorgio Topa, Wilbert Van der Klaauw, and Basit Zafar. 2016. "The Price Is Right: Updating Inflation Expectations in a Randomized Price Information Experiment." *Review of Economics and Statistics* 98(3):503–523.

Atkinson, Adele, and Flore-Anne Messy. 2011. "Assessing Financial Literacy in 12 Countries: An OECD/INFE International Pilot Exercise." *Journal of Pension Economics and Finance* 10(4):657–665.

Baerg, Nicole, Dominik Duell, and Will Lowe. 2019. "Inflation Expectations as Public Opinion?" Working Paper.

Baerg, Nicole, Julia Gray, and Jakob Willisch. 2019. "Opportunistic, Not Optimal, Policy: A Power-Sharing Explanation for Central Bank Independence in Post-Communist Countries." Working Paper.

Baerg, Nicole Rae, and Mark Hallerberg. 2016. "Explaining Instability in the Stability and Growth Pact: The Contribution of Member State Power and Euroskepticism to the Euro Crisis." *Comparative Political Studies* 49(7):968–1009.

Baerg, Nicole, and Colin Krainin. 2016. "Committees and Discretionary Vagueness." Working Paper.

Baerg, Nicole, and Will Lowe. 2018. "A Textual Taylor Rule: Estimating Central Bank Preferences Combining Topic and Scaling Methods." *Political Science Research and Methods* 1–17. Advanced Online Publication

Baron, David P., and John A Ferejohn. 1989. "Bargaining in Legislatures." *American Political Science Review* 83(4):1181–1206.

Barro, Robert J. 1977. "Unanticipated Money Growth and Unemployment in the United States." *American Economic Review* 67(2):101–115.

Barro, Robert J., and David B. Gordon. 1983. "A Positive Theory of Monetary Policy in a Natural-Rate Model." *Journal of Political Economy* 91(4):589–610.

Bearce, David. 2009. *Monetary Divergence: Domestic Policy Autonomy in the Post-Bretton Woods Era*. University of Michigan Press.

Bernhard, William, J. Lawrence Broz, and William Roberts Clark. 2002. "The Political Economy of Monetary Institutions." *International Organization* 56(4):693–723.

Blinder, Alan S. 2007. "Monetary Policy by Committee: Why and How?" *European Journal of Political Economy* 23(1):106–123.

Blinder, Alan, Michael Ehrmann, Marcel Marcel Fratzscher, Jakob De Haan, and David Jansen. 2008. "Central Bank Communication and Monetary Policy: A Survey of Theory and Evidence." *Journal of Economic Literature* 46(4):910–945.

Blinder, Alan, and J. Morgan. 2005. "Are Two Heads Better Than One? An Experimental Analysis of Group vs. Individual Decisionmaking." *Journal of Money, Credit and Banking* 37(5):789–812.

Bloom, Nicholas. 2009. "The Impact of Uncertainty Shocks." *Econometrica* 77(3):623–685.

Bodea, Cristina. 2017. "When Are Women Elevated to Central Bank Boards? Institutions, Politics and Development." Working Paper.

Bodea, Cristina, and Raymond Hicks. 2015. "Price Stability and Central Bank Independence: Discipline, Credibility, and Democratic Institutions." *International Organization* 69:35–61.

Bowles, Samuel, Steven N. Durlauf, and Karla Hoff. 2006. *Poverty Traps*. Princeton University Press.

Bruno, Michael. 1993. *Crisis, Stabilization, and Economic Reform: Therapy by Consensus*. Oxford University Press.

Bryan, Mike, and G. Venkatu. 2001a. "The Curiously Different Inflation Perspectives of Men and Women." *Federal Reserve Bank of Cleveland Commentary*, 1101.

Bryan, Mike, and G. Venkatu. 2001b. "The Demographics of Inflation Opinion Surveys." *Federal Reserve Bank of Cleveland Commentary*, 1105, pp. 1–4.

Bulíř, Aleš, Martin Čihák, and David-Jan Jansen. 2014. *Does the Clarity of Inflation Reports Affect Volatility in Financial Markets?* Number 14-175. International Monetary Fund.

Cagan, Phillip. 1956. "The Monetary Dynamics of Hyperinflation." In *Studies in the Quantity Theory of Money*, ed. Milton Friedman. University of Chicago Press. 25:117

Carrillo, Paul E., and M. Shahe Emran. 2012. "Public information and inflation expectations: Microeconometric evidence from a natural experiment." *Review of Economics and Statistics* 94(4):860–877.

Carroll, C. 2003. "Macroeconomic Expectations of Households and Professional Forecasts." *Quarterly Journal of Economics* 118(1):269–298.

Cavallo, Alberto. 2012. "Online and Official Price Indexes: Measuring Argentina's Inflation." Working Paper. MIT Sloan.

Chang, Kelly H. 2003. *Appointing Central Bankers: The Politics of Monetary Policy in the United States and the European Monetary Union*. Cambridge University Press.

Chappell, Henry W., Thomas M. Havrilesky, and Rob Roy McGregor. 2000. "Monetary Policy Preferences of Individual FOMC Members: A Content Analysis of the Memoranda of Discussion." *Review of Economics and Statistics* 79(3):454–460.

Chappell, Henry W., Rob Roy McGregor, and Todd A. Vermilyea. 2005. *Committee Decisions on Monetary Policy: Evidence from Historical Records of the Federal Open Market Committee*. MIT Press.

Chappell, Henry W., Rob Roy McGregor, and Todd A. Vermilyea. 2008. "Regional Economic Conditions and Monetary Policy." *European Journal of Political Economy* 24(2):283–293.

Chen, Ying. 2011. "Perturbed Communication Games with Honest Senders and Naive Receivers." *Journal of Economic Theory* 146(2):401–424.

Clague, Christopher, Philip Keefer, Stephen Knack, and Mancur Olson. 1999. "Contract-Intensive Money: Contract Enforcement, Property Rights, and Economic Performance." *Journal of Economic Growth* 4(2):185–211.

Crawford, Vincent P., and Hans Haller. 1990. "Learning How to Cooperate: Optimal Play in Repeated Coordination Games." *Econometrica* (May 1): 571–595.

Crawford, Vincent P., and Joel Sobel. 1982. "Strategic Information Transmission." *Econometrica* 50(6):1431–51.

Crowe, Christopher, and Ellen E Meade. 2007. "The Evolution of Central Bank Governance around the World." *Journal of Economic Perspectives* 21(4): 69–90.

De Bruin, Wändi Bruine, Charles F. Manski, Giorgio Topa, and Wilbert Van Der Klaauw. 2011. "Measuring Consumer Uncertainty about Future Inflation." *Journal of Applied Econometrics* 26(3):454–478.

Dhir, Aaron A. 2015. *Challenging Boardroom Homogeneity: Corporate Law, Governance, and Diversity*. Cambridge University Press.

Dincer, Nergiz, and Barry Eichengreen. 2014. "Central Bank Transparency and Independence: Updates and New Measures." *International Journal of Central Banking* (Mar):189–253.

Ehrmann, Michael, Sylvester Eijffinger, and Marcel Fratzscher. 2012. "The Role of Central Bank Transparency for Guiding Private Sector Forecasts *Scandinavian Journal of Economics* 114(3):1018–1052.

Ehrmann, Michael, and Marcel Fratzscher. 2007. "Communication by Central Bank Committee Members: Different Strategies, Same Effectiveness?" *Journal of Money, Credit and Banking* 39(2–3):509–541.

Ehrmann, Michael, and Marcel Fratzscher. 2009. "Explaining Monetary Policy in Press Conferences." *International Journal of Central Banking* 5(2):42–84.

Ehrmann, Michael, and Marcel Fratzscher. 2010. "Politics and Monetary Policy." *Review of Economics and Statistics* 93(3):941–960.

Eijffinger, Sylvester, Ronald Mahieu, and Louis Raes. 2017. "Inferring Hawks and Doves from Voting Records." *European Journal of Political Economy* 51:107–120.

Enøe, Claes, Marios P. Georgiadis, and Wesley O. Johnson. 2000. "Estimation of Sensitivity and Specificity of Diagnostic Tests and Disease Prevalence When the True Disease State Is Unknown." *Preventive Veterinary Medicine* 45(1):61–81.

Erhart, Szilárd, and Jose-Luis Vasquez-Paz. 2007. "Optimal Monetary Policy Committee Size: Theory and cross country evidence." MNB Working Papers.

ESCB, Organisation. 1992. "Treaty on European Union - Protocol on the statute of the european System of Central Banks and of the European Central Bank—Chapter III: Article 11: The Executive Board." *Official Journal C 191* 29(7):70.

Fracasso, Andrea, Hans Genberg, and Charles Wyplosz. 2003. "How Do Central Banks Write? An Evaluation of Inflation Targeting Central Banks." *Geneva Reports on the World Economy Special Report* 2.

Francis, Bill, Iftekhar Hasan, Jong Chool Park, and Qiang Wu. 2015. "Gender Differences in Financial Reporting Decision Making: Evidence from Accounting Conservatism." *Contemporary Accounting Research* 32(3):1285–1318.

Frechette, Guillaume R., John H. Kagel, and Steven F. Lehrer. 2003. "Bargaining in Legislatures: An Experimental Investigation of Open Versus Closed Amendment Rules." *American Political Science Review* 97(2):221–232.

Frieden, Jeffry A. 1991. "Invested Interests: The Politics of National Economic Policies in a World of Global Finance." *International Organization* 45(4):425–451.

Friedman, Jerome, Trevor Hastie, and Robert Tibshirani. 2001. "The Elements of Statistical Learning." New York: Springer series in statistics.
Gaines, Brian J., James H. Kuklinski, and Paul J. Quirk. 2007. "The Logic of the Survey Experiment Reexamined." *Political Analysis* 15(1):1–20.
Gavin, William T., and Rachel J. Mandal. 2000. "Inside the Briefcase: The Art of Predicting the Federal Reserve." *Regional Economist* (Jul):4–9.
Gerlach-Kristen, Petra. 2006. "Monetary Policy Committees and Interest Rate Setting." *European Economic Review* 50(2):487–507.
Gerlach-Kristen, Petra. 2008. "The Role of the Chairman in Setting Monetary Policy: Individualistic vs. Autocratically Collegial MPCs." *International Journal of Central Banking* 4(3):119–143.
Gerlach-Kristen, Petra, Ellen Meade, et al. 2010. Is There a Limit on FOMC Dissents? Evidence from the Greenspan Era. Technical report.
Gersbach, Hans, and Volker Hahn. 2008. "Should the Individual Voting Records of Central Bankers Be Published?" *Social Choice and Welfare* 30(4):655–683.
Gilligan, Thomas, and Keith Krehbiel. 1987. "Collective Decision-Making and Standing Committees: An Information Rationale for Restrictive Amendment Procedures." *Journal of Law, Economics and Organization* 3: 287–335.
Gilligan, Thomas W., and Keith Krehbiel. 1989. "Asymmetric Information and Legislative Rules with a Heterogeneous." *American Journal of Political Science* 33(2):459–490.
Goffman, Erving. 1963. "Stigma: Notes on a spoiled identity." *Jenkins, JH & Carpenter*, Simon and Schuster.
Goodfriend, Marvin. 1999. The Role of a Regional Bank in a System of Central Banks. In *Carnegie-Rochester Conference Series on Public Policy*, Vol. 51, pp. 51–71. Elsevier.
Greenspan, Alan. 2008. *The Age of Turbulence: Adventures in a New World.* Penguin.
Gul, Ferdinand A., Bin Srinidhi, and Anthony C. Ng. 2011. "Does Board Gender Diversity Improve the Informativeness of Stock Prices?" *Journal of Accounting and Economics* 51(3):314–338.
Hallerberg, Mark. 2002. "Veto Players and the Choice of Monetary Institutions." *International Organization* 56(4):775–802.
Hallerberg, Mark, and William Roberts Clark. 2002. "Political Business Cycles in EU Accession Countries." *European Union Politics* 3(2):231–250.
Hallerberg, Mark, and Joachim Wehner. 2018. "When Do You Get Economists as Policy Makers?" *British Journal of Political Science* 1–13. Advanced Online Publication
Helleiner, Eric. 1994. *States and the Reemergence of Global Finance: From Bretton Woods to the 1990s*. Cornell University Press.

Helleiner, Eric. 2014. *The Status Quo Crisis: Global Financial Governance after the 2008 Meltdown*. Oxford University Press.

Hix, Simon, Bjørn Høyland, and Nick Vivyan. 2010. "From Doves to Hawks: A Spatial Analysis of Voting in the Monetary Policy Committee of the Bank of England." *European Journal of Political Research* 49(6):731–758.

Hoff, Karla, and Joseph Stiglitz. 2001. "Modern Economic Theory and Development." *Frontiers of Development Economics* (Mar):389–459.

Hong, Lu, and Scott E. Page. 2004. "Groups of Diverse Problem Solvers Can Outperform Groups of High-Ability Problem Solvers." *Proceedings of the National Academy of Sciences of the United States of America* 101(46):16385–16389.

Howell, Llewellyn D. 2011. "International Country Risk Guide Methodology." East Syracuse, NY: PRS Group.

Jackman, Simon. 2005. "Pooling the Polls over an Election Campaign." *Australian Journal of Political Science* 40(4):499–517.

Jansen, David-Jan. 2011. "Does the Clarity of Central Bank Communication Affect Volatility in Financial Markets: Evidence from Humprey-Hawkins Testimonies." *Contemporary Economic Policy* 29(4):494–509.

Johnson, J. 2016. *Priests of Prosperity: How Central Bankers Transformed the Postcommunist World*. Cornell Studies in Money. Cornell University Press.

Kaplan, Stephen B. 2013. *Globalization and Austerity Politics in Latin America*. Cambridge University Press.

Kaplan, Stephen B. 2017. "Partisan Technocratic Cycles in Latin America." *Electoral Studies* 45:219–229.

Krishna, Vijay, and John Morgan. 2001. "A Model of Expertise." *Quarterly Journal of Economics* 116(2):747–775.

Krishna, Vijay, and John Morgan. 2008. "Contracting for Information under Imperfect Commitment." *RAND Journal of Economics* 39(4):905–925.

Kydland, Finn E., and Edward C. Prescott. 1977. "Rules Rather Than Discretion: The Inconsistency of Optimal Plans." *Journal of Political Economy* 85(3):473–492.

Linzer, Drew A. 2013. "Dynamic Bayesian Forecasting of Presidential Elections in the States." *Journal of the American Statistical Association* 108(501):124–134.

Lombardelli, Clare, James Proudman, and James Talbot. 2005. "Committees versus Individuals: An Experimental Analysis of Monetary Policy Decision Making." *International Journal of Central Banking*. (May):181:205.

Loughran, Tim, and Bill McDonald. 2011. "When Is a Liability Not a Liability? Textual analysis, Dictionaries, and 10-Ks." *Journal of Finance* 66(1):35–65.

Lusardi, A., and O. Mitchell. 2008. "Planning and Financial Literacy: How Do Women Fare?" *American Economic Review* 92(8):413–417.

Mackintosh, James. 2014. "ECB Division on Wording Fails to Impress." http://www.ft.com/intl/cms/s/0/c76327ae-7bd4-11e4-a695-00144feabdc0.html.

Maier, Philipp. 2010. *How Central Banks Take Decisions: An Analysis of Monetary Policy Meetings.* Chapter 10 in *Challenges in Central Banking: The Current Institutional Environment and Forces Affecting Monetary Policy.* New York: Cambridge University Press.

Mainwaring, Scott, and Christopher Welna. 2003. *Democratic Accountability in Latin America.* Oxford University press.

Malmendier, Ulrike, and Stefan Nagel. 2015. "Learning from Inflation Experiences." *Quarterly Journal of Economics* 131(1):53–87.

Maltzman, Forrest, James F. Spriggs, and Paul J. Wahlbeck. 2000. *Crafting Law on the Supreme Court: The Collegial Game.* Cambridge University Press.

Mankiw, N. Gregory, Ricardo Reis, and Justin Wolfers. 2003. "Disagreement about Inflation Expectations." *NBER Macroeconomics Annual* 18:209–248.

March, James G. 1962. "The Business Firm as a Political Coalition." *Journal of Politics* 24(4):662–678.

Meade, Ellen E. 2010. "Federal Reserve Transcript Publication and Regional Representation." *Contemporary Economic Policy* 28(2):162–170.

Meade, Ellen, and D. N. Sheets. 2005. "Regional Influences on FOMC Voting Patterns." *Journal of Money, Credit, and Banking* 37:661–677.

Meade, Ellen E., and David Stasavage. 2008. "Publicity of Debate and the Incentive to Dissent: Evidence from the US Federal Reserve." *Economic Journal* 118(528):695–717.

Menz, Jan Oliver, and Phillip Poppitz. 2013. "Households' Disagreement on Inflation Expectations and Socioeconomic Media Exposure in Germany." Discussion Paper Deutsche Bundesbank (27/2013).

Meseguer, Covadonga. 2010. *Learning, Policy Making, and Market Reforms.* Cambridge University Press.

Mikhaylov, Slava, Michael Laver, and Kenneth R. Benoit. 2012. "Coder Reliability and Misclassification in the Human Coding of Party Manifestos." *Political Analysis* 20(1):78–91.

Minozzi, William. 2011. "A Jamming Theory of Politics." *Journal of Politics* 73:301–315.

Mirkov, Nikola, and Gisle James Natvik. 2016. "Announcements of Interest Rate Forecasts: Do Policymakers Stick to Them?" *Journal of Money, Credit and Banking* 48(5):901–920.

Mishkin, Frederic S. 1995. "The Rational Expectations Revolution: A Review Article of: Preston J. Miller, ed.: The Rational Expectations Revolution, Readings from the Front Line." Working Paper 5043 National Bureau of Economic Research.

Morris, Stephen, and Hyun Song Shin. 2002. "Social Value of Public Information." *American Economic Review* 92:1521–1534.

Morris, Stephen, and Hyun Song Shin. 2007. "Optimal Communication." *Journal of the European Economic Association* 5(2–3):594–602.

Murphy, Kevin M., Andrei Shleifer, and Robert W Vishny. 1989. "Industrialization and the Big Push." *Journal of Political Economy* 97(5):1003–1026.

O'Donnell, Guillermo A. 1998. "Horizontal Accountability in New Democracies." *Journal of Democracy* 9(3):112–126.

OECD. 2011. "Consumer Price Index: Methodological Issues." http://stats.oecd.org/mei.html

Oshima, Yusuke, Yoichi Matsubayashi et al. 2018. "Monetary Policy Communication of the Bank of Japan: Computational Text Analysis." Technical report.

Owens, Ryan J., and Justin P. Wedeking. 2011. "Justices and Legal Clarity: Analyzing the Complexity of US Supreme Court Opinions." *Law and Society Review* 45(4):1027–1061.

Ray, Debraj. 1998. *Development Economics*. Princeton University Press.

Riboni, Alessandro, and Francisco J. Ruge-Murcia. 2010. "Monetary Policy by Committee: Consensus, Chairman Dominance or Simple Majority?" *Quarterly Journal of Economics* 125(1):363–416.

Riboni, Alessandro, and Francisco Ruge-Murcia. 2008. "The Dynamic (in) Efficiency of Monetary Policy by Committee." *Journal of Money, Credit and Banking* 40(5):1001–1032.

Rodriguez-Clare, Andres. 1996. "The Division of Labor and Economic Development." *Journal of Development Economics* 49(1):3–32.

Rogoff, Kenneth. 1985. "The Optimal Degree of Commitment to an Intermediate Monetary Target." *Quarterly Journal of Economics* 100(4):1169–1189.

Romer, Thomas, and Howard Rosenthal. 1978. "Political Resource Allocation, Controlled Agendas, and the Status Quo." *Public Choice* 33(4):27–43.

Rosa, Carlo, and Giovanni Verga. 2007. "On the Consistency and Effectiveness of Central Bank Communication: Evidence from the ECB." *European Journal of Political Economy* 23:146–175.

Rozkrut, Marek, Krzysztof Rybiński, Lucyna Sztaba, and Radosław Szwaja. 2007. "Quest for Central Bank Communication: Does It Pay to Be Talkative?" *European Journal of Political Economy* 23(1):176–206.

Sargent, Thomas J. 1982. The Ends of Four Big Inflations. In *Inflation: Causes and Effects*, pp. 41–98. University of Chicago Press.

Sargent, Thomas J., and François R. Velde. 2003. *The Big Problem of Small Change*. Princeton University Press.

Sargent, Thomas J., and Neil Wallace. 1982. "The Real-Bills Doctrine versus the Quantity Theory: A Reconsideration." *Journal of Political Economy* 90(6):1212–1236.

Sargent, Thomas, Noah Williams, and Tao Zha. 2009. "The Conquest of South American Inflation." *Journal of Political Economy* 117(2):211–256.

Scheve, Kenneth. 2004. "Public Inflation Aversion and the Political Economy of Macroeconomic Policymaking." *International Organization* 58(1):1–34.

Schillemans, Thomas. 2008. "Accountability in the Shadow of Hierarchy: The Horizontal Accountability of Agencies." *Public Organization Review* 8(2):175.

Schonhardt-Bailey, Cheryl. 2013. *Deliberating Monetary Policy*. MIT Press.
Schonhardt-Bailey, Cheryl. 2014. "Monetary Policy Oversight in Comparative Perspective: Britain and America during the Financial Crisis." Political Science and Political Economy Working Paper.
Schonhardt-Bailey, Cheryl. 2017. "Nonverbal Contention and Contempt in UK Parliamentary Oversight Hearings on Fiscal and Monetary Policy." *Politics and the Life Sciences* 36(1):27–46.
Shapiro, Carl, and Hal R. Varian. 2013. *Information Rules: A Strategic Guide to the Network Economy*. Harvard Business Press.
Shih, Victor. 2008. *Factions and Finance in China: Elite Conflict and Inflation*. Cambridge University Press.
Shirai, Sayuri. 2014. "Communication and Forward Guidance in a World of Unconventional Monetary Policy: The Case of the Bank of Japan." Remarks by Ms. Sayuri Shirai, Member of the Policy Board of the Bank of Japan, at the 2014 Monetary Policy Forum New York City (Accessed: 2014 12 03). http://www.bis.org/review/r140304c.pdf.
Sibert, Anne. 2003. "Monetary Policy Committees: Individual and Collective Reputations." *Review of Economic Studies* 70(3):649–665.
Sibert, Anne. 2006. "Central Banking by Committee." *International Finance* 9(2):145–168.
Sibert, Anne. 2009. "Is Central Bank Transparency Desirable?" *Journal of the European Economic Association* 7(4):831–857.
Soto, Alonso. 2013. "Brazil Central Bank Aims for Simple after Communication Fumbles." *Reuters* (Accessed June 7: 2015) http://www.reuters.com/article/2013/08/29/brazil-cenbank-communication-idUSL2N0GT1I920130829.
Štajner, Sanja, Nicole Baerg, Simone Paolo Ponzetto, and Heiner Stuckenschmidt. 2016. Automatic Detection of Speculation in Policy Statements. In *Workshops on Natural Language Processing and Computational Social Science*. Association for Computing Machinery.
Staton, Jeffrey K., and Georg Vanberg. 2008. "The Value of Vagueness: Delegation, Defiance, and Judicial Opinions." *American Journal of Political Science* 52(3):504–519.
Stein, Jeremy C. 1989. "Cheap Talk and the Fed: A Theory of Imprecise Policy Announcements." *American Economic Review* 79(1):32–42.
Stubbs, Amber. 2011. MAE and MAI: Lightweight Annotation and Adjudication Tools. In *Proceedings of the 5th Linguistic Annotation Workshop*, pp. 129–133. Association for Computational Linguistics.
Thatcher, Mark, and Alec Stone Sweet. 2002. "Theory and Practice of Delegation to Non-Majoritarian Institutions." *West European Politics* 25(1):1–22.
Thornton, Daniel L., and David C. Wheelock. 2014. "Making Sense of the Dissents: A History of FOMC Dissents." *Federal Reserve Bank of St. Louis Review* 96(3):213–227.

Tucker, Paul. 2018. *Unelected Power: The Quest for Legitimacy in Central Banking and the Regulatory State*. Princeton University Press.

Tverdova, Yuliya V. 2012. "The Formation of Economic Perceptions in Post-Communist Countries of East Central Europe." *Political Behavior* 34(1):137–158.

Tversky, Amos, and Daniel Kahneman. 1974. "Judgment under Uncertainty: Heuristics and Biases." *Science* 185(4157):1124–1131.

Weidmann, Jens. 2018. "Central Bank Communication as an Instrument of Monetary Policy." Lecture by Dr Jens Weidmann, President of the Deutsche Bundesbank and Chairman of the Board of Directors of the Bank for International Settlements, at the Centre for European Economic Research, Mannheim, May 2, 2018 (Accessed: November 20, 2018). https://www.bis.org/review/r180511a.htm.

Woodford, Michael. 2005. "Central Bank Communication and Policy Effectiveness." Available at http://www.nber.org/papers/w11898.

Index

accountability 13, 29
  horizontal vs. vertical 155–157
actors 11, 15, 16, 48, 57–61, 152–154, *see also* committee chair, median committee member, households, Board of Governors
  differing preferences of 60*fig*
Adolph, Christopher 30, 166
Africa 121
age, of consumer
  impact on inflation expectations by 109
agreement frequency 7
Aksoy, Yunus 26
Argentina 23, 121, 126
Armantier, Olivier 40, 41

Baerg, Nicole Rae 88, 162
Bank of England 21*fig*, 22, 47
Bank of Ireland 22
Bank of Israel 47
Bank of Japan 19, 21*fig*, 22
bank presidents, regional, *see also* FOMC, central bank committees
bank presidents, regional 9, 32, 58
bargaining models 45, 48, 50, 52, 150
  current adaptation of 52–56
Bernanke, Ben 4, 22, 51, 56, 79
  agreement frequency under 8
bias
  vs. preference distance 61*fig*
biases, *see also* preferences, preference distance
  opposing 89*fig*
blackout period
  purpose of 7
Blinder, Alan 26, 35
Board of Governors, 79, 81, *see also* FOMC, central bank committees
  voting rights of 33
Bodea, Cristina 30
Brazil 36, 121, 123
Bulíř, Ales 37
Bundesbank (German central bank) 101
Bush, George W. 79

Canada 121
capital restrictions 23
Carrillo, Paul E. 39
Cavallo, Alberto 119
central bank appointments
  committee composition and 68
  horizontal accountability and 157–159
  political factors in 161–163
central bank committees, *see also* MPCs, Board of Governors
  as political 11–14, 151
  committee appointments 68
  composition of 12–14, 31*fig*, 29–32, 75, 157, 162
  decision-making protocols 34*fig*, 32–35, 51
  design of 18
  government oversight of 13, 14, 18, 55, 158
  impact of preferences 58–61
  impact of size 25–29
  independence of 16, 18, 155–157
  policy consensus through 8, 34, 69, 151
  voting rule variations 33–34
central bank communication, *see also* policy communication
  functions of 35
  market responses to 10, 16
  public expectations and 101–102
  public vs. private sources of 36, 57
  strategic vagueness vs. information precision 50–52
  theoretical models of 38–39

central bank communications
  policy changes in 20, 21*fig*, 24*fig*
central bank independence 16, 18, 155–157
central bank preferences, *see* preferences
Central Bank Transparency Index 24*fig*
Central Europe 121
Chang, Kelly H. 32, 162
Chappell, Henry W. 31
cheap talk communication models 38
Čihák, Martin 37
Cleveland Federal Reserve Bank 126
committee biases, *see* biases,
committee chair 16, 46, 57, 150, 151
  aligned vs. opposing preferences of 60*fig*
  bias vs. distance 61*fig*
  role of in deliberations 12, 42, 48, 79, 166
committee composition, *see* composition, diversity
Committee on Banking, Housing, and Urban Affairs (US) 156
Committee on Financial Services (US) 156
communication models
  theoretical 38–39
communication policies
  changes to central banks 20, 21*fig*, 24*fig*
  improvements to central banks 19–23
communism 116
composition, *see also* diversity
  central bank appointments and 68
  information precision and 12–14
  of central bank committees 31*fig*, 75, 157, 162
  strategic vagueness and 63
  variations in 29–32
computational social science 16
consensus economics 126
consumer price index (CPI) 126n, 126
contract intensive money (CIM) 138
Convertibility Program (Argentina) 121
corporate governance
  diversity in (future research) 165–166
credibility
  governments and 137–138, 147, 155
Czech Republic 37
data analysis
  committee diversity and policy statement uncertainty 92–96
  committee preferences and policy statement uncertainty 150–152
  inflation expectations vs. information precision in Latin America 138–142, 147–148, 154
  policy statement uncertainty and households' inflation expectations 114–116, 152–154
  preference distance and policy statement editing 96–98
data sources
  central bank preferences (Baerg & Lowe) 88
  Cleveland Federal Reserve Bank 126
  curated dictionary 83
  Factiva 128
  FOMC meeting transcripts 75–77, 82–83
  GESIS Online Panel Pilot (GOPP) 105
  international country risk data set 143
  primary textual reports 16
  Reuters news articles 18, 134
  unstructured textual information 75, 83
De Grauwe, Paul 26
decision-making protocols 24, 34*fig*, 32–35, 51
deflation 125, *see also* inflation, disinflation
delegation
  as solution to inflation 157–159
descriptive statistics
  inflation expectations 109–114
Dewachter, Hans 26
Dhir, Aaron A. 30
dictionary (study methodology) 83–86, 95
Dincer, Nergiz 23
disinflation 125, *see also* inflation, deflation
dissenting opinions 7, 33, 56, 72, 90, 152
  transparency and 22
dissenting opinions (study methodology) 90

distance, *see* preference distance
diversity, *see also* composition
accountability and 157
committee preferences and 75
in corporate governance (future research) 165–166
information precision and 12–14, 69, 162
policy statement uncertainty and 92–96
study methodology 88–90
Draghi, Mario 10, 23

East Germany 116
eastern Europe 121
ECB 10, 21*fig*, 23, 33, 101, 160
economic policies
time-inconsistent nature of 147
Ecuador 40
education levels
financial literacy and 103, 116
Ehrmann, Michael 99, 129
Eichengreen, Barry 23
empirical testing
exogenous variations to 78–79
political variables in 79
sample period 77–78
equilibrium outcomes 39–42, 49–53, 63–69
Erhart, Szilárd 27
Eurobarometer 105
European Central Bank, *see* ECB
European Debt Crisis 102
European Social Survey 105
Exchange Rate Agreements and Exchange Rate Restrictions (IMF) 137
exchange rate regime 121–123

Factiva 128
federal funds rate 2n, 24, 81, 87
Federal Open Market Committee, *see* FOMC
Federal Reserve Act (1913) 2
financial literacy
impact on inflation expectations 41, 103–105, 109, 116
Financial Policy Committee (UK) 156
FOMC 1, 17, 51
communication policy improvements 19–22
decision-making protocols 24, 33, 34*fig*, 51
meeting transcripts 75–77, 82–83
operation of 2, 76, 80–82
policy statement uncertainty and member diversity 92–96, 99
preference diversity 88–90
voting rights 76, 95
voting rules 78
foreign direct investment (FDI) 23
forward guidance 4, 22
Fracasso, Andrea 37
Fratzscher, Marcel 99, 129
frontier markets 23

game sequence 62–63
game-theoretic models 39
Gavin, William T. 4
Geithner, Timothy 51, 56
Genberg, Hans 37
Gerlach-Kristen, Petra 26
German central bank (Bundesbank) 101
Germany 116, 121
Gersbach, Hans 26
GESIS Online Panel Pilot (GOPP) 105
Governing Council 160
government oversight
of central bank committees 13, 14, 18, 55, 158
Gray, Julia 162
Great Inflation 78
Great Moderation 77
Great Recession 22, 78, 149
Greenspan, Alan 2, 79
agreement frequency under 7
Gul, Ferdinand A. 166

Hahn, Volker 26
Hallerberg, Mark 88
heterogeneity 12–14, *see also* diversity
Hicks, Raymond 30
Hoenig, Thomas 51, 56
homogeneity 12–14, *see also* diversity
Hong, Lu 30

horizontal accountability
central bank appointments and 157–159, 162
vs. vertical accountability 155–157
households (public)
inflation expectations and 42, 57, 58, 71, 80, 111, 114, 115*table*, 126, 147, 150, 153
policy communication and 4, 8, 12, 15, 36, 39, 57
Hyun Song Shin 52

IFS (international financial stability) 5
inflation, *see also* deflation, disinflation
reasons for variation in 147
solutions for 121–124, 157–159
inflation aversion, *see also* inflation preferences
"hawks" vs. "doves" 32, 88
inflation expectations, *see also* macroeconomic outcomes
committee preferences and 58–61
education level and 116
factors in 109–114, 115*table*
financial literacy and 41, 103
forward-looking vs. backward-looking 123
government credibility and 137–138, 147, 155
households and 42, 57, 58, 71, 80, 111, 114, 126, 147, 150, 153
information precision and 39–42
policy statement uncertainty and 114–116, 152–154
public information and 69–71
"Rational Expectations Revolution" 123
study methodology 105–107
survey experiment 16, 17, 118–120
variations in 103–105
vs. information precision in Latin America 125, 138–142, 147–148, 154
inflation forecasts 126
inflation preferences, *see* preferences
inflation rates
historical global variations in 122*fig*, 121–123
inflation stabilization policies
central bank information and 123–124
Latin America 121–123
information environment 18, 35, 138, 140, 146, 147, 155
information precision, *see also* strategic vagueness
committee composition and 12–14
definition of 47
diversity and 69
inflation expectations and 39–42
preference distance and 59
strategic vagueness and 50*fig*, 50–52
study methodology 50, 83–87
survey experiment 16, 17, 102, 120
vs. inflation expectations in Latin America 125, 138–142, 147–148, 154
institutional design 37, 63, 65
institutional environment 10, 14, 15
interest rates
federal funds rate 2n, 24, 81, 87
MPCs and 2, 6, 53, 80, 105
international country risk data set 143
international financial stability (IFS) 5
International Labour Organization 126
International Monetary Fund (IMF) 121, 137
Israel 121

Jansen, David-Jan 37
Jordan 23
judicial politics
in statement vagueness (future research) 163–165

Kaplan, Stephen B. 162
Kocherlakota, Narayana 58
Krishna, Vijay 39
Kroszner, Randall 9

Latin America 121
inflation article text (Reuters) 131*table*
inflation expectations vs. information precision in 125, 139*table*, 138–142, 144*table*, 147–148, 154

Latin America (*continued*)
inflation stabilization policies in 121–123
Latvia 23
Levenshtein distance measure 87
Linguistic Inquiry and Word Count (LIWC) 85, 164
Lombardelli, Clare 26
Loughran, Tim 86, 165
Lowe, Will 88

machine learning 16, 83, 129
macroeconomic outcomes, *see also* inflation expectations
committee vs. single entity 17, 25, 159
information precision and 69
information precision vs. inflation expectations 39–42
Maier, Philipp 30
Maltzman, Forrest 163
Mandal, Rachel J. 4
March, James G. 151
market responses
to central bank communication 10, 16
McDonald, Bill 86, 165
McGregor, Rob Roy 31
Meade, Ellen E. 19, 31, 55
median committee member 17, 57, 150
aligned vs. opposing preferences of 60*fig*
bias vs. distance 61*fig*
role of in deliberations 12, 48, 166
voting rights of 48
Menz, Jan Oliver 128
Mexico 123
Middle East 121
Minozzi, William 38
Mirkov, Nikola 42
monetary policy, *see also* FOMC,. individual banks
in political studies 166
Monetary Policy Committee (UK) 156
monetary policy committees, *see* MPCs
monetary policy statements, official
committee preferences and statement uncertainty 150–152
households' inflation expectations and 152–154
increasing importance of 7
information precision and 73
policy bargaining over 32–35, 45, 51, 63
uncertainty vs. households' inflation expectations 114–116
Morgan, John 26, 35, 39
Morris, Stephen 52
MPCs, *see also* central bank committees, Board of Governors
decision-making 34*fig*
decision-making by 1
homogeneous vs. heterogeneous 12–14
interest rates and 2, 6, 53, 80, 105
policy statement uncertainty and member preferences 150–152
size distribution 28*fig*
Multipurpose Annotation Environment (MAE) 84

natural language 4
Natvik, Gisle James 42
new and revised statement (NS) 82
Ng, Anthony C. 166

Organisation for Economic Co-operation and Development (OECD) 104
Outright Monetary Transactions (OMT) 102
Owens, Ryan J. 164

Page, Scott E. 30
policy bargaining 32–35, 45, 51, 63
policy communication, *see also* central bank communication
as strategic process 8–10
households and 4, 8, 12, 15, 36, 39, 57
increasing importance of 6–7
policy consensus
institutional environment and 10, 14
through committee deliberations 8, 34, 69, 151
policy language
impact of 102

policy statement editing
preference distance and 96–98
policy statement uncertainty
committee diversity and 92–96
FOMC member diversity and 99
impact of voting rules on 89*fig*, 90, 93, 99
inflation expectations and 152–154
policy statements, *see* monetary policy statements
Poppitz, Phillip 128
preference distance *see also* biases,
information precision and 59
Levenshtein distance measure 87
policy statement editing and 96–98
study methodology 90
vs. bias 61*fig*
preferences, *see also* committee chair, median committee member
committee diversity and 64
FOMC diversity and 75–76
"hawks" vs. "doves" 32, 35, 59, 88
in committee deliberations 6, 11, 12, 42, 48–49, 58–61, 65, 68, 95
Proudman, James 26

quantitative easing (QE) 10

"Rational Expectations Revolution" 123
Real Plan (Brazil) 123
Report to the FOMC on Economic Conditions and Monetary Policy 81
Reuters news articles 18, 124, 129, 131*table*, 134, 135, 146, 155
Riboni, Alessandro 33, 52, 53
Rogoff, Kenneth 68, 157, 158
"roll-call" vote 6, 17, 26, 31, 51, 79, 81, 82, 90
Romer, Thomas 39, 45, 52, 73
Rosenthal, Howard 39, 45, 52, 73
rotational voting 33, 99
future research in 159–161
Ruge-Murcia, Francisco J. 33, 52, 53

Sargent, Thomas 58, 123
Scheve, Kenneth 31
Schonhardt-Bailey, Cheryl 55, 154
Securities and Exchange Commission (SEC) 166
sensitivity analysis
inflation expectations vs. information precision 116
inflation expectations vs. information precision in Latin America 143–146
Shahe Emran, M. 39
Sheets, D. Nathan 31
Shih, Victor C. 30, 162
Sibert, Anne 26
spatial bargaining model 39, *see also* bargaining models
Spriggs, James F. 163
Srinidhi, Bin 166
Stasavage, David 19, 55
statistical analyses 16, 17, 98, 146
status quo statement (SQ)
status quo statement 82
Statute of the European System of Central Banks 161
strategic vagueness 12, 47, 50*fig*, 49–52, 58, 63, 150, *see also* information precision
study methodology
amendments to policy statements 87–88
dissenting opinions 90
inflation expectations 69–71, 105–107
inflation expectations vs. information precision in Latin America 125–138, 139*table*, 144*table*, 146
information precision 50, 83–87, 102
preference distance 90
preference diversity 88–90
survey experiment
inflation expectations 105–107, 118–120
inflation expectations vs. information precision 16, 17
information precision 102
Sveriges Riksbank (Sweden) 22

Talbot, James 26
"text as data"
analysis of 7, 16, 75, 83

textual information
  data source 16, 75, 83
Tombini, Alexandre 36
transparency 13, 14, 20*fig*, 21*fig*, 19–23, 24*fig*, 53–55, 156, 167
Tucker, Paul 158

United States 37, 51, 121
unsupervised classification 129
US Federal Reserve (Fed) 19, 20*fig*
US financial crisis (2008) 22, 78
utility functions 61*table*, 61

Vasquez-Paz, Jose-Luis 27
Venezuela 121, 123
Vermilyea, Todd A. 31
vertical accountability
  vs. horizontal accountability 155–157
Volker, Paul
  agreement frequency under 7
voting
  agreement frequency 7
  Board of Governors 33
  ECB decision-making protocols 33
  FOMC decision-making protocols 24, 33, 34*fig*, 51
  future research in rotational 159–161
  impact of transparency on 19
  influence of voting members 8n, 12, 17, 76, 79, 81, 83, 89, 90*fig*, 90, 93*table*, 93, 94*table*, 96, 98*table*, 98, 151
  median committee member 48
  "roll-call" vote 6, 17, 26, 31, 51, 79, 81, 82, 90
voting rights
  FOMC 76, 95
voting rules
  FOMC 78
  impact on policy statement uncertainty 89*fig*, 90, 93, 99
  variations in 33–34

Wahlbeck, Paul J. 163
Wedeking, Justin P. 164
Weidmann, Jens 101
West Germany 116
Willisch, Jakob 162
Wyplosz, Charles 37

Yellen, Janet 9